GEORGE FARMER SCHOOL LIBRARY

CLASS ....242..............

No. ......01551...............

GEORGE FARMER LIBRARY   REF.
04574
LOWER SCHOOL ASSEMBLY BOOK

THE
LOWER SCHOOL ASSEMBLY
HANDBOOK

THE LOWER SCHOOL ASSEMBLY HANDBOOK

David Self

HUTCHINSON
London   Melbourne   Auckland   Johannesburg

Hutchinson Education

An imprint of Century Hutchinson Ltd
62–65 Chandos Place, London WC2N 4NW

Century Hutchinson Australia Pty Ltd
PO Box 496, 16–22 Church Street, Hawthorn,
Victoria 3122, Australia

Century Hutchinson New Zealand Ltd
PO Box 40–086, Glenfield, Auckland 10, New Zealand

Century Hutchinson South Africa (Pty) Ltd
PO Box 337, Bergvlei, 2012 South Africa

First published 1987
Reprinted 1988

© David Self 1987

Typeset in 11 on 12pt Meridien by
D. P. Media Limited, Hitchin, Hertfordshire

Printed and bound in Great Britain by
Mackays of Chatham

British Library Cataloguing in Publication Data
The Lower school assembly book.
   1. Schools——Exercises and recreations
   2. Schools——Prayers
  I. Self, David
   377'.1   BV283.S3
ISBN 0-09-173050-3

Contents

Introduction — 11

THEMES

1 The inner me — 17
  Readings about the individual
  1: Who do you think you are? — 17
  2: What kind of liar are you? — 18
  3: Africa's plea — 19
  4: The rebel — 20
  5: Bad tempers — 21

2 Yourself and all the others — 23
  Readings about getting on with family and friends
  1: Parents, brothers and sisters — 23
  2: First day — 25
  3: The ball: justice or prudence? — 27
  4: Sympathy — 29
  5: Getting on with friends — 32
  6: How to be a good listener — 34
  7: Kindness — 36

3 Fables for our times — 39
  1: Aesop's fables — 39
    Sour grapes — 39
    Forewarned is forearmed — 39
    What a piece of work is man! — 40
  2: The bear who let it alone — 40
  3: Dividing the camels — 41
  4: The mango tree — 43
  5: The old woman at the bus stop — 45
  6: The tiger who would be king — 47
  7: warty bliggens the toad — 48

4 Living – and partly living 51
Readings to encourage an appreciation of life
1: Living with blindness 51
2: If only I could walk 53
3: Trees for life 55
4: A healthy heart 57
5: Why do people smoke? 60
6: Alcohol abuse 63
7: Drugs: a case history 64
8: Cry for my lost son 66

5 Today's society 71
1: The defeat of the male 71
2: Equal rights 73
3: Too much tv? 78
4: Heroes off the screen 79
5: Addicted to gambling 81
   A Amusement arcades 81
   B Horse racing 82
6: Emergency service 83
7: Homeless – in the search for work 85
8: The soup run 88
9: Acid rain 90

6 The wider world 93
1 Flood 93
   Yakub Ali's story 93
   Survivors and casualties 96
   Any answers? 97
2: Drought in Ethiopia 100
3: How much is a packet of rice? 103
4: Home for the dying *(for two voices)* 105

7 Human rights – and prisoners of conscience 108
1: Terror in Iran 108
2: Prisoner of conscience 110
3: In Buchenwald 111
4: Speaking out 112
5: We have never been free 113
6: Human rights *(for two or more voices)* 116
7: We will never die 118
8: People, not enemies 119

Contents

8	**Lessons from the past**		**122**
	1: The Great Fire of London		122
	The fire takes hold		122
	Fighting the fire		124
	The fire continues to rage		125
	2: Useful work		127
	3: A Wesleyan childhood		128
	4: England's first woman doctor		130
	5: George and the chocolate factory *(for ten voices)*		132
	6: Jesse Boot, chemist *(for four voices)*		138
	7: One hundred years ago *(for five voices)*		141
9	**Stories from the faiths**		**147**
	1: In the beginning		147
	A The Chinese creation story		147
	B The Greek creation story		149
	C The Christian view of creation		151
	D The creation		152
	2: The blind men and the elephant		155
	3: Confucius and friends		156
	4: David and Goliath		159
	5: Amritsar		161
	6: Hannah Senesh		163
	The plan		163
	Into Hungary		166
	The execution		168
	Blessed is the match		171
10	**The Christian way**		**173**
	1: The magic picnic *(for seven voices)*		173
	2: One man		178
	3: Prayer		179
	4: Footprints		180
	5: Army without guns		181
	6: In the street		183
11	**Stories from the world of Islam**		**184**
	1: Young Muhammad		184
	2: The call of the Prophet		186
	3: Ramadan		189
	4: The Hijra		191
	5: Suleman the Humble		193

Contents

6:	Be my guest	197
7:	Daud conquers Jalud	200

12 Looking ahead — 202
- 1: Options — 202
- 2: Equality for all — 204
- 3: In the dock (*for eight voices*) — 206
- 4: After the bomb — 209

SEASONAL READINGS
(*See also A Calendar of Readings, page 275*)

Autumn term — 213
- 1: Rosh Hashanah — 213
- 2: Therese of Lisieux (*3 October*) — 214
- 3: Divali — 217
- 4: Remembrance Sunday — 219
- 5: St Martin (*11 November*) — 220
- 6: Hugh of Lincoln (*17 November*) Part 1 — 223
- Part 2 — 226

CHRISTMAS
- 7: The Christmas tree — 228
- 8: Father and son — 229
- 9: The worm turns — 231
- 10: The massacre of the innocents (*28 December*) — 233

Spring term — 236
- 1: Winter celebrations (*for four voices*) — 236
- 2: Chinese New Year — 238
- 3: Robert Burns (*25 January*) — 240
- 4: Winter weather (*for three voices*) — 243
- 5: St Valentine's Day (*14 February*) — 244
- 6: Carnival (*Shrovetide*) — 247
- 7: St Joseph (*19 March*) — 249
- 8: Mothering Sunday (*Mid-Lent Sunday*) — 251
- 9: Passover — 253

EASTER
- 10: Pontius Pilate — 255
- 11: The crucifixion — 257
- 12: Good Friday: the one o'clock news — 260

Contents

Summer term 262
   1: Road to Emmaus 262
   2: Ballad of the Bread Man 263
   3: The Sikh uniform (*Baisakhi, 13 April*) 266
   4: Shavuot 268
   5: Seaside holiday (*for seven voices*) 270

A Calender of readings 275

Acknowledgements 282

Index of authors and topics 286

Introduction

The night before I sat down to write this introduction, a Sunday school teacher was interviewed on television. 'I can't tell them to love their neighbour,' she said. 'I've got to tell them to be cautious.' Despite the harsh realities of what some see as an increasingly brutish society, there does however remain a place for idealism as well as pragmatism and for many, the school assembly is still a very special forum where ideals (and yes, warnings) may be shared and a sense of community developed.

This is despite ever increasing demands from other quarters for precious time within the school day and from voices both inside and outside the educational world arguing that school assembly (and especially the school act of worship) is now an out-moded concept. Furthermore, it is despite the enormous hurdles that have to be overcome in order actually to get a secondary school to assemble. Just how difficult it is was made abundantly clear by a survey conducted by *The Times Educational Supplement* towards the end of 1985 and on which I reported for that paper in December of the same year.*

The TES survey polled a representative sample of 10 per cent of all secondary schools in England and Wales. Questionnaires were completed by 73.7 per cent of those schools, a remarkably high return rate for such surveys. It immediately confirmed the impossibility for many schools of holding a single, full-school assembly. As the survey revealed, less than one-third of wholly maintained schools possess a space in which all their pupils can conveniently

---

*The Times Educational Supplement, 20th December 1985.

Introduction

gather. What is perhaps more surprising is that only 6 per cent of those schools with an adequate hall (1.9 per cent of the total) elect to use that space for assembly on a daily basis and only two out of three of them reported holding a full-school assembly on even a weekly basis.

The many schools which do not possess a space convenient for full-school assemblies are therefore presumably quite justified in holding assemblies on another basis and the survey revealed just how widespread is the custom of holding upper and lower school assemblies and of the even commoner system of separate assemblies for 'years' or combinations of two year groups.

It appears that this kind of pattern of one or two year assemblies or, more simply, a 'lower school assembly' occurs in over three-quarters of the secondary schools in England and Wales. It is for leaders of such assemblies and of course similar assemblies in Scotland that this anthology of readings has been specially compiled.

The Lower School Assembly Book is a resource, not a course. Not every passage will be suitable in every context and it is not suggested that the user reads steadily through it, day by day or week by week. However, it is hoped that assembly leaders will find plenty of passages which appeal to them and to those they address. In selecting the readings, I have drawn on my experience over ten years as a teacher responsible for school assembly, my continuing work on BBC religious education and assembly programmes and on my other work in education and religious broadcasting.

I have chosen passages which have a wide and immediate aural appeal and which 'come off the page' easily. I hope I have included ones which will entertain, stimulate or even provoke. I have not included anything I would be embarrassed to stand up and read aloud myself. I have let the writers' voices be heard unadapted, rather than rewriting them in some kind of bland prose.

It is hoped that the passages will seem equally apposite in schools where assembly is also an act of worship and in schools where it is not. As an anthology, it is of course complete in itself, but it is also complementary to two earlier books, *Anthology for Assembly* and *The Assembly Handbook* (both Hutchinson). Indeed, it is the gratifying popularity of

Introduction

these books that has led in part to the compilation of this present collection and I have been conscious of the need not to duplicate material provided in the earlier volumes. I have also tried to correct any earlier imbalances: there is, for example, a larger number of Muslim narratives in this collection than in the earlier ones. (Indeed, bearing in mind that it is especially for the younger age range of the secondary school, I have preferred the narrative to the more philosophical.) Should a user fail to find a passage on a particular theme or for a specific season in this book, then he or she should find it in *Anthology for Assembly* or *The Assembly Handbook*. 'A Calendar of Readings' (pages 275–81) provides references to all three books.

Rehearsal is advised before any reading, and some thought might be given as to who is the best available reader (or readers) for a particular passage. No matter how much at home you feel reading to the assembly, remember that even a professional actor or reader prefers to have time to rehearse; that is, to check that he or she understands the meaning of what is to be read, to absorb its mood and tone, to appreciate the writer's viewpoint and to note where pauses and changes of pace are necessary.

The passages have been arranged thematically and a sequence of readings can be selected for use within one assembly or over a series of linked assemblies. In many schools, it is quite common to stage semi-dramatized presentations and a number of suitable scripts are included. References to these will be found in the topic index (page 288).

In almost every case, two introductions have been provided for each passage. The first is a background note for the leader's use. The second will serve as a ready-made introduction which can be simply read aloud to introduce the passage to the assembly when time does not permit the devising of a more locally relevant introduction.

The terms BCE and CE have been used in preference to the exclusively Christian terms BC and AD. These stand for Before the Common Era and Common Era.

The gathering together of a number of people for assembly places a heavy responsibility on those who lead that assembly. I hope this collection will lighten the load a little and help the arrangement of assemblies which nurture an awareness of values and the needs of others; which develop a sense of community; and which create a feeling of wonder, mystery, joy and, yes, idealism.

THEMES

1
The inner me
Readings about the individual

1: WHO DO YOU THINK YOU ARE?

A poem that encourages wonderment at the complexity and marvel of the human body. A follow-up might be to ask listeners to think (or perhaps write about) what else goes to make up a human being: aspects of personality, etc., and to ponder that, even given the ingredients of a human body, no scientist could manufacture one.

Who (or what) do you think you are? And what are you made of? Bone, flesh, blood, yes. But what else?

Who do you think you are
    and where do you think you came from?
From toenails to the hair of your head you are mixed
    of the earth, of the air,
Of compounds equal to the burning gold and amethyst
    lights of the Mountains of the Blood of Christ at
    Santa Fe.
Listen to the laboratory man tell what you are made
    of, man, listen while he takes you apart.
Weighing 150 pounds you hold 3,500 cubic feet of
    gas—oxygen, hydrogen, nitrogen.
From the 22 pounds and 10 ounces of carbon in you is
    the filling for 9,000 lead pencils.
In your blood are 50 grains of iron and in the rest of
    your frame enough iron to make a spike that would
    hold your weight.
From your 50 ounces of phosphorus could be made
    800,000 matches and elsewhere in your physical
    premises are hidden 60 lumps of sugar,

20 teaspoons of salt, 38 quarts of water, two ounces of lime, and scatterings of starch, chloride of potash, magnesium, sulphur, hydrochloric acid.
You are a walking drug store and also a cosmos and a phantasmagoria treading a lonesome valley, one of the people, one of the minions and myrmidons who would like an answer to the question, 'Who and what are you?'

Carl Sandburg

2: WHAT KIND OF LIAR ARE YOU?

A reminder that almost everyone tells lies at some time, and a suggestion that some lies matter more than others.

Today we are thinking about lies – and liars. What kind of liar are you? Do you, for example, lie about things you have forgotten? Or because you like exaggerating?

Do you tell 'white lies', lies for which there is an excuse – like not telling someone something that's true, but which would hurt them? Do you lie to get out of trouble? Or to cheat other people?

And which of these different kinds of lie is worst? What kind of liar are you?

What kind of a liar are you?
People lie because they don't remember clear what they saw.
People lie because they can't help making a story better than it was the way it happened.
People tell 'white lies' so as to be decent to others.
People lie in a pinch, hating to do it, but lying on because it might be worse.
And people lie just to be liars for a crooked personal gain.
What sort of a liar are you?
Which of these liars are you?

Carl Sandburg

The inner me

3: AFRICA'S PLEA

A poem asking for independence and the right to develop individuality. As well as being seen as a plea made for the African continent (or the Black races), it can be interpreted on a personal basis.

'Why can't you be like other people?' 'Why can't you be like that nice boy/girl?' If ever anyone has said anything like that to you, you'll understand this poem. It's asking people to let you be yourself, not just a copy of others.

I am not you —
but you will not
give me a chance,
will not let me be *me*.

'If I were you' —
but you know
I am not you,
yet you will not
let me be *me*.

You meddle, interfere
in my affairs
as if they were yours
and you were me.

You are unfair, unwise,
foolish to think
that I can be you,
talk, act
and think like you.

God made me *me*.
He made you *you*.
For God's sake
Let me be *me*.

Roland Tombekai Dempster

4: THE REBEL

Jesus, the Prophet Muhammad, even the Buddha . . . they were all (in their different ways) rebels. So were many of the great secular leaders and teachers. Yet rebels are . . . well, inconvenient! The last verse of this poem is a useful starting point for class or group discussions which could precede or follow a reading of this poem in assembly (and, perhaps, a home-made presentation on the same subject).

Do you admire or fear people who 'do different'? Are they a nuisance or necessary? And have you ever been a rebel? Was that a good time – or a bad time?

When everybody has short hair,
The rebel lets his hair grow long.

When everybody has long hair,
The rebel cuts his hair short.

When everybody talks during the lesson,
The rebel doesn't say a word.

When nobody talks during the lesson,
The rebel creates a disturbance.

When everybody wears a uniform,
The rebel dresses in fantastic clothes.

When everybody wears fantastic clothes,
The rebel dresses soberly.

In the company of dog lovers,
The rebel expresses a preference for cats.

In the company of cat lovers,
The rebel puts in a good word for dogs.

When everybody is praising the sun,
The rebel remarks on the need for rain.

When everybody is greeting the rain,
The rebel regrets the absence of sun.

When everybody goes to the meeting,
The rebel stays at home and reads a book.

When everybody stays at home and reads a book,
The rebel goes to the meeting.

When everybody says, Yes please,
The rebel says, No thank you.

When everybody says, No thank you,
The rebel says, Yes please.

It is very good that we have rebels,
You may not find it very good to be one.

D. J. Enright

5: BAD TEMPERS

A passage about the loutishness that afflicts some adolescents. It is a passage which may be a little 'difficult' for some listeners, but a carefully prepared reading will unlock its meaning and relevance.

As we grow up, we sometimes go through a period of time when we become bad-tempered, when we fight and are quarrelsome. This is a time that can be particularly upsetting to the grown-ups who love you, such as your parents. This is one man's memory of the time when he was thirteen.

I had reached the stage when boys stick together to hide the shame of their inexperience, and turn without knowing it against their parents and the laws of the house. My rough friendships were an indirect challenge to my father and mother, a hidden gesture of rebellion. I played a great deal of football; it was as if my body demanded explosive action. The place where we played was called the Craftie; it was a little field of grass, worn bare in patches, close by the slaughter house. To us in our raw and unhappy state the slaughter house had an abominable attraction, and the strong stench and sordid colours of blood and intestines seemed to follow us in our play. Our language and manners grew rough; even our friendship had an acrid flavour. There were savage fights in the Craftie, and the boys, crying with rage, would have killed each other if they could; yet behind their fury there was a sort of sad shame and frustration.

I do not know why boys of this age, the age of awakening puberty, should turn against everything that was pleasant in their lives before and rend it in a fit of crude cynicism. Perhaps it comes from their first distorted knowledge of the actual world, which is not the world of childhood, and a divination that all their childish games in which they played at being grown-up were of no use, something sterner being needed. Or it may be merely that I was unlucky in my friends, for I had far less wordly knowledge at the time than town boys of my age, and I was always perfectly prepared to be friendly with anyone who was friendly with me. I remember one fine summer day spent with another boy in wandering along the Wideford Burn, picking flowers and looking at birds' nests, without a single rough word. Why did I not have more days like that one in which I was perfectly happy, instead of all those days in the Craftie, when I was really miserable, though I did not know it? The Craftie seemed to hypnotize us; we kicked the football in hatred; there was a deep enmity in the bond between us.

Edwin Muir

2
Yourself and all the others
Readings about getting on with family and friends

1: PARENTS, BROTHERS AND SISTERS

A passage about relationships within the family; with parents and siblings.

How do you get on with your brothers and sisters? (That is, if you have any.) Do you have good or bad relationships with them? All of us have a whole number of different relationships – with people we meet just once or twice, with best friends and within our families. And it's family relationships that we're thinking about today . . .

First of all, there is the relationship which one has with one's mother and father. The parents give the child care, food, protection and – most important of all – the love which all children need. The child gives its parents the pleasure of having a child of their own, the admiration and love which children have for their parents and so on. They all get something which they need out of the relationship, their feelings are good ones and so the relationship between child and parents grows closer.

Of course things are seldom perfect, so relationships in any family have their ups and downs. There are probably times when you think your Mum and Dad are rotten to you. There are times, no doubt, when they wonder how they had a child as annoying as you. But, underneath these bad feelings, you and they know that you have a lot to give to each other; and the bad feeling doesn't usually last.

When we are babies our needs are few and simple ones – food, warmth, safety. To have these needs looked after is the first sign the baby receives of being loved. This is hugely important to the small child – and often to the same child as it grows older – that the relationship which develops is smooth and happy, because this helps the child to learn how to relate with people generally.

Sad to say, not all parents are able to give this early love and care to their children and the relationship which grows is not smooth or happy. When this is so – when the child can't get good feelings from its parents – it may find that making relationships with other people is hard throughout its life. It never learns how to relate.

When you were a tiny baby, no one else mattered to you except your mother: it was she who looked after you, cared for you and gave you the good feelings. You soon found that your father also played a big part in this and your earlier relationships were with these two people only. But if you had brothers and sisters they, too, became important quite early in your life. For your first few years they were the main people around your own age with whom you had any contact.

If you have bigger brothers or sisters you will remember how important they seemed to you when you were small. Perhaps they still do. If your brothers or sisters were younger than you, you will remember that you had special feelings about them, too – not always friendly but special all the same. If sisters or brothers were close enough to your own age to play with you and play your kind of games, they did a lot to affect the way you thought and behaved about things.

Later on in life, brothers and sisters usually mean a good deal to each other, even if they don't like each other much. They are often the first people we turn to if we need help. We generally have a rather special relationship with them, and as uncles and aunties they have a special relationship with *our* children. I know that some people – older or younger ones – hate their sisters or brothers. Even so, they wouldn't dislike them so much if they didn't mean something to each other.

So we learn about relationships in the first place from our brothers and sisters as well as from our parents.

Bill Stewart

2: FIRST DAY

A reading to remind second and third years what it was like to be 'new'.

As senior citizens of this school, you probably look down on the new first years . . . But do you remember what it was like to be new yourself, especially if you knew almost no one else in the school? This is to remind you how lonely and lost you can feel when you're new – and to make you think what you might do to help those who are new.

I'd never seen Cronton School until the morning I started there. My mother took me in the car, dropping me at the gate.

She grinned at me and said, 'Now it's up to you.'

I walked straight in, looking forward in an odd, excited way to being the same as the other kids. The school was just as my mother had described it, a grouping of shoe box shapes made of concrete and glass, with the brilliant green of an overgrown playing field stretching away behind it towards the distance where the hills were.

I walked along the front of the school and round a corner and I was in the playground. In front of me were hundreds of boys doing the things I had never done. They were wrestling and rolling and screaming and shouting. They were darting and dashing so swiftly that the patterns of their movements made me dizzy while their noise deafened me.

In a corner of the playground I met loneliness for the first time in my life. Loneliness isn't being alone but wondering why you have to be alone. I had rarely known other kids, I had always been alone, yet in those first moments at school I felt loneliness flood through me as I watched the hundreds of boys. My brain ached as their uproar beat against it. They and I were all wearing the same uniform, but they were different from me. They were rough savages, screaming their war cries and rushing into brutal battle, and they were happy in a way I had never known. They were happy shouting at each other, wrestling each other, hating each other.

Then one of them spotted me and, like a dog catching a strange scent, he swerved and stopped in front of me. He was smaller than I was and younger and his thick glasses gave him the look of an owl.

'You a new kid?' he asked.

I nodded.

'What's your name?'

'Stewart,' I said. He was shooting his questions at me like bullets and I didn't like them.

'Stewart what?' he asked.

'Jimmy Stewart.'

'Jimmy Stewart,' he said as if tasting the name. Then he went into a convulsive dance and starting screaming, '*Jimmy Stewpot! Jimmy Stewpot!*'

I was so astonished that I just stared at him and didn't at first see the other boys his voice had attracted. They came gathering round and while he went on jerking like a Dervish, they studied me. He was red-faced and hoarse, his spectacles on the end of his nose, he was a nightmare of a boy yet they watched me.

'He's a new kid!' he yelled. 'His name's Jimmy Stewpot!'

I could see dozens of pairs of eyes and I knew how zoo animals must feel on Sunday afternoons when people press close to the cages. There was a dull kind of interest in all the eyes, interest and animosity, but no friendliness. I felt lonelier than ever.

Reginald Maddock

3: THE BALL: JUSTICE OR PRUDENCE?

This excerpt from David Line's novel, Run for your Life, *suggests the importance of standing up to bullies and of seeing that younger and weaker people are not put upon. It also asks whether we should always stand up for our rights or sometimes take the easy way out. The obvious follow-up to this reading is to ask whether 'the little kid' (his family is Hungarian and he is called Istvan Szolda) was right or foolhardy to try to get his ball back.*

A story today about bullying and seeing justice is done. It takes place one rainy evening. A group of bullies are beating up a first year boy in a dark alley. Along comes the storyteller, an older boy called Woolcott.

As far as I could see, he was letting them. He wasn't struggling or yelling or anything. He was just kneeling there sobbing, and doing that pretty quietly.

I said, 'All right, break it up.'

It was dark in the alley and they had to peer at me.

'Get lost,' one of them said, uncertainly.

'Yeah, vanish.'

'Scramaroo.'

They let go of him all the same.

I could see they were younger than me, and smaller, which was all right except one of them had some kind of cosh in his hand, a piece of hosepipe or something.

'I know you!' this one yelled suddenly, just about the same moment I realized I knew him, too. He was a tough young kid with an elder brother who'd made my life a misery at another school. 'You're Woolcott, ain't you? I know where you live, Woolcott. Better shove off if you don't want trouble.'

'Yeah, shove.'

'Buzz off. He's ours.'

I said to the kid, 'Get up.'

'You leave him alone,' the kid with the cosh said. 'He started it. He hit one of us.'

'Yeah, he was throwing things.'

'Were you throwing things?' I said to the kid.

He just shook his head, still sobbing.

'Yes, you did, you rotten little liar! He caught Harris, didn't he, Harris?'

'Right here,' Harris said, pointing to his temple. 'I've still got a headache.'

I said, 'What did he throw?'

'He threw a ball. He threw it flipping hard, too. We was in the timber yard and he run away before we could see who done it.'

'How do you know it was him, then?'

'He told us.' Harris said triumphantly. 'He come up and laughed and told us right out, didn't he?'

'Yeah.'

'Yeah, right out, he did. He done it last Thursday and he come up just now and said it was him. Laughing, too.'

'I only asked for my ball back,' the kid said. It was the first time he'd spoken, and I looked at him twice because it was with a foreign accent. 'I saw them playing with it and I came up and apologized and asked for it back. It was only an accident. I didn't mean to hit anybody. It went over the wall by mistake.'

'Yeah, you rotten little liar, you threw it.'

'No, please, I didn't. It's the only ball I've got.'

'The only one you had.'

I said, 'Give him his ball back.'

'You take a jump.'

'Give him it back, quick.'

They were ganging up round me, and the one with

the cosh was fingering it, so I made a quick snatch before he was ready and got it off him.

I said, 'Give him his ball.'

One of them pulled a ball out of his pocket and dropped it on the ground, and the kid picked it up.

'My brother'll murder you,' the kid with the brother said.

'Give him his satchel, too.'

'He'll jump about on you. He'll tear you in little pieces. He'll give you such a crunching – '

I said, 'If those are your bikes jump on them quick.'

Their bikes were leaning up against the alley wall and they got on them and pushed off.

'I wouldn't like to be you,' the kid with the brother said.

He said something else, too, but I didn't catch it. They were all laughing as they rode off.

I picked up the kid's cap from the puddle and stuck it on his head.

I said, 'You're a bit of a case, aren't you? What do you want to tell them you did it for?'

'They had my ball,' the kid said, still sobbing. 'I thought they might hit me, but they ought to give it back.'

'Give it back! Look, you want to keep away from that lot,' I said. 'They'd do you up just for fun. Risk a good hiding for a rotten old ball you can buy anywhere for ninepence?'

David Line

4: SYMPATHY

One of the greatest gifts is knowing how to say the right thing, when to say it – and when it is safe to joke. A passage to encourage sympathy for others.

As you know, it's very easy to hurt someone by saying the wrong thing at the wrong time. There are times when some-

one's in the mood for a joke, even to be laughed at. Other times they just don't feel like it. It's important that we stop to think which sort of mood a person is in – and to think what we can say to cheer up someone who's feeling 'down'. The writer of this passage is now an actress.

Even if you're the sort of person who usually takes no notice of what other people say or think about you, there are still times when they can really hurt you. If you've got skin like a baby and somebody calls you crater-face it doesn't affect you at all. If the same person calls you the same thing the day you've sprung an enormous spot on your chin it makes you feel terrible.

    Times like that, when you're feeling vulnerable, a bit of praise works wonders. It doesn't even have to have any bearing on your situation. Once, when I was about nine my father lost his job and couldn't get another one. We were evicted from our house and sent to live in the poor ward of a local hospital. This ward contained about a hundred beds divided from each other by grey blankets hung on ropes. It was full of women and children. No fathers were allowed. Mine slept in the park and got shaved in the public lavatory every day. I was terribly ashamed of living in the hospital. I had always thought only poor old loonies went there, not ordinary people like us. Every afternoon I used to sneak the long way round coming home from school so nobody would see where I lived. I know it shouldn't have mattered to me but it did. Anyway one day this girl in my class, Jean Meredith, followed me home. I didn't see her but next day everyone in my class knew I lived in the hospital. I tried to pretend I didn't care but just a few odd remarks to the girl sitting next to me about being careful what she caught really hurt. I couldn't wait for the day to end and I thought I would never go back to that school again even if I had to play truant every day.

    That afternoon we had English and we were reading

a play. Our class teacher, Miss Sansom, picked people to go to the front of the class and act it. She told me to read Dick Whittington. The part of the play we did that afternoon was where he was on the road to London in his rags. He feels hopeless and decides to give up the idea of going to London, and return home. I suppose I read it with feeling because I was poor too and life was looking pretty hopeless for me. When Miss Sansom rang the classroom bell, pretending to be the bells of London and one of the boys said 'Turn again Whittington, Lord Mayor of London', I was overcome with joy. It seemed like it was really me it was happening to. Then the lesson finished and I was just me again, still humiliated. Before she started the next lesson Miss Sansom held her hand up for silence. 'Lesley,' she said, 'Have you ever thought of being an actress when you grow up? I think you'd be a very good one.' Everybody looked at me. I went bright red. I thought it was like Dick Whittington hearing the bells, but this time it really was for me. What she said didn't change anything: I still had to go home to the hospital. But that day and many days after I walked home with a wonderful feeling inside me.

When I was about fifteen I was in Miss Winter's class. She wasn't too bad as teachers go. I usually liked her cynical sense of humour and gave her back as good as I got and she didn't mind. The only day she went wrong was when I came in with a new hair cut and she teased me about it being cut round a pudding basin. Everybody was laughing and I was pretending to join in but I felt terrible. My Mum had cut my hair and I knew it looked awful. Miss Winter kept on and on, and I managed to fix a permanent grin on my face although I wished I could just disappear. My grin grew falser and falser and my mouth started twitching. Suddenly I knew that if I didn't get out of the classroom I would burst into tears in front of everyone and then I'd look even more of a fool. I dived for the door, rushed to the cloakroom and locked myself in the lavatory for half an hour. When I'd pulled myself together I went back and told her I'd suddenly felt sick. She was very nice about it and seemed to believe it, but she didn't mention my hair again.

I suppose it's a matter of how well you understand other people. I'm very bad at seeing what kind of a mood somebody's in, and I'm always saying the wrong thing. In fact people like Miss Sansom, who have the gift of knowing exactly the right thing to say to help someone when they're down, are very rare.

Lesley Davies

5: GETTING ON WITH FRIENDS

A second passage about personal relationships. (See also page 23.)

How do you get on with your friends? If you've got a really good friend, do you have to worry how you get on with him or her? Or doesn't it matter what you do or say when you're with that person? Today we're thinking about how we get on with our friends. Let's begin by thinking about how babies get on with other babies.

Small babies don't play with other children. They may play in the same place as others, but they play their own games and don't take much notice of the other children around. But the age of about two and a half years marks the beginning of a really special time in our lives, when we begin to mix more and more with other children and less and less within our family. Parents still count for a lot, but it is mostly with other children that we play. This is when brothers and sisters become really important, since it may be with them that we play most.

When we are very young, relationships are much simpler than when we get older. You and little Jane or Johnnie found at this time that you could get fun and help from each other and you were soon best friends.

Perhaps, very soon, you found you had got all the fun and help from each other that you could get – so you stopped being friends, or, at all events, became less friendly. Or perhaps the better you knew each other the more you found you could get from each other, so you stayed close friends for years.

You didn't worry much about hurting each other's feelings. When you – or Jane, or Johnnie – lost interest in another person you just stopped playing with them. You could quarrel one minute and be best friends again the next.

As we get older, relationships get more complicated. We find it harder to forget quarrels – pride or shame may prevent us. We also find it harder to offend people by dropping them when they cease to interest us. We think, 'I don't like Jane much nowadays, but she relies on me so I can't just stop talking to her.' Or we say to ourselves, 'John loves me but I don't love him any more. All the same, I don't want to hurt him and if I tell him how I feel he will be very unhappy. What *can* I do?'

There are two reasons for this change in the way we look at things. One is that, when we are little, we are still very much involved with ourselves – in a way very selfish. We don't really care how other people feel so long as we feel good, and if we don't feel good we don't worry about other people's feelings. As we grow older we learn that other people have feelings too, and we have to give good feelings as well as getting them. So we feel *bad* if we think we aren't giving enough, and now we have to decide what *is* enough.

The other reason is that we also learn to take some notice of what other people think about us – whether they see us as good or bad, nice or nasty. We begin to behave in ways which other people think are nice, or at least we are bothered about what they will think if we're nasty. We often behave in one way and think in quite another way because we know that, if we do as we really want to do, other people will think less of us.

And again we have to decide when and whether this is sensible.

One result of our *not* being able to handle life and its relationships well is that we make enemies. Babies don't make enemies, at least in the usual sense of the word. Very young children may squabble or fight over a toy, or because one wants to do what the other doesn't, but once the squabble is over they forget it. Their feelings are simple, whether they are bad or good ones.

Older children and grown-ups have less simple feelings and their quarrels, too, are less simple – but the quarrels are about much the same things. John has something Jane wants – a possession, a position, someone else's love, even a particular good feeling – and Jane can't get it. Or Jane acts in a way in which John doesn't want to act, and so he doesn't want Jane to act in that way either. They may not fight, because other people will think they are silly; or they may quarrel and make things worse. Either way, they will give each other *only bad* feelings – and they will become enemies unless these bad feelings can be replaced in some way by good ones.

Bill Stewart

6: HOW TO BE A GOOD LISTENER

These excerpts are taken from an American best-seller, The Friendship Factor, *and offer advice on how to be a good friend by being a good listener.*

How often has anyone said to you, 'Your trouble is, you don't listen!'? And how often have you wanted a good friend, someone whom you could really trust and who would listen to you? People who are good listeners make good friends and win friends for themselves – so what makes a good listener?

Good Listeners Listen with Their Eyes

According to communication experts, even when our mouths are closed we are saying a lot. When people speak to you, they are receiving lots of messages about how interested you are. Remember: The surest way to be interesting is to be interested, and the intensity of your interest can be measured by the way your body talks.

Eye contact is one of the surest indicators. If you are staring at the wall or glancing at other people, the speaker gets a strong impression of how little you care about the conversation. On the other hand, if you look a person directly in the eye as he or she speaks, you will be amazed at how quickly he or she gets the compliment.

Good Listeners Dispense Advice Sparingly

During the darkest hours of the American Civil War, President Abraham Lincoln wrote to an old friend and fellow lawyer, Leonard Swett, in Springfield, asking him to come to Washington. Lincoln said he had some problems he wanted to discuss.

Swett hurried to the White House, and Lincoln talked to him for hours about the advisability of issuing a proclamation freeing the slaves. He went over the arguments for and against such a move and then read letters and newspaper articles, some denouncing him for not freeing the slaves and others denouncing him for fear he was going to free them. After talking far into the evening, Lincoln shook hands with his old neighbour, said good night, and sent him back to Illinois without even asking for his opinion. Lincoln had done all the talking himself. That seemed to clarify his mind. 'He seemed to feel easier after the talk,' Swett said. Lincoln hadn't wanted advice. He had merely wanted a friendly, sympathetic listener to whom he could unburden himself.

When people bring you problems, they may appear to want your opinion. They may even say they need advice. But more often than not, they will thank you for simply listening. Because you help them get the problem outside themselves and on the table between you, the issues become clear and they are able to arrive at their own decision.

Good Listeners Never Break a Confidence

One of the signs of deepening friendships is that people trust you with secrets. Little by little, you are handed morsels of information with which you could do them harm. Then they wait to see how you handle the trust. If you handle it well, they breathe a sigh of relief and tell you more.

So the cardinal rule for every person who desires deeper relationships is: Learn to zipper your lip. Nothing causes people to clam up and to abandon your friendship more quickly than to discover that you have revealed a private matter.

If you are a leaky repository, others are sure to learn of it. When you tell one other person a fact told you in secret, you identify yourself to the listener as an untrustworthy confidant. A man does not have to be very smart to conclude that if you would tell him someone *else's* secret, you'll probably tell someone else *his* secret.

Alan Loy McGinnis

7: KINDNESS

An excerpt from the autobiography of the Russian poet, Yevgeny Yevtushenko (see also page 119). He was born in 1933 and his poems were first published in 1952. He is particularly noted for his poem, 'Babiy Yar', an attack on Soviet anti-semitism.

This is a true story written by a young Russian about himself. He describes a time when he was fifteen and working as a labourer in Siberia which is a particularly cold and harsh area of Russia.

One day I discovered I had lice. My clothes were teeming with the filthy vermin. I was in despair, I didn't know what to do.

I ran off into the steppe and climbed down into an abandoned dig. There I took off my clothes and set about killing the lice. Somewhere high above me the grass rustled, the birds sang and the clouds billowed; while I stood hating myself, naked, alone, shivering with cold and disgust at the bottom of my pit with the frogs giving me scornful looks.

I couldn't change my clothes because I had no others.

Suddenly I started as it grew darker in the pit and, looking up through the rectangular opening, saw a young peasant woman, bare-footed and with a yoke slung over her shoulders, standing on the edge.

I leant hard against the side of the pit, wishing I could vanish into the earth, and sobbed with shame, covering my face with my hands.

There was a soft thud as the woman jumped down.

She pulled my hands away from my face. Intensely blue eyes between long black lashes looked at me with a warm kindness which is much better than pity.

'What are you crying for, you silly child?' asked the woman. 'Come along with me.'

I pulled on my clothes somehow and, hanging my head in confusion, followed her.

She lit the stove in her bath house, scrubbed me like a child, steamed my clothes and put me to bed.

That night as I lay on a wooden trestle-bed under a sheepskin coat, she came over in her nightdress and sat on the edge of the bed.

'Feeling better now, you silly? How could you get in such a state? You mustn't be afraid of people, people will always help you if you're in trouble.'

She stroked my hair.

I jerked back and began to cry again. I was so repulsive to myself, I felt I could only be repulsive to everyone else.

'What a fuss. I suppose you've got it into your head that you're disgusting. You're not in the least.'

She lay down by me under the sheepskin, her big

strong body with its clean, bath-house smell of birch leaves pressed against mine.

I shall never forget her.

Ever since then I have known that if all the values in this world are more or less questionable, the most important thing in life is kindness.

Yevgeny Yevtushenko

3
Fables for our times

1: AESOP'S FABLES

We know very little about Aesop except that by the fifth century BCE his was a familiar name in Greece and he was spoken of as 'the author of (all) the fables'. In fact, what are known as Aesop's Fables are probably a collection of different people's stories.

Aesop's Fables are not particularly 'moral' (one or two are distinctly amoral and merely guides to self-preservation). The lessons they generally teach are those of wisdom, prudence and worldly wisdom. They have a wide appeal to young and older children. If the latter are alerted to the fact that these are 'stories with a meaning', they may not need the moral pointing out but may appreciate deducing it for themselves.

Sour grapes

A hungry fox tried to reach some clusters of grapes which he saw hanging from a vine trained on a tree, but they were too high. So he went off and comforted himself by saying: 'They weren't ripe anyhow.'

In the same way some men, when they fail through their own incapacity, blame circumstances.

Forewarned is forearmed

A farmer was confined to his homestead by bad weather. Unable to go out and find food, he began by eating his sheep; and as the storms still continued, it was the goats' turn next. Finally, since the rain did not cease, he was driven to slaughtering his plough oxen.

At this the dogs, who had been watching what he did, said to each other: 'We had better make ourselves scarce. If the master doesn't spare even the oxen which share his labour, how can we expect him to keep his hands off us?'

Beware above all of people who do not shrink from ill-using their friends.

What a piece of work is man!

(Zeus was regarded by ancient Greeks as the greatest of the gods.)

According to tradition the animals were fashioned before man, and Zeus endowed them with various powers, such as strength, and swiftness of foot or wing. Man, standing naked before him, complained that he alone was left without any such endowment. 'You do not appreciate what has been given you,' said Zeus. 'You have received the greatest gift of all – the gift of reason, which is all-powerful in heaven and on earth, stronger than the strong, swifter than the swift.' This made man realize what had been vouchsafed him, and he departed with adoration and thanksgiving.

Although all men have been favoured by God with the gift of reason, some are insensible of this privilege and choose rather to envy creatures which lack the faculties of perception and rational thought.

Aesop

2: THE BEAR WHO LET IT ALONE

A fable by James Thurber (see also page 47). This one teaches the importance of moderation.

This story has a moral – a 'meaning'. As you listen, try to make up your mind what that moral is.

In the woods of the Far West there once lived a brown bear who could take it or let it alone. He would go into a bar where they sold mead, a fermented drink made of honey, and he would have just two drinks. Then he would put some money on the bar and say, 'See what the bears in the back room will have,' and he would go home. But finally he took to drinking by himself most of the day. He would reel home at night, kick over the umbrella stand, knock down the bridge lamps, and ram his elbows through the windows. Then he would collapse on the floor and lie there until he went to sleep. His wife was greatly distressed and his children were very frightened.

At length the bear saw the error of his ways and began to reform. In the end he became a famous teetotaller and a persistent temperance lecturer. He would tell everybody that came to his house about the awful effects of drink, and he would boast about how strong and well he had become since he gave up touching the stuff. To demonstrate this, he would stand on his head and on his hands and he would turn cartwheels in the house, kicking over the umbrella stand, knocking down the bridge lamps, and ramming his elbows through the windows. Then he would lie down on the floor, tired by his healthful exercise, and go to sleep. His wife was greatly distressed and his children were very frightened.

MORAL: *You might as well fall flat on your face as lean over too far backward.*

James Thurber

3: DIVIDING THE CAMELS

This story is a Sufi tale. Sufism is a sect of Islam. Sufis seek to come close to God through self-denial, prayer and other spiritual exercises. Sufis have also sought to know God through such practices as fire-walking and gyratory dancing (the 'whirling Dervishes'). Sufism has sometimes been at odds with orthodox Islam but many Sufis have been respected teachers and storytellers.

It is important in life to know whom to trust and whom to respect. How do you decide if someone is wise or not? This is a story, or parable, about a Sufi, an Eastern religious teacher, a group of his followers, or disciples, and how they found a wise teacher.

There was once a Sufi who wanted to make sure that his disciples would, after his death, find the right teacher of the Way for them.

He therefore, after the obligatory bequests laid down by law, left his disciples seventeen camels, with this order:

'You will divide the camels among the three of you in the following proportions: the oldest shall have half, the middle in age one-third, and the youngest shall have one-ninth.

As soon as he was dead and the will was read, the disciples were at first amazed at such an inefficient disposition of their Master's assets. Some said, 'Let us own the camels communally,' others sought advice and then said, 'We have been told to make the nearest possible division,' others were told by a judge to sell the camels and divide the money; and yet others held that the will was null and void because its provisions could not be executed.

Then they fell to thinking that there might be some hidden wisdom in the Master's bequest, so they made inquiries as to who could solve insoluble problems.

Everyone they tried failed, until they arrived at the door of the son-in-law of the Prophet, Hazrat Ali. He said:

'This is your solution. I will add one camel to the number. Out of the eighteen camels you will give half — nine camels — to the oldest disciple. The second shall have a third of the total, which is six camels. The last disciple may have one-ninth, which is two camels. That makes seventeen. One — my camel — is left over to be returned to me.'

This was how the disciples found the teacher for them.

Idries Shah

4: THE MANGO TREE

A story intended to encourage sibling affection.

In India, there is a time in March when all girls pray for their brothers: that no harm will come to them. Today's reading is an Indian story that reminds us that we should remember our brothers and sisters and pay attention to them when they ask us to do something that really matters to them.

In a small town, there was a small house in which lived a young man, his wife, and the young man's sister. This small house had a small garden at the back in which grew a small mango tree. One day the young man's wife came to him and said, 'Look here, I'm fed up with our situation. Your sister . . .'

'Have you come here to complain about my sister again?'

'What can I do? I know it's quite useless . . . my complaints fall on deaf ears, anyway . . . I'm just . . . so angry with your sister. I get up early in the morning, draw water from the well, light the fire in the kitchen, cook breakfast, wash and scrub pots . . .'

'Don't go on,' said the brother. 'I've heard it all before.'

'And what does your lazy sister do all day? Nothing . . . nothing . . . she lolls about in the garden, watering her mango tree, talking to it, clearing away dead leaves, and feeding it manure and mulch . . .'

'That isn't all she does. She comes in and talks to me. Just an hour ago, she was playing chess with me.'

'Just because she adores you, doesn't mean you should ignore her faults. You must tell her to leave that . . . silly mango tree alone, and come and help me with the housework. I really think we should marry her off.

That might teach her to be a bit more responsible.'

Since the sister was of marriageable age, the brother could not really object. He knew though, that he would miss her very, very much.

A marriage was arranged. When all the ceremonies were over, and the sister was about to leave with her groom to lead a new life in a new town, she turned to her sister-in-law and said, 'Dearest sister-in-law, I'm going to miss my mango tree so much. Would you please do me a great favour and look after it for me? Please water it well and clear the weeds that grow in its shadow.'

'Oh, well, yes, yes,' answered the sister-in-law.

Once the sister had left, the sister-in-law turned to her husband and yelled, 'Did you hear that? Did you *hear* that? Did you hear your selfish sister? She didn't say that she was going to miss you. She didn't say that she was going to miss me. She *did* say that she was going to miss her mango tree!' She decided then that she was going to ignore the mango tree. The mango tree irritated her just as much as her husband's sister had. Now she could be rid of both.

As the days passed, the unwatered, uncared for mango tree started drying up and its leaves began to fall.

At the same time, the brother, who had been a strong, robust and healthy young man, began to lose his appetite and get thinner and weaker.

One day, a letter arrived. It was from the sister and said, 'Dearest brother and sister-in-law. I hope all is well and that my tree is green and that my brother is in good health.'

The remaining leaves of the mango tree were quite yellow by this time, but the sister-in-law wrote back, 'Dearest sister. Your tree is fine, but your brother has not been feeling so good.'

Soon another letter arrived from the sister. 'Are you sure my tree is green? And how is my brother?'

Fables for our times

The mango tree only had one brown leaf left on it now, and the brother was so sick that the doctors said that he could not live. So the sister-in-law wrote back. 'Your tree is fine, but the doctors have given up all hopes for your brother.'

When the sister received this letter, she raced back to her small hometown and went straight into the small garden to water her small tree. As she watered it, cleared the weeds around it, and mulched it, it began slowly to turn green.

The brother too, began to recover.

As more leaves returned to the tree, the brother's cheeks got pinker and his eyes became brighter. Within a month, the tree was healthy and strong.

And so was the brother.

It was only then that the sister turned to her sister-in-law and said, 'Now do you understand? It was not the tree that I loved, but my brother. It was not the tree whose welfare I was concerned with, but my brother's. The tree and my brother share a common soul. It was my duty to look after them both.'

Madhur Jaffrey

5: THE OLD WOMAN AT THE BUS STOP

A true story told by a Roman Catholic priest, designed to make its listeners decide what moral it teaches them. That is, do we resign ourselves to the thought in the last paragraph or, if not, for what must we be prepared?

The storyteller in today's reading is a Roman Catholic priest. (Priests in that church do not, of course, marry.) As you listen to it, decide what lesson it has to teach us – and see if you think what the priest says at the end is inevitable.

She was a dear old soul of 89. It was a bitterly cold day, and there she was standing in a bus queue just outside my kitchen window. A bus had just gone and she would have at least twenty minutes to wait for the next.

I had just made a pot of tea, and so went out and invited her to come and share it with me before the fire. I plied her with tea and biscuits, and then took her out and helped her on to the next bus with quite a glow of affection for the dear old soul.

Two days later I met the old lady's daughter in the town, and began preening myself for the expected words of thanks. They did not come. Instead, there flowed a stream of abuse. Who did I think I was? Wasn't I even capable of making a cup of tea, without dragging in a poor old woman to make it for me? Wasn't I ashamed of making an old lady miss her bus so as to minister to my selfish needs? Just because I was a priest, did I think that everyone had to wait on me hand and foot? The passers-by slowed down to lap it up. Condemnation glinted in their eyes and disgust curled their lips. Again I had quite warm feelings for the old lady, but of a different kind.

It happened to me. It has happened to you. Some well-intentioned action is distorted and misrepresented out of all recognition. Your humility is portrayed as arrogance; your generosity as self-seeking greed. The trouble is that such treatment may well dry up yet another source of goodness in the world. I regret to say that I never invited the old lady to tea again. Heaven alone knows what I might be accused of next time.

The sad truth is that we are all so ready to judge without waiting for possession of all the truth. Facts are almost an impediment to judgement. And if people do something fine in the name of religion, they can almost expect a harsher judgement than anyone else. I recall one good young lady who was convinced that the only reason why nuns run homes for unmarried mothers was so that later the nuns could cook and eat the babies. I patiently suggested that perhaps this was untrue, and she replied: 'It is true, it was in the papers.' Nothing would convince her otherwise.

And so we all grow measured and cautious in what

we do for others — and the world becomes a colder place to live in.

Father Robert Manley

6: THE TIGER WHO WOULD BE KING

A fable by James Thurber which warns of the dangers of greed, power-seeking and/or war.

You may wish to explain the following word to your listeners: gibbous — between half and full moon

This story has a moral — a 'meaning'. As you listen, try to make up your mind what that moral is.

One morning the tiger woke up in the jungle and told his mate that he was king of beasts.

'Leo, the lion, is king of beasts,' she said.

'We need a change,' said the tiger. 'The creatures are crying for a change.'

The tigress listened but she could hear no crying, except that of her cubs.

'I'll be king of beasts by the time the moon rises,' said the tiger. 'It will be a yellow moon with black stripes, in my honour.'

'Oh, sure,' said the tigress as she went to look after her young, one of whom, a male, very like his father, had got an imaginary thorn in his paw.

The tiger prowled through the jungle till he came to the lion's den. 'Come out,' he roared, 'and greet the king of beasts! The king is dead, long live the king.'

Inside the den, the lioness woke her mate. 'The king is here to see you,' she said.

'What king?' he inquired, sleepily.

'The king of beasts,' she said.

'I am the king of beasts,' roared Leo, and he charged out of the den to defend his crown against the pretender.

It was a terrible fight, and it lasted until the setting of

the sun. All the animals of the jungle joined in, some taking the side of the tiger and others the side of the lion. Every creature from the aardvark to the zebra took part in the struggle to overthrow the lion or to repulse the tiger, and some did not know which they were fighting for, and some fought for both, and some fought whoever was nearest, and some fought for the sake of fighting.

'What are we fighting for?' someone asked the aardvark.

'The old order,' said the aardvark.

'What are we dying for?' someone asked the zebra.

'The new order,' said the zebra.

When the moon rose, fevered and gibbous, it shone upon a jungle in which nothing stirred except a macaw and a cockatoo, screaming in horror. All the beasts were dead except the tiger, and his days were numbered and his time was ticking away. He was monarch of all he surveyed, but it didn't seem to mean anything.

MORAL: *You can't very well be king of beasts if there aren't any.*

James Thurber

7: WARTY BLIGGENS THE TOAD

One of don marquis' archy the cockroach poems – a warning against thinking oneself to be the centre of the universe.

You may wish to explain the following words to your listeners:
cosmos – *universe*
cerebrum – *(front part of) brain*

We all like to think that we are very important. We are in many ways but there is a danger in thinking that we are so important that everything else and everyone else exist just for our sake. We are not the centre of the universe. The speaker in this poem is called archy. He's a cockroach.

i met a toad
the other day by the name
of warty bliggens
he was sitting under
a toadstool
feeling contented
he explained that when the cosmos
was created
that toadstool was especially
planned for his personal
shelter from sun and rain
thought out and prepared
for him

do not tell me
said warty bliggens
that there is not a purpose
in the universe
the thought is blasphemy
a little more
conversation revealed
that warty bliggens
considers himself to be
the centre of the said
universe
the earth exists
to grow toadstools for him
to sit under
the sun to give him light
by day and the moon
and wheeling constellations
to make beautiful
the night for the sake of
warty bliggens

to what act of yours
do you impute
this interest on the part

Themes

of the creator
of the universe
i asked him
why is it that you
are so greatly favoured

ask rather
said warty bliggens
what the universe
has done to deserve me
if i were a
human being i would
not laugh
too complacently
at poor warty bliggens
for similar
absurdities
have only too often
lodged in the crinkles
of the human cerebrum
          archy.

don marquis

4
Living – and partly living Readings to encourage an appreciation of life

1: LIVING WITH BLINDNESS

An excerpt from the autobiography of Tomi Keitlen, a blind woman who skis, plays golf and does photography as a hobby.

Which do you think is harder: to have been blind since birth or to lose your sight as a young grown-up? This is part of the introduction to a book written by a blind woman.

I was not always blind. I did not lose my sight completely until 1955, when I was thirty-three years old. This is an advantage and a disadvantage. On the minus side, I am sharply aware of the beauty that is lost to me. On the plus side, I can draw upon a storehouse of visual memories. I know what the world looks like, and this is a tremendous help in finding my way about it. People ask me if I see anything, or if I live in a black void. Once I would have asked this question myself. Now I know how foolish it is.

When I wake in the morning I see light, because there is light. If the sun is shining I see it from the warmth on my face; or I see rain when it patters on the windows. I see if grass is green or brown by the way it smells and feels. I see birds by the flutter of their wings and the music of their songs. I know by the time of day when the sun is setting. I know from my calendar whether the moon is crescent or full. And when I turn out the lights at night to go to sleep, I see darkness.

No blind person needs to live in blankness. I see my home, my furniture, my paintings, because I furnished it myself in the style and colours I wanted. I see my friends by their affection. I see Phyllis, my daughter, in many ways. My memory shows me how she was. And I keep track of the way she grows by her words, her thoughts, her touch, her walk, her love. A few years ago I asked Phyllis for a picture of herself. She chose one that showed her picking potatoes in an open field; she wears dungarees and a flannel shirt; her bare feet toe into the earth; her hair is tousled, she holds a half bitten potato between her teeth and a dozen more in her arms. She picked that photo, she said, 'because there are so many things in it you can see.' We made a huge enlargement, and Phyllis guided my finger as I traced out her description of it. The picture hangs over my bed. Each morning I look at it.

My other senses did not become sharper after I lost my sight. I did not develop any 'sixth sense'. There is no truth to these old wives' tales. But I did learn to use my remaining four senses properly again. Each of us does this naturally when we are youngsters. Remember the smell of spring, of wet cement, of sawdust? The feel of grass and mud under bare feet? The brittle sound when the thin crust of ice on a puddle cracks in winter? The sense of eerie pressure in the air just before a thunderstorm? The taste of a snowflake?

When we grow up we take the easy way – we rely on sight. The other senses dull from disuse. We think of the loss of sight as a catastrophe. (Deafness, by comparison, is almost a subject for joking; yet communication is the essence of life, and it is much harder for the deaf to communicate than for the blind.) Only when sight goes does one realize how much of the world can come to one through the other senses.

I am not trying to convince you that 'it's fun to be

blind'. I cannot read a book or a newspaper when the spirit moves me; I must wait until someone can read it to me or until the book is available on record. I can't buy accident insurance; I must pay a special premium rate for life insurance, and even so I cannot get double indemnity. Despite the laws that permit a guide dog to accompany its blind master anywhere, I am often humiliated by being refused admission to restaurants. A hospital once refused me as a patient because my dog would have to be with me. The dog's presence, I was told, would be a 'traumatic experience to the nurses'.

Most infuriating of all is the constant battle to be treated as a normal person, to avoid being segregated as one of 'the blind'. My biggest problem is not blindness, but society's attitude towards it. Once when I was looking for a job an employment agency kept suggesting I work with a blind service organization.

'Why do you keep pushing me in that direction?' I asked.

'Well,' said the interviewer, 'your experience makes you valuable, and besides you're – '

He stopped short.

'I'll finish it for you,' I said. 'I'm blind too, so that's where I belong.'

Tomi Keitlen (with Norman M. Lobsenz)

2: IF ONLY I COULD WALK

An excerpt from the novel of this name which features a teenage girl suffering from spina bifida and her attempts to establish 'ordinary' friendships.

In this passage, there are two main characters. Dave is just an ordinary teenage boy. Penny lives nearby but goes to a different school. She is just an ordinary teenage girl, except that she suffers from an illness which keeps her in a wheelchair. Dave has asked her out for the first time. The reading ends with Dave saying that people should be taught a lesson. As you listen, think what that lesson is.

'Can you get out of your wheelchair in your house?' Dave asked as he steered the chair round an empty coke tin lying on the pavement.

'I can move about a bit by supporting myself on my arms but I can't stand,' said Penny.

'What's wrong with you exactly?' Dave enquired in a puzzled voice.

'Spina bifida,' Penny replied.

'Spiner what?' asked Dave. 'Sorry,' he added as he jerked the chair over a stone.

'It means my muscles don't work below my waist because something's wrong with the lower part of my backbone. I was born like that,' Penny explained. 'That's why I look a mess.'

'You must be joking,' said Dave. 'You're really pretty with your golden hair, don't worry about that.'

Penny's freckled face went scarlet. Dave didn't sound as if he was trying to be kind.

Dave was speaking the truth for although Penny believed she looked odd, except that her legs were rather shapeless she looked just like anyone else.

'I wouldn't mind being pushed about in the chair,' Dave said. 'No, I suppose I'd get fed up after a bit,' he decided.

Penny was silent. No one had ever talked about her handicap like this before. Most people took care not to mention it but if they did they spoke in an awkward way as if it embarrassed them. But Dave spoke quite openly making it sound ordinary.

They turned into the main road. Almost at once they reached a big, modern shopping centre. Whenever she had the chance Penny would look into the shop windows. She would gaze at dresses attractively displayed, at televisions, radios and cassette players jammed together, at rows of fashion shoes in which she would never walk, at shelves of bread giving off a delicious smell of baking. When she was among crowds of shoppers Penny felt she was part of the world, part of everyday life.

Among so many people Dave found it hard to manage the wheelchair. He caught a man's heel with one of the wheels. The man swore at Dave. Dave swore back.

Now as Dave weaved the chair among the shoppers Penny hoped he wasn't feeling sorry he had brought her out. Suddenly a woman grabbed her little girl and dragged her towards a shop.

'I wouldn't have run your little girl over, I was nowhere near her, missis,' said Dave loudly.

The woman didn't answer. Penny explained that people often stared at her and then moved away fast. She glanced at Dave's face. He looked as if he didn't believe her. A little further on Dave stopped outside a café called Dick's Eating Place.

'Ever been here?' Dave asked.

'No,' said Penny as a woman with two children came out of the café. The woman looked hard at Penny then turned away hurrying the children before her.

'Go on, run!' roared Dave, 'you might catch a deadly illness, you never know!'

The woman didn't actually run but she grabbed both children and walked on as fast as she could.

Dave was furious. 'People like her need to be taught a lesson.'

Myra Schneider

3: TREES FOR LIFE

A reading to remind us of the importance of trees and the interdependence of all forms of life.

Today we are thinking about why trees are so important and why we need to conserve them and replace those that die.

A tree supports life in many different ways. It is central

to the feeding pattern of many living things. An essential part of conservation is an understanding of the idea that all living things are dependent on each other. On our earth there is a tremendous variety of forms of life, which all have to share what the earth provides. You and I are no exception. We must share the environment with all of the world's animals, plants and all other living organisms. We are all dependent on each other for survival. We breathe oxygen, which is continually added to the air by trees and other green plants. In turn, we breathe out carbon dioxide which is needed by trees and green plants for their own energy. Eventually, all plant and animal life dies. When leaves, plants and creatures decay they can put back essential goodness into the soil for new life to use. Both humans and animals depend on plants for food. Without plant life there would be no animals – without plants and animals, no food for humans.

Berries and nuts gleaned from the forests formed a substantial element in the diet of our early ancestors. Today, trees throughout the world still provide an incredible range of edible goods which are one of the most nutritious and valuable components of our modern diet. Fruits and nuts are available in abundance and the modern world's well-developed systems of growing, harvesting, trading and transportation allow those of us in cooler lands easy access to fruits from warmer places – for instance, peaches, figs, nectarines, oranges, grapefruits, lemons, limes, tangerines and apricots, plus the dozens of tropical tree fruits such as mangoes and papayas. In our own climate, growers produce a wide range of foods in the fruit family, such as apples, pears, plums and cherries.

Let us consider now the importance of trees in supplying our other needs – first, at a practical level. Our world would be a very different place without wood and wood products, of which paper is the most important. Indeed, it is almost impossible to imagine our modern society without timber, books, newspapers, magazines, pencils and toilet rolls, to name but a few of the countless everyday articles that are derived from trees. Looking back into history we can, indeed, wonder how our civilization would have progressed to its present state without tree products. Primitive societies used wood for tools, weapons, drinking vessels and for fires; branches made huts and leaves their thatch. It would be fascinating to study the use of timber through the ages – for homes, furniture, tools, weapons, boats, fences and an almost infinite number of other needs of humankind. Hence the dramatic reduction in areas of natural forest with the passage of time.

In our present, sophisticated society, trees are as vital as ever. Despite the increasing availability of plastics and metals which can replace wood in many of its uses, trees are still needed in even greater quantities, both for direct use as timber and also for wood products and derived products.

Products derived by special treatments

Soap   *Disinfectant*   *Cellophane*
Paper   *Animal feeds*   *Glues*
Paint   *Lacquers*   *Varnish*
Dyes

The lives of animals, plants and people are clearly inter-related through the existence of trees. The loss of trees in our country and throughout the world is serious.

Joy Palmer

4: A HEALTHY HEART

These passages come from a booklet published by the Flora Project for Heart Disease Prevention (24–28 Bloomsbury Way, London WC1A 2PX). Although a commercially-funded organization, many of their publications are informative and reasonably objective.

Everyone would like to be fit and healthy. Fit, healthy people have more energy, look and feel better, and can generally get more out of life. For most of us though, staying fit and healthy is our own responsibility.

Here are four rules for staying fit and healthy – and keeping your heart healthy.

Don't smoke

Your body was just not designed to take in large quantities of fumes, so it's not surprising that smokers suffer much more than non-smokers from many serious diseases – especially heart disease, lung cancer and bronchitis.

But doctors have shown that it's never too late to give up or cut down on smoking. If you really can't stop, cutting down is still very worthwhile. Even if you can only manage to smoke a few less a day, it helps to reduce your risk from the serious diseases associated with cigarettes.

Keep the right weight

It stands to reason that if you pile more weight on to your body than it was designed to carry, you'll put it under a lot of strain.

In fact, if you are overweight, you may get tired easily and you'll be more likely to suffer from conditions like high blood pressure and heart disease.

But if you are the right weight you'll look better, feel better and give your body a chance to work better for you.

There is a great deal of information on ways to help you maintain your correct weight. The important thing is to *make sure* you know which foods are the most fattening – and then concentrate on cutting down on these. Often, fattening foods are the least 'filling'. For example, biscuits, cakes, sweets and chocolates are much more fattening than boiled or jacket potatoes, wholemeal bread, vegetables and fruit.

If you think you have a weight problem, consult your doctor.

Cut down on fatty foods

You are what you eat. This famous remark is very true of food and health. Because it's not just eating too much that's bad for you, but eating the wrong *kinds* of food.

Especially important is the type and amount of *fat* you eat. And many doctors now believe we eat too much saturated animal fat – which is found not only in the obvious things like fatty meat, butter, some margarines and lard, but in things like cakes, biscuits and chocolate.

Don't worry! Eating sensibly doesn't mean giving up all the meals you like. A few sensible guidelines are:

a) Where possible, choose lean meat, and cut off any visible fat. Make more use of chicken and fish. Grill rather than fry.
b) Use butter and hard fats sparingly, preferably use a soft margarine high in essential polyunsaturated fats. In general, cut down on cream and the top of the milk.
c) Use oils high in polyunsaturated fats for cooking, e.g. corn oil, sunflower oil, safflower oil. Avoid lard and other hard fats.
d) Eat more vegetables and fruit of all kinds.

Exercise regularly, especially in the holidays

Your body was designed to be active. If you use it regularly, your heart, lungs and circulation will benefit, and you'll feel fitter, too.

In the past, most people used to get enough exercise in their daily lives. But nowadays most of us – especially as we get older – need to set aside a bit of time if we want to stay fit. Just a few short exercise periods a week should be all that's needed.

5: WHY DO PEOPLE SMOKE?

Pleasure, relaxation, habit, addiction are all reasons why adults smoke. But what about young people? Why do (or don't) they smoke?

Today's reading is about smoking. Now, you may be thinking to yourself that if the dangers of smoking are so well known nowadays, why do people still smoke? Well, nearly all the grown-up smokers you see around you started before they were old enough to understand or care about damaging their health. They got into the habit, and now they feel there would be a big gap in their lives if they gave it up.

But what about when they were young?

JOE is twenty-four. He gets through about twenty cigarettes a day, though he used to smoke a lot more. He gave up for four months once, and found it hell. He was jittery, on edge and bad tempered, so he started again. This is his story:

'I started smoking at school at the age of twelve. I did it because at that age I wanted to look big, and more grown-up. I wanted to impress the girls too. Also it was against the rules, and that made a big difference. We were told by our teachers that anyone caught with a packet of cigarettes would be expelled, so it was an exciting thing to do. I think if the teacher had said, "OK, let's all have a smoke", we would have said "no way".

'The first time I smoked I threw up all over the place, but I had another one because I thought it looked good standing on the corner of the street. The trouble is that when you're very young your biggest ambition is to be older and to be able to say that you are going down the pub with friends, having a drink and a smoke. At that age statistics don't mean a thing. It's all image. By the age of sixteen I realised I couldn't give up. Before that it had never crossed my mind that I was "a smoker", and that I probably would be all my life. I certainly didn't want to be, but you get hooked. The thing is a lot of people who don't smoke tell you there's no pleasure in it. I say nonsense. Smoking definitely feels good, and it's very relaxing. But you don't start smoking because you need to feel relaxed. You start to smoke because you want to look good. Then you get dependent on what it does for you, and you can't give it up.'

MARGARET is now seventeen, and she has been smoking since she was thirteen. She and a friend used to hide from their parents on the stairs outside their flats smoking. Margaret says, 'My mum and dad smoke, and I just thought it's what adults do. I started smoking to look grown-up. I used to save lemonade bottles and things to get enough money for fags. Then I got caught by my mum and she was furious. That put me off for a while, but then all my friends in school were smoking — hiding in the toilets and passing the cigarettes along the line, and I took it up again.

'My mum and dad hate me smoking though they smoke a lot themselves. It's probably because they've got to the stage of knowing what it does to you. I wouldn't like to see a picture of my lungs now, but I can't see them so I'm not really bothered, though I do get a bad cough every winter. I get fed up with smoking when I've got no money left for other things, but I've got no will power and I don't think I could stop now.'

EILEEN's story is a bit different. She is now sixteen and she too started smoking at thirteen. But she has never really liked it. 'I got in with a crowd and they were all smoking. I couldn't be the only one left out. And at discos and things you can't sit with a bar of chocolate in your hand. For me it's the action, not the cigarette. I don't enjoy smoking — it makes me sick, and I know inside it's a horrible habit. But when all your friends are smoking, it's hard to resist the pressure.'

Eileen found it difficult to resist the pressure, but there are lots of people who don't smoke. Some have never felt tempted to try. Some have tried and felt too bad to try again. And some have very positive reasons for not smoking...

LINSEY MACDONALD is seventeen. About six years ago she took up running seriously, and when she was only sixteen she won a bronze medal at the Olympic games in Moscow. She broke the British 400 metre record, and recently she broke the British record for the 600 metres as well. Linsey says:

'I have never smoked because I was always interested in sports. You have to be at your peak of health if you want to be any good in sport, and you can never reach that peak if you smoke. I've never been under any pressure to try it. Some of my friends at school do smoke, but I think they're the odd ones out. I think it could be classed as old-fashioned nowadays. It's not necessarily the done thing any more. That's my experience anyway.'

JANE is now twenty-six, and she has never been a smoker. 'It sounds strange, but I don't smoke for the very reason people do start smoking. When I was younger at parties and things I thought people who were just starting looked silly puffing smoke in and out quickly, not knowing how to hold a cigarette and a glass at the same time, and getting smoke in their faces so that their eyes watered. I knew I'd probably be the same, and I didn't want to make a fool of myself. Then you get past the stage where everyone is experimenting and people don't pressurise you any more anyway. The main advantage of not smoking is that when you go out with friends it makes you feel good to be the one who isn't skint. You can usually pay your way when others are often hanging around wondering whether anyone will pay for them.'

Sue Armstrong

6: ALCOHOL ABUSE

Alcohol abuse is on the increase; there are said to be half a million alcoholics in the country. It is a problem that involves ever younger people. Many under-age drinkers are reported as having had their first alcoholic drink during school hours. This passage has been included because it is informative rather than sensational.

Many people think 'a drink' (meaning alcohol) doesn't do you any harm. It's fun. 'We all like a drink,' we say. But what is alcohol and what does it do?

Many people who condemn hard drugs find alcohol socially acceptable. Teetotallers (those who do not drink alcohol at all) are frequently regarded as rather eccentric. Yet it can be argued that alcohol causes as much ill health and social disturbance as any other drug and should be reckoned a major evil in our society.

Way back in the earliest times men have known and used the effects of alcohol. Probably the most common was by chewing certain plants and then spitting them out. The spittle (owing to its enzyme ingredient amylase) had the effect of converting starch into sugar. In Bolivia and Peru the best beer (chicha) is still made from maize that has been well chewed by the Indian women. In other parts of the world malt came to be used to replace spittle.

In the Middle Ages, beer was the most common drink. It consisted of about one part alcohol to twenty parts water, a relatively harmless mixture. It was a Franciscan friar, Raymond Lilly, who died in 1315, who discovered how to distil wines and beers. Wine is about four times as strong as beer, and spirits consist of about half alcohol and half water.

Alcohol is absorbed into the blood stream immediately, thus reaching every cell in the body. It is not a stimulant but a sedative, and has a depressant effect on the brain. Drinkers may feel a freedom from social inhibition and enjoy a more cheerful frame of mind, but alcohol also diminishes the powers of judgement and the ability to make rational thought. Addiction grows slowly, and people can often fool themselves that they are less dependent on alcohol than in fact they are.

Taken in excess over a long period, alcohol can have serious consequences for the individual, both mental and physical. It can cause cirrhosis of the liver and alcoholic gastritis. There are about 500,000 alcoholics in this country.

Perhaps the social effects of alcohol are even more terrible. The dreadful plight of a family where father or mother is a chronic alcoholic is well-known. Their financial situation is often grim, but worse is the violence that so often accompanies extreme drunkenness.

On the road, drunken drivers are at best a danger, at worst a death-trap.

Because even just a few drinks impair physical and mental functioning, the commonest hazard to the alcoholic is physical injury, for instance from falling or from driving badly. About one-third of drivers and up to a quarter of all adult pedestrians killed in road accidents have blood alcohol levels above the legal limits.

In the nineteenth century, temperance preachers used to talk in severe tones about 'demon drink'. Probably most people would laugh today — but is it really so funny?

Angela Cotton

7: DRUGS: A CASE HISTORY

Obviously this is a passage to be used with discretion, especially in the lower school. Drugs do however remain a problem that is not solved by being ignored.

You probably think you will be able to say 'No' if anyone tries to tempt you into drug taking. But you need to be warned that the first time you are offered drugs it is most unlikely to be by a dirty man in a raincoat pestering you on the way home from school. It will be by someone you know at a party, disco or amusement arcade. *You'll be teased and called a coward if you say no. This is the story of a boy who said yes.*

'I first started taking drugs when I was about fifteen. At that age in the groups I mixed with it was just the thing to do. Then I wanted to keep on trying something new all the time. It made me feel more grown up. There may be a price to pay, but you don't think about that. Anyway, you feel that it will be paid a long time in the future.

'When I left school I couldn't get a job, and I had very little to do. Taking drugs was an exciting life-style and it filled the time.

'I'd like to make it clear I wanted it myself. No pusher pushed it on to me. I don't blame anyone. And I got fixes among my friends.

'Some people seem to think that the only drug addicts are down and outs and doss people. It isn't true. There are lots of them at the universities. We don't necessarily look like drop-outs either. I used to hate my greasy hair and leather jackets. You don't have to be a sensational problem to be a drug addict.

'The first time I took heroin I was sick. People said, "Oh, it's all right, you'll get over it". Soon I found it was the feeling I really wanted. Many people say that they take heroin and they feel they can do it again and again. After a while, though, it's not something you do because you want to, but because you have to. And you know all the time the risk you run. A few years ago heroin came much purer than it does now. You don't know whether there is talcum powder or weed-killer in it. I even heard of one girl who took a dose with strychnine in it. She became totally mentally disabled.

'When you come off you feel terribly depressed. I've spent hours and hours wandering around Hyde Park thinking and thinking what I'm going to do with myself. You get all thrown up emotionally too. I've thrown up abominable behaviour in pubs. There are great swings of mood. Sometimes I'd be laughing around, another I'd be curled up in a ball, shaking.

'One awful side to it is that you can hardly escape becoming a criminal. Some of the girls take the easy way out and become prostitutes. I just couldn't do that. I took to thieving. I remember I was even able to feel disgusted with myself when I stole from my parents.

'Gradually, all decency goes. Your home doesn't matter. Your studies don't matter. Your exams don't matter. Your face, dress, don't matter. You become a drug — with a body attached.

'At last I decided I wanted to be done with it. I didn't go to a doctor. I went to a little house in the country with friends. It's hard going on your own, although my friends were wonderful. People who feel they need more trained help go to a drug dependency unit.

'The hardest thing about coming off for me was that I lost all the friends I had before and during the time I became an addict. Most of my family didn't want to know me.

'On heroin life is very narrow. You can only think of your little smack and where you will get it. Afterwards, you notice the grass is green, the road winds, the sky is blue.'

Angela Cotton

8: CRY FOR MY LOST SON

Each user of this book must make his or her own decision about whether it is appropriate to use this passage in a particular assembly. This is a true, personal account taken from the Dublin Evening Herald *of what it is like to be the mother of a drug addict.*

Brian was a Dublin man who was a heroin addict for all his adult life.

But his fourteen years on drugs, at one stage taking over £700 worth a week, and his fight to get off them were as much a struggle against hardship and pain for his mother as they were for himself.

Throughout those years, she stood by him – until last November, off heroin, he committed suicide.

He left her a note asking her to take care of herself, telling her he would always love her.

She feels strongly that he took his life because he craved for heroin and wanted to spare her and his family any more pain. A month after he died, she sat down and wrote how she felt about it all in a small copybook.

This is her story.

I write this for my son, Brian, a drug addict for fourteen years.

He died aged twenty-nine years in November 1985, not a drug addict as you will know if you read my story. For when he died he was off drugs for a year after being in a clinic.

Why am I writing? You may ask, so what? I want the whole world to know what it is like to see the son you love destroy himself with heroin, the hell he lived through, my fourteen years of hell watching him.

My son was a healthy baby, like my other two sons and daughter. He was a very happy child – did the same things other little boys did, playing football, marbles, going fishing.

I don't want sympathy for me or my dead son. Maybe my story will help other addicts if they are not too far gone to stop. This story is also for those who said – not to my face – my son is a junkie.

To me, it was like having a crippled child or somebody dying of cancer. Only worse. You can't look after them and if they don't agree with what you try to tell them, there is nothing you can do.

You feel so helpless just watching them destroy themselves. If he was sick or crippled I could have had him treated.

Yes, my son committed suicide. You will know from my story why.

When he reached his teens he got into bad company. When he was fifteen years old, he was tall for his age, over six feet. He used to hang around St Stephen's Green and got mixed up with the drug family there. I did not know at that time he was on drugs. A friend told me he was hanging around the Green.

I worked on Grafton Street at the time and used to look for him. Sometimes I'd find him, sometimes not.

I only found out for sure about his drug problem when he was nineteen. His father found out and put him out of the house. His father died seven years ago, RIP. He had a heart problem.

So I started into the nightmare of my son going missing for weeks at a time. He would come into my job. I would give him money for food and buy him clothes as he used to be so shabby.

Sometimes he would come home with me. Other times, he said he would meet me, then would not turn up. I used to be so upset. I could not sleep.

I used to search for him, getting taxis at all hours. I got to know the boys he used to hang around with. Most of them are dead now.

Some of them used to tell me where he was. Others would not.

I remember going to an address one night. I found my son with six other guys stoned out of their heads. I could not get him to come home.

I used to pay a hostel for him by the week, knowing he might make it there at night as it was in the city centre.

So all my years of battle with my son had to end in death. I loved my son so much. He was special to me, always the perfect gentleman with perfect manners.

When he was younger, he was expelled from two schools, not because he knew nothing. A headmaster told me he had a super brain but was behind in class.

He was big for his age and wanted to be the leader. But he was harmless. The only harm he was to himself.

Living – and partly living

When he was twenty he went into a clinic for his addiction. A doctor told me he wouldn't see twenty-one. But he came out of the clinic and for nine months seemed to be all right. So the years went by. Sometimes he was stoned and sometimes he was all right. But in 1982, he met somebody who got him into chequebooks . . . forging cheques.

From then on he was drugged day and night. I tried talking to him, pleaded with him but he would not listen. This went on for a year then the law caught up with him and he was sent to prison.

I used to visit him. He cried to me once and explained about heroin.

He said it was like a god.

I had been ill before he went to prison and used to wonder why he went out of the house every morning, leaving me without a cup of tea or any shopping.

I found out he was running out every morning to get a fix. I thought he did not care about me. In fact he really loved me. But the craving for his heroin was stronger.

I had some good times too. That is what I want to remember about him.

He loved parties and always had a joke. He made our home so alive. He would always be shouting "Ma", and if he did not like what I was wearing, he would say as he was the type who dressed well.

He was the type who, if he walked into a room, people turned to look. He was very handsome and girls just fell over him.

On that last Friday night, he went to the local pub with his brother. They both had four pints and came home. Brian had his supper, said "Goodnight Ma" and went to bed. That was the last time I saw him alive.

The next morning was a dark and drizzly day. I slept late as all that week I was ill with the 'flu. Brian was doing the housework and bringing me food.

I came downstairs, made myself a cup of coffee and

smoked a cigarette. I looked at the clock and it was lunchtime. I said to myself I had better call Brian and see did he want anything to eat.

I went into his room and called him. But he would not answer. So I shook him. Still no answer. I pulled back his curtains and noticed he was a funny colour. He was still breathing. Once, he opened his eyes and then closed them again.

I phoned for an ambulance. My other son went with Brian to the hospital.

He phoned me later on and said Brian was in intensive care. What he did not tell me until well after Brian had died was that the doctors told him on arrival he was clinically dead.

That evening, I kept phoning the hospital to be told there was no change. I could not understand. I thought he would be pumped out and that he would be all right.

I was in Brian's room when I noticed a writing pad and pen on his dressing table. I went over and opened it and there was a goodbye note to me.

He told me to take care of myself and that he loved me. I knew from that note that he had had it planned.

He was on a machine for five days, but finally he died.

5
Today's society

1: THE DEFEAT OF THE MALE

An excerpt from Betsy Byars' humorous novel, The Eighteenth Emergency. *It is a warning to would-be macho males and perhaps an encouragement to all women.*

Today we have part of an American story about a boy called Mouse. His real name is Benjamin Fawley. One recess (school break), he and some other boys have what they think is a very clever idea.

One recess long ago the boys had decided to put some girls in the school trash cans. It had been one of those suggestions that stuns everyone with its rightness. Someone had said, 'Hey, let's put those girls over there in the trash cans!' and the plan won immediate acceptance. Nothing could have been more appropriate. The trash cans were big and had just been emptied and in an instant the boys were off chasing the girls and yelling at the tops of their lungs.

It had been wonderful at first, Mouse remembered. Primitive blood had raced through his body. The desire to capture had driven him like a wild man through the school yard, up the sidewalk, everywhere. He understood what had driven the cave man and the barbarian because this same passion was driving him. Putting the girls in the trash cans was the most important challenge of his life. His long screaming charge ended with him red-faced, gasping for breath – and with Viola Angotti pinned against the garbage cans.

His moment of triumph was short. It lasted about two seconds. Then it began to dim as he realized, first, that it *was* Viola Angotti, and second that he was not going to be able to get her into the garbage can without a great deal of help.

He cried, 'Hey, you guys, come on, I've got one,' but behind him the school yard was silent. Where was everybody? he had wondered uneasily. As it turned out, the principal had caught the other boys, and they were all being marched back in the front door of the school, but Mouse didn't know this.

He called again, 'Come on, you guys, get the lid off this garbage can, will you?'

And then, when he said that, Viola Angotti had taken two steps forward. She said, 'Nobody's putting *me* in no garbage can.' He could still remember how she had looked standing there. She had recently taken the part of the Statue of Liberty in a class play, and somehow she seemed taller and stronger at this moment than when she had been in costume.

He cried, 'Hey you guys!' It was a plea. 'Where are you?'

And then Viola Angotti had taken one more step, and with a faint sigh she had socked him in the stomach so hard that he had doubled over and lost his lunch. He hadn't known it was possible to be hit like that outside a boxing ring. It was the hardest blow he had ever taken. Viola Angotti could be heavyweight champion of the world.

As she walked past his crumpled body she had said again, 'Nobody's putting me in no garbage can.' It had sounded like one of the world's basic truths. The sun will rise. The tides will flow. Nobody's putting Viola Angotti in no garbage can.

Later, when he thought about it, he realized that he had been lucky. If she had wanted to, Viola Angotti could have capped her victory by tossing his rag-doll body into the garbage can and slamming down the lid.

Then when the principal came out on the playground calling, 'Benjamin Fawley! Has anybody seen Benjamin Fawley?' he would have had to moan, 'I'm in here.' He would have had to climb out of the garbage can in front of the whole school. His shame would have followed him for life. When he was a grown man, people would still be pointing him out to their children, '*That's* the man that Viola Angotti stuffed into the garbage can.'

Betsy Byars

2: EQUAL RIGHTS

A story to encourage girls to seek rights they do not always see as theirs and to help boys to see what is unfair about an inequality.

If an advert says, 'Paper boy wanted', should a girl be allowed to apply for the job? And, if she gets it, should she be paid the same as a boy?

'Can't you read?'

The man was looking at me and reaching under the counter as if he was going for his gun. He came up with another of his signs to spread over the front of a paper. ' "Only two children at a time allowed in this shop",' he read out loudly.

I looked across at the two kids in the corner. They were pretending to pick Penny Chews while they gawped at the girls on the magazines. OK, I made three, but I wasn't there for the same reason as them. Couldn't he recognize business when he saw it?

'I'm not buying,' I said, 'I've come about the job.'

He frowned at me, in between watching the boys in the corner. 'What job?' he said. He was all on edge with three of us in the shop.

' "Reliable paper boy wanted",' I told him. ' "Enquire within". It's in the window. I'm enquiring within.'

'Hurry up, you two!' he shouted. And then he

frowned at me again as if I was something from outer space.

' "Reliable paper *boy* required", that says. If I'd meant "boy *or girl*" I'd have put it on, wouldn't I? Or "paper *person*"!' He did this false laugh for the benefit of a man with a briefcase standing at the counter.

'Oh,' I said, disappointed. 'Only I'm *reliable*, that's all. I get up early with my dad, I'm never off school, and I can tell the difference between the *Sun* and the *Beano*.'

'I'm glad someone can,' the man with the briefcase said.

But the paper man didn't laugh. He was looking at me, hard.

'Where d'you live?' he asked.

'Round the corner.'

'Could you start at seven?'

'Six, if you like.'

'Rain or shine, winter or summer?'

'No problem.' I stared at him, and he stared at me. He looked as if he was deciding whether or not to give women the vote.

'All right,' he said, 'I'll give you a chance. Start Monday. Seven o'clock, do your own marking-up. Four pounds a week, plus Christmas tips. Two weeks' holiday without pay . . .'

Now that he'd made up his mind he smiled at me over-doing the big favour.

'Is that what the boys get?' I asked. 'Four pounds a week?'

He started unwrapping a packet of fags. 'I don't see how that concerns you. The money suits or it doesn't. Four pounds is what I said, and four pounds is what I meant. Take it or leave it.' He looked at Briefcase again, shaking his head at the cheek of the girl.

I walked back to the door. 'I'll leave it, then,' I said, 'seeing the boys get five pounds, *and* a week's holiday with pay.' I knew all this because Jason used to do it. 'Thanks anyway, I'll tell my dad what you said . . .'

'Please yourself.'

I slammed out of the shop. I was mad, I can tell you. Cheap labour, he was after; thought he was on to a good thing for a minute, you could tell that.

The trouble was, I really needed a bit of money coming in, saving for those shoes and things I wanted. There was no way I'd get them otherwise. But I wasn't going to be treated any different from the boys. I wouldn't have a shorter round or lighter papers, would I? Everything'd be the same, except the money.

I walked the long way home, thinking. It was nowhere near Guy Fawkes, and Carol Singing was even further away. So that really only left car washing – and they leave the rain to wash the cars round our way.

Hearing this baby cry gave me the idea. Without thinking about it, I knocked at the door where the bawling was coming from.

The lady opened it and stared at me like you stare at double-glazing salesmen, when you're cross for being brought to the door.

' "Baby-play calling",' I said – making up the name from somewhere.

The lady said, 'Eh?' and she looked behind me to see who was pulling my strings.

' "Baby-play",' I said. 'We come and play with your baby in your own home. Keep it happy. Or walk it out – not going across main roads.'

She opened the door a bit wider. The baby crying got louder.

'How much?' she asked.

That really surprised me. I'd felt sorry about calling from the first lift of the knocker, and here she was taking me seriously.

'I don't know,' I said. 'Whatever you think . . .'

'Well. . . .' She looked at me to see if she'd seen me before; to see if I was local enough to be trusted. Then I was glad I had the school jumper on, so she knew I could be traced. 'You push Bobby down the shops and get Mr Dawson's magazines, and I'll give you twenty pence. Take your time, mind . . .'

'All right,' I said. 'Thank you very much.'

She got this little push-chair out, and the baby came as good as gold — put its foot in the wheel a couple of times and nearly twisted its head off trying to see who I was, but I kept up the talking, and I stopped while it stared out a cat, so there wasn't any fuss.

When I got to the paper shop I took Bobby in with me.

'Afternoon,' I said, trying not to make too much of coming back. 'We've come down for Mr Dawson's papers, haven't we, Bobby?'

You should have seen the man's face.

'Mr Dawson's?' he asked, burning his finger on a match. 'Number 29?'

'Yes, please.'

'Are you . . . ?' He nodded at Bobby and then at me as if he was making some link between us.

'That's right,' I said.

He fumbled at a pile behind him and lifted out the magazines. He laid them on the counter.

'Dawson', it said on the top. I looked at the titles to see what Mr Dawson enjoyed reading.

Worker's Rights was one of them. And *Trade Union Times* was the other. They had pictures on their fronts. One had two men pulling together on a rope. The other had a woman bus driver waving out of her little window. They told you the sort of man Mr Dawson was — one of those trade union people you get on television kicking up a fuss over wages, or getting cross when women are treated different to men. Just the sort of bloke I could do with on my side, I thought.

The man was still fiddling about with his pile of magazines.

'Oh, look', he said, with a green grin. 'I've got last month's *Pop Today* left over. You can have it if you like, with my compliments . . .'

'Thanks a lot,' I said. Now I saw the link in his mind.

He thought I was Mr Dawson's daughter. He thought there'd be all sorts of trouble now, over me being offered lower wages than the boys.

'And about that job. Stupid of me, I'd got it wrong. What did I say — *four* pounds a week?'

'I think so,' I said. 'It sounded like a four.'

'How daft can you get? It was those kids in the corner. Took my attention off. Of course it's *five*, you realize that. Have you spoken to your dad yet?'

'No, not yet.'

He stopped leaning so hard on the counter. 'Are you still interested?'

'Yes. Thank you very much.'

He came round the front and shook hands with me. 'Monday at seven,' he said. 'Don't be late . . .' But you could tell he was only saying it, pretending to be the big boss.

'Right.' I turned the push-chair round. 'Say ta-ta to the man, Bobby,' I said.

Bobby just stared, like at the cat.

The paper man leaned over. 'Dear little chap,' he said.

'Yeah, smashing. But Bobby's a girl, not a chap, aren't you, Bobby? At least, that's what Mrs Dawson just told me.'

I went out of the shop, while my new boss made this funny gurgling sound, and knocked a pile of papers on the floor.

He'd made a show-up of himself, found out too late that I wasn't Mr Dawson's daughter.

I ran and laughed and zig-zagged Bobby along the pavement. 'Good for us! Equal rights, eh, Bobby? Equal rights!'

But Bobby's mind was all on the ride. She couldn't care less what I was shouting. All she wanted was someone to push her fast, to feel the wind on her face. Boy or girl, it was all the same to her.

Bernard Ashley

3: TOO MUCH TV?

A warning that too much television can kill not only the art of conversation but also relationships.

How much of the time is the television on at your home? Not enough? Too much? Always? And do you ever get the feeling that, if it is on all the time, you can't have a proper talk with a member of your family when you want to? This poem is a warning that having the television on all the time may stop us really getting to know each other.

Teevee

In the house
of Mr and Mrs Spouse
he and she
would watch teevee
and never a word
between them spoken
until the day
the set was broken.

Then 'How do you do?'
said he to she,
'I don't believe
that we've met yet.
Spouse is my name.
What's yours?' he asked.

'Why, mine's the same!'
said she to he,
'Do you suppose that we could be – ?'

But the set came suddenly right about,
and so they never did find out.

Eve Merriam

4: HEROES OFF THE SCREEN

Young people often idolize (and idealize) their sporting, pop and screen heroes and heroines. This excerpt is from the novel A Star for the Latecomer *which is about a girl called Brooke Hillary who goes to an American performing arts school (as in* Fame*).*

We all have our different heroes: sporting stars, pop stars, stars on television and in films. Sometimes we think they are perfect. Sometimes we think their lives must be ideal. But being a star doesn't mean the freedom to do just as you like and it doesn't necessarily bring happiness. In this reading, an American girl, Brooke Hillary, goes to a cinema to see a film which stars her idol, Marilyn Monroe.

The movie began and there was Marilyn up there on the screen, bigger than life, and she was moving in that sensuously innocent way she had. She was beautiful as always. She had that face, those eyes, the adoration of so many men wanting her; and whenever I saw her I wished that someday I would be like her. Then I remembered she grew up in an orphanage because her mother hadn't wanted her. No matter how much money and success she had, Marilyn wasn't supposed to have been very happy. *A star needs someone who really believes in her*, I thought, and then wondered about the people around Marilyn who made her grow into what she became. A star and a suicide. I found my thoughts drifting to my mother, about evenings when I would go out on a date, how I would ask her, 'Mom, do I look all right?'

'Of course you look all right, sweetheart. You're a beautiful girl,' she'd say. But I never felt beautiful.

She'd be sitting in the living room reading or watching television in her special chair, or sewing or just talking with my father. And she would catch me looking at myself in the hallway mirror trying to analyse my profile and small chin. She'd always catch me.

'No,' she'd say. 'You can look from now till doomsday, but you have to feel pretty inside,' she'd say, pointing towards her heart.

'I know that,' I said defensively, many times. But I didn't know how to find that place she was pointing to.

A close shot of Marilyn came on the screen, and her look was gentle, like that of a young girl in a grown-up body. It was as though she was smiling right at me, and the shot of her face, although fleeting on the screen, seemed frozen in time. Marilyn was smiling and telling me a secret. I think there are a few times in your life when some sort of truth comes thundering down on you, and on this day, in that little theatre, I thought that this was one of those times. Marilyn Monroe, behind the pounds of heavy masking powder and magical Hollywood lashes, was peering outside her image and looking right at me, Brooke Hillary, and telling me something so real that it was frightening. I could see that she had another life beneath that veneer. What she really had to say was more of a scream. Marilyn had had acting teachers tell her what to do, people who invited her to stay at their houses, men who married her, men and all of Hollywood to tell her who she was and what she had to be. But she was something else underneath, someone I saw for a second when she smiled.

Underneath this successful star was an unsuccessful woman who committed suicide. She must have been very lonely, no matter how much adoration she received. I have read that sometimes people attempt to take their own lives as a last desperate try to call out, 'Somebody help me! I need help!' No one had heard her calling out. Maybe no one had been listening to her calls for a long time. Marilyn might not have met the end she did if people hadn't tried to make her into something she wasn't. According to an article I read about her, she was very shy and it took her three hours to get dressed and put on her make-up just so she would look like the person we knew as Marilyn

Monroe. She must have been a very different person from the Hollywood image she portrayed.

Bonnie and Paul Zindel

5: ADDICTED TO GAMBLING

A reading that shows how apparently harmless teenage fruit machine and video game gambling can develop into a serious addiction.

In one year, recently, over £3,000 million was staked in betting shops. Every year hundreds of adults get into serious trouble (such as divorce, debt and even prison) – because they lose their money by gambling. There's an organization called Gamblers' Anonymous which sets out to help these people. It reported recently that 75 per cent of those who ask for their help started gambling before they were fourteen.

A Amusement arcades

Some days, twelve-year-old Simon has a packet of crisps for lunch, other days he has nothing. It isn't that his mother forgets to give him his lunch money. She gives it to him, but he has another use for it.

Every evening Simon and his friends go to the local amusement arcade. Simon always makes his way first to the Space Invaders game. The other boys spread out among various video games and fruit machines, which they all enjoy. Afterwards they go to a late-night café where they spend more money on one-armed bandits and lukewarm cups of tea!

This has been Simon's life-style for around eighteen months. He says he spends about two pounds every evening.

The money comes from various sources. Some Simon is more willing to talk about than others. 'I do a bit of gardening for my Gran, and there's my lunch money.' But he doesn't mention the fifty pence pieces he steals from his classmates' coat pockets.

Simon says his parents know about his trips to the arcade but not how frequent they are. 'Some evenings I tell them I'm off to football practice. They don't notice if there's no mud on my boots when I get back home,' he says.

Simon finds it difficult to explain why he's addicted to Space Invaders. 'It sort of fascinates me, gives me a feeling of excitement. I love everything about the game – the challenge, the colours, the noise.'

Yet Simon doesn't regard himself as an addict. 'What I'm doing is quite harmless,' he claims. 'At least I don't waste my money on fags and drink like some of my mates do.'

Gambling is increasing at an alarming rate among children. Many are becoming so hooked on gambling machines and video games that they play truant from school and become involved in petty theft. Unlike betting shops and casinos, where children are not allowed, machines and games are easily accessible in cafés and amusement arcades.

Research shows that children who start gambling in this way often graduate to betting shops and gaming clubs when they grow older.

B Horse racing

Horses are the great passion in David's life. Although he doesn't ride or own a horse, he regularly loses every pound in his pocket backing them at races.

Today he has a broken marriage and a prison sentence behind him. Ahead, he hopes, is a happier life – if he can keep off the racecourse and out of the betting shop.

David's gambling started innocently enough in the school playground, with marbles, when he was just six-years-old. Toffees and wine gums were the winnings! At nine he and his friends were playing Black Jack for pennies. As he grew older the gambling increased. Mornings were spent in amusement arcades and afternoons in the betting shop. He dodged school whenever he could, and when he started work he would disappear for hours, sometimes even days. Not surprisingly he reckons he's been hired and fired from at least twenty jobs!

When he was twenty-five, David had a chance to make a fresh start. He married and got a job as a trainee salesman in a car showroom. His charm and persuasive manner were ideal for the job. 'If you're not born that way, it's a knack you quickly acquire as a gambler,' he says. 'When you're often owing money, you have to be able to talk your way out of a sticky situation.'

After his marriage David stopped gambling for a few months. 'Then the itch started again. At first it was the odd fifty pence or one pound but it didn't stop there. Soon I was losing most, occasionally all of my week's wages. I even stole some of my wife's jewellery, including her engagement ring. She'd been very understanding till then, but I think that was the last straw.'

The end for David came when he sold a car for almost £4,000 and 'borrowed' the money to pay off his gambling debts. But he gambled that away too and was sent to prison.

Vanora Leigh

6: EMERGENCY SERVICE

The role of the Salvation Army emergency services within the United Kingdom is now accepted as the norm by the general public, who offer the Army their financial and moral support, enabling it to substantiate its claim, 'Where there's a need – there's The Salvation Army.' The following reports are examples of many incidents in which the emergency services have been involved.

When there's an accident, we expect the police, fire brigade, ambulance and rescue services to turn up. It's their job; something they're paid to do. Very often members of the Salvation Army also turn up, quite voluntarily, to help in different ways – like these:

Inferno

Fire brigade appliances rushed to a group of terraced houses in the city of Westminster. Four people had already perished in the flames, and many families were homeless. Firemen came to grips with a raging inferno, and police tried to sort out traffic chaos built up by early-morning commuters.

Amidst the frustration and chaos Salvation Army officers applied their own brand of expertise. The first of thirty families arrived at the Goodwill Centre, Hoxton, finding a place of safety and refuge. Tears were dried and fears subsided as, within the warmth of the centre, love and care were given to shocked and numbed people — many of whom could not understand the English language.

The national co-ordinator was asked to speak to a family who lost their son in the inferno. This was difficult because of the language barrier, but a hug and a squeeze of the hand were quickly interpreted as a caring and understanding gesture. For over twenty-four hours the evacuated people were fed, cared for and re-clothed by salvationists.

Lifeboat Disaster

Sixteen seamen lost their lives in a lifeboat disaster. Policemen and coastguards kept watch in winter conditions along the coastline of deserted beaches in the hope of finding survivors. The local corps officer and soldiers travelled to these difficult and sometimes almost impossible situations with soup, bread and a 'God bless you', as the watchers were encouraged to stay at their posts.

Two Salvation Army officers visited every family in the village who had been affected by the disaster. They prayed and tried to comfort those who had lost loved ones in their attempts to save lives from a stricken vessel.

Today's society

Bandstand Bombed

A terrorist bomb exploded in a bandstand in a London park. Six soldiers in the band lost their lives and eighteen persons were injured. Police headquarters alerted the national co-ordinator for emergency services at National Headquarters and soon an emergency mobile unit was given an escort as it made its way into the park. More than 300 police and military personnel were on duty, and refreshments were supplied as they commenced their task. Veteran police officers were grateful not only for the refreshments but also for the encouragement and counsel given to them by the salvationists. Those who had the gruesome task of searching for pieces of bodies were thankful for words of comfort as they returned from searching for what had once been their comrades and colleagues.

At the place where pathologist and forensic scientists worked, salvationists assisted with mortuary work. A casualty clearing desk was manned by them and relatives were counselled. Salvationists could feel and share the pain and the anguish of the rescuers who came to the Army's mobile unit for a short respite. The time given for sympathy and comfort was essential as the rescuers showed something of their grief for their lost comrades and friends.

Captain Joe Burlison

7: HOMELESS – IN THE SEARCH FOR WORK

This article is taken from a Shelter publicity leaflet and is a true account of how unemployment (and the search for work) can result in homelessness. It will serve both to increase awareness of the problems of others and as a warning.

80,000 households (or families) are officially accepted as homeless each year. Many more, especially single homeless people, are not even counted, never mind helped. The homeless are not simply tramps or people who don't 'fit in'. This is the true story of a man called David Moore, who, because he was unemployed, left his home in Scotland in search of work.

David Moore was unemployed with little hope of a job in his native Scotland. A letter offering work with a construction gang in England seemed just what he needed. Accommodation was offered as well. Being single and desperate for work, he jumped at the chance.

A long coach journey brought him to Bedford at dawn on Saturday, 17th June, with two heavy suitcases containing virtually all his belongings. The letter said that he would be met at 8.30 am and taken to the place where he was to stay. He was still waiting at the bus station at eleven o'clock that night and he had spent what little money he had.

'So,' in David's own words, 'I slept down on the embankment on the Saturday night. There was no alternative. On Monday I went to the Social Security and explained the situation and asked whether they could let me have a travel warrant back to Scotland. I made it clear that I only wanted to borrow the money and that my sister would lend me the money to pay for it as soon as I got back. But it was no good, they just said, "We don't issue warrants for people to travel up and down the country at will," and they wouldn't accept that I only wanted to borrow the money.

'I thought about hitching, but it would've been impossible with those two cases. And I couldn't leave them behind, or else I'd have nothing but what I stood up in.' David Moore then explained that he had not eaten since Saturday and that he needed money to buy food. This request was also refused. He was, however, told to sign on at the Labour Exchange as a preliminary to obtaining a Social Security payment as soon as his papers came through from Scotland. He comments: 'It was like hitting a blank wall. I spent five-and-a-half hours in those offices to go out as wise as I went in . . .'

David was alone in a strange town with just seven

pence in his pocket. He walked the streets all day and slept in the open or in derelict buildings at night. By Tuesday he was desperately hungry.

'I kept going to the DHSS but they wouldn't help until they got my records from Scotland. So the only thing I could think of was to go to the police station. I explained the situation and asked them for a bed in the cells hoping that I would get a breakfast in the morning. They just smiled and said: "No, we only keep the cells for special guests." '

Each day David would go to the railway station where he had his belongings in a locker which he could not afford to secure. He would wash, shave and change his clothing. The only people he talked to were those in a similar position to himself. No one knew where he could get help. Then he met someone sleeping rough who told him where he could get food. It was at a children's home run by nuns.

'I was starving and yet I was reluctant to go there. I felt embarrassed having to do this. I have never experienced anything like this before – having to beg for my food. But they were sympathetic and helpful. They gave me food and asked me to call back every day. But I never did that – I called back every *other* day, just enough to sustain myself.

By the end of the week he was still homeless and without money. He tried every agency he could think of 'even though I knew I was going to get a knock back, but I would not have felt content unless I had tried.' No one offered any help. At the Housing Department he asked for emergency accommodation and they looked at him, 'as though I had three heads or something.'

By this time, David Moore began to realise that his situation could drive him to steal in order to survive. He was also getting weak.

Then, after eleven days someone took him seriously.

'It was the week on the Wednesday after I arrived in Bedford. There were two girls doing a survey into general housing conditions down at the dole office. I was one of the fortunate ones to get stopped. I explained that I had no accommodation and was sleeping rough and getting no assistance here in Bedford. They wrote down an address – the Bedfordshire Housing Aid Centre, which is part of Shelter.'

It was clear that David Moore needed help immediately. We contacted everyone we knew and by evening he had a room of his own and a bed to sleep in. It was only then he received a Social Security payment.

Before he left Scotland, David did not believe that what he came to experience could happen to anyone in Britain:

'I always thought that the Welfare State would help anyone who needed it. But I was starving and no one took any notice, except Shelter. Out of the eleven days I genuinely went six of those days without anything to eat – just water – and that is true.'

Shelter

8: THE SOUP RUN

One of The Salvation Army's most vital activities is the midnight soup run, aiming to reach men and women who are homeless and destitute and who sleep rough in London's streets. (This passage will have most impact if it is used on a particularly cold day.)

Every night in London, many homeless people sleep rough on the streets, perhaps huddled up in a doorway and (if they're lucky) with a bit of sacking or cardboard for protection against the cold. Every night they are given some help by members of the Salvation Army, or Salvationists as they are known.

It is 10.30 pm and three Salvationists are hard at work in the kitchen of the Hoxton Goodwill Centre. There are no banners or bonnets and no uniforms. Workers are dressed for rough tough work and are busy emptying cans of soup into huge cauldrons heating on the stove – donations have helped supply the vast number used each night. Soon a great steaming urn full of soup is lifted into the van. Dozens of loaves follow and piles of warm clothing — shirts, jackets, shoes, trousers and pullovers.

The little blue van heads towards the midnight haunts of the homeless who sleep rough. The first stop is just off fashionable Oxford Street. There is nobody to be seen, but suddenly the piles of cardboard by the wall begin to move and fall away — not rubbish ready for the next morning's garbage truck, but men sleeping in and under cardboard boxes. Terry from Glasgow, Harry from Warrington, George from Liverpool. Soon some twenty men are waiting for supper. Everybody knows the Captain and his team. The approach is deceptively casual. Men are made to feel at ease. There is no preaching, no reproach. Recipients are almost unaware that they are being treated kindly, feeling warmed and cheered as they drink the soup and eat the bread. It is simply taken from the wrapper and handed out, but as an observer said it was like celebrating Communion as he sensed the presence of Christ.

The next stop is underneath the arches at Charing Cross. Men are no longer allowed to sleep there, but wait for the soup, bread and perhaps a warm pullover. Afterwards they wander off to Temple Gardens on the Victoria Embankment. Here tolerant police turn a blind eye. Beds are built from cardboard cartons and boxes, on and under benches and on the tulip-fringed grass. Early next morning the beds will be deposited in the great skips waiting to take the rubbish away from the elegant hotels that overlook the gardens. The following evening the habitual itinerants will collect new boxes from the piles of refuse. This may seem unreal, but it happens, and The Salvation Army along with other groups and charities is committed to serve.

A Salvation Army officer tells of his experience: 'Not all those whom we serve on the soup run are willing to come to our van for help, so there are times when we must spend a little time looking for them. Most of them will use a "skipper" which can be a room or space in the cellar of some old house or an attic in some disused warehouse. Skippering can be quite a nerve-racking experience, as one is not only confronted with the darkness and emptiness of an old place, but also with broken floorboards, strange surrounds and even rats. The unexpected can happen. I remember sliding down a cellar to look for an addict and found myself in the dark, up to my waist in stagnant water full of old cabbages.'

If asked why he risks himself in such a way the officer would say, 'We get to the place where we have to stop thinking rationally at times and let our experience and emotions take over. The people we deal with stopped thinking rationally a long time ago.'

The Salvation Army

9: ACID RAIN

Acid rain destroys stone, pollutes rivers and lakes, rots metal, causes bronchitis, kills forests and harms crops. This passage may help the next generation learn to feel responsible for the environment.

One of the greatest achievements of the human race has been to control fire and use the heat produced to alter natural materials and to provide power for light, warmth and machines. Unfortunately, much waste is also produced: unburnt particles, called hydrocarbons, and gases which form when chemicals such as sulphur and nitrate mix with oxygen in the air.

When petrol burns in an engine, or fuel is burnt in a furnace, the exhaust fumes are waste. They contain harmless water and carbon dioxide, together with one or more of sulphur dioxide, nitrogen oxide and carbon monoxide. These are usually harmful to plants and creatures, including people.

The gases react with the water present in the air to form

acids such as carbonic, sulphuric and nitric acids. When this acidic water falls to the ground in the form of rainfall, it is known as 'Acid Rain'.

It was October 1984 and Robin Heid was angry. He was so incensed that he climbed up a giant smoke-stack at the Gavin Power Plant in Ohio, USA, tied a banner around the top and then jumped off. He parachuted to safety, only to be arrested for trespassing. His banner remained aloft. It said 'STOP ACID RAIN NOW'.

Robin Heid was a protestor. He belonged to an organization called Greenpeace. Most of us do not go to such extremes as Robin and other active members of Greenpeace. If we wish to protest about something we usually grumble and do nothing much about it. If we feel really strongly we write to the papers, to our local councillors or to our MP. Letter writing does have an effect, especially if enough people write about the same thing. They can join together to protest.

In Norway and Sweden there is a joint 'Stop Acid Rain Campaign' organization. Together with the Friends of the Earth it organized an International Acid Rain Week in April 1984 and 1985. In the USA the American Lung Association adds its protest over polluted air.

Is any notice taken of angry people by those who can alter matters? The answer can be yes.

Fog, mist, steam and cloud all consist of small droplets of water floating in the air. When fog occurs naturally, it is troublesome enough. When unburnt carbon bits, which we call soot, and yellow sulphur particles mix with it, then it becomes a choking, smoky fog.

The fogs of London which began in Victorian times became world famous. They were called 'pea-soupers' because they seemed to be as thick as soup and were often a greenish-yellow colour in the gas lamplight of that time. Thriller stories made much of the terrors lurking in the swirling fog.

People began to protest about such fog in London and other cities. Doctors realized that many chest complaints, notably bronchitis, were caused or made worse by the smoke-laden fog and the word *smog* was used to describe this air pollution. The culprit guilty of producing the smog was coal. Nearly all houses were heated with open, coal-burning fires and from their chimneys poured thick, black smoke laden with sulphurous fumes.

In the late 1940s more and more people began to protest. Politicians joined the protestors but nothing much was done to improve the air. In 1952 London had many days of terrible, choking smog. It was so bad that bus conductors had to walk in front of their buses carrying flaming torches so that the driver could follow the way. Thousands of people had difficulty in breathing and many bronchitis sufferers became so ill that they died. London came almost to a halt.

The newspapers wrote, and the people of London said, 'Enough is enough.' In 1956 Parliament passed a Clean Air Act which permitted the setting-up in the urban areas of smoke-controlled zones in which no smoke might be emitted. The Government gave grants to people to alter their heating systems especially to take smokeless fuel such as coke and anthracite.

Not all of the country has smokeless zones and so in some areas smoke pollution continues. Nevertheless, most cities in Britain now have clean, smoke-free air. The carbon bits that floated in the air and caused the fog are gone, but not the invisible gases which are the ingredients for Acid Rain.

Angry people stopped the smoke. Now others, like Robin Heid, are protesting with their message 'STOP ACID RAIN'. It is time, they say, to stop the gases also.

Philip Neal

6
The wider world

1: FLOOD

A tropical cyclone (or hurricane) and the resulting tidal waves caused terrible flooding and casualties in Bangladesh in May 1985. Figures must, to a large extent, rely on guesswork but conservative estimates suggest that over 10,000 died and 250,000 were made homeless.

This particular storm was by no means unique: a far worse storm killed 100,000 in 1970. Whenever a cyclone occurs in the Bay of Bengal, it sweeps huge amounts of water northwards into the narrow end of the bay. When it combines with a high tide, waves of ten feet or more sweep towards the mouth of the Ganges, drowning the people and animals on the low-lying, silt islands in the estuary.

These passages illustrate both individual human suffering and the more general aspects of such tragedies. Among the questions they raise are why people live in such areas (the soil is especially fertile); whether better warnings can be given; what relief is of most help; and what must be done in future. It is also hoped that they will develop an understanding of and sympathy for the way in which the less fortunate people on this planet must live.

Yakub Ali's story

(Begin by linking the topic to any local or recent flooding.)

A flood in this country can be a nuisance; it can cause a lot of damage. It might even cause some loss of life. Floods can be very much worse in other countries. In 1985 (as in other years), a terrible cyclone or hurricane hit Bangladesh, blowing in from the Bay of Bengal. As it reached the tiny, low-lying islands off the coast, it swept huge waves over the land.

Ten thousand people died. A quarter of a million lost their homes. This is the story of one family.

'It was a hot, humid day and overcast,' recalled Yakub Ali, a forty-year-old farmer on the tiny Bangladeshi island of Urirchar. 'First came the dark and the menacing clouds. Soon the wind started whistling ominously. Then the heavy rains began to fall.' At first, Yakub thought with relief that the torrents might disperse the stifling heat, which can exceed 100°F at this time of year. But the downpour quickly gained greater and still greater force. As the alarmed farmer walked out of his hut, he came upon his neighbours gathering in the night. There was frightened talk that Danger Signal No. 9, a cyclone warning calling for immediate evacuation, had been announced on the radio. It was news to Yakub.

On the previous day, Indian meteorologists had alerted the Bangladesh government in Dhaka that a killer storm was sweeping toward the country's myriad offshore islets and southern flatlands along the Bay of Bengal. Danger Signals Nos. 4 and 5, warning of winds racing above 50 mph, had been hoisted in the port of Chittagong, and fishermen and other sailors had been urged to stay close to the shore. Hourly warnings were broadcast on state-run radio and television, advising residents in the imperilled areas to seek shelter instantly. But most of the impoverished squatters who crowd the islets are too poor to own radios, and many of those who heard the warnings may have shrugged them off as a false alarm.

As wind and water gathered force, however, Yakub Ali knew that something ominous was on the way. Hurrying back to his homestead, he awoke his wife, his ten-year-old son and his younger brother and urged them to come along to Urirchar's only concrete building, a two-storey Forestry Department complex, a little more than half a mile away. By then the tide had begun to rise. Yakub and his family started running: all around them, people were racing for safety.

A few minutes later, still hundreds of yards from the Forestry building, Yakub felt himself lifted by a towering wave. Frantically he looked around for his family, but all was lost in the darkness behind blinding sheets of rain. 'Everything was dark – rain, rain. I was floating for several hours,' he recalled of the hours he passed at sea before sailors from a naval vessel pulled him to safety. 'I am a good swimmer, but it was terrible. I really do not know how I survived. And where,' he asked, tears in his eyes, 'where are my near and dear ones?'

The same question haunted all of Urirchar after the night of the raging elements. While the sea crashed over the twenty square mile island, whose highest point is only ten feet above sea level, families were torn asunder. In desperation, people clung to the rafters of the Forestry Department building or to trees or to anything else not swept away by the terrifying storm.

By the time dawn came and the murderous storm had headed farther north, the afflicted area was stripped clean. Thatched huts and small shops, animals and people had been swept beneath the waves; thousands of fishing boats had vanished. Whole settlements had been swamped or washed into the sea. Across the length and breadth of Urirchar there hung an eerie silence, broken now and then by the wails of survivors. Only a few houses remained, among them the Forestry Department building. Of some 10,000 residents of the islet, mostly peasant farmers and a few shopkeepers, up to 7,000 were dead or missing. The flat, wet land was dotted with corpses and the carcasses of cattle; vultures and crows feasted. Upon the muddy waves of the Bay of Bengal floated hundreds upon hundreds of blackened, bloated bodies.

Time Magazine

Survivors and casualties

This is another report on the 1985 cyclone and flooding in the Bay of Bengal.

It was the middle of the night, and Abdul Hadi and his family were sound asleep. Outside their tin-roofed hut on the tiny island of Urirchar, off the coast of Bangladesh, gale force winds and heavy rain lashed the landscape. All at once a wall of water more than twelve feet high slammed into the building. Hadi grabbed a pair of logs, put them under his armpits and caught hold of two of his young sons. The surf swept them more than three miles out to sea and then miraculously brought them back to land again. The three survived, but Hadi's wife and four other children were lost. He eventually found a daughter's body in a pond. Five days later, Hadi was lining up at a relief centre for biscuits and water — and material to build a new home.

'Where else can I go?' he said. 'What Allah has done is done.'

For many people in Bangladesh, that sort of stoicism was the only possible response to the cyclone that subsided early last week after ravaging their country. Relief officials totting up the damage from the storm and deadly tidal bores that had hit over the weekend, estimated that at least 10,000 people had been killed and more than 250,000 left homeless. Those figures were mostly the result of guesswork, however, and some observers believed that the actual body count was possibly higher. In 1970 a cyclone that struck the country killed somewhere between 300,000 and one million people, one of the worst natural disasters of modern times. As in that earlier case, the brunt of this cyclone (the term used in the Indian Ocean region for a hurricane) had been borne by the delta region of Bangladesh, an area dotted with hundreds of low-lying islands. In some cases the storm appeared to have washed away whole villages and even entire islands.

Meanwhile, the survivors were confronted with a new threat from disease. The storm had contaminated streams and freshwater wells over an area of 1,961 square miles. The tainted drinking water had already led to outbreaks of diarrhoeal disease – officials staunchly denied it was cholera – that reportedly killed fifty people.

Still, the dazed survivors all had harrowing stories to tell. A wiry farmer named Nasir ul-Haq, seventy, vividly recalled the ordeal of his twelve member family. As the wave hit, he found himself clinging to the roof of his house along with his ninety-year-old mother. After several hours of drifting, Nasir watched helplessly, as she weakened and finally disappeared beneath the surface. Rescued by a boat, Nasir returned to find that two children and two grandchildren were missing. Another daughter was hospitalized on Sandwip. Now the remaining members of the family were painstakingly searching for their household items, which had been scattered across the landscape. All the while Nasir's wife, a sad-eyed woman in a worn blue sari, crouched under a crude lean-to near a primitive stove, rocking back and forth on her heels and weeping.

Newsweek

Any answers

This report on the Bangladeshi disaster considers what might have been done to lessen the tragedy. What other solutions do you think there might be?

Though the storm itself could hardly have been prevented, there were inevitable questions about whether the government had taken adequate steps to ensure the safety of the inhabitants along the coast. The authorities had known for days that a cyclone was brewing – and no one could have doubted the potential hazards that the storm posed. The waters of the Bay of Bengal provide almost perfect conditions for spawning killer cyclones, which need heat from the sea surface to sustain themselves, and tend to follow warm currents. Even the shape of the Bay acts as a kind of funnel for the storms with, as one meteorologist puts it, 'Bangladesh as a bull's-eye right at the end.' As the storm approaches the mainland, water begins to pile up in a 'cyclone surge,' which is then raised even higher in tidal bores as the water is forced into channels between the delta's islands. The net result of this movement is to raise the sea level by at least ten feet, which is more than enough to overwhelm the islets formed by the annual floods of the Ganges and Brahmaputra rivers.

One cruel irony was that despite its poverty, Bangladesh has one of the most sophisticated storm-alert systems in the world. The first sign of the cyclone came on the morning of May 23 when a bank of computers at the headquarters of the Bangladesh Space Research and Remote Sensing Organization (Sparsso) in a northern suburb of Dhaka printed out a satellite photograph taken over the Bay of Bengal. The violet-coloured picture showed an ominous development: a swirling white knot of clouds forming almost due west of Rangoon. As the storm gathered strength, it began heading slowly northward. The head of Sparsso, Dr Farooq Aziz Khan, took the unusual step of releasing the satellite photo to the local newspapers in Dhaka, which also carried small stories about the storm. While the word was spreading, the cyclone continued building up until it was packing winds of more than 75 mph and covering an area larger than Bangladesh itself.

By that time the government had started broadcasting warnings over state radio every half hour. The trouble was that most of the residents along the southern coast are too poor to own radios. Many of those who did hear the announcements simply disregarded them, recalling the numerous false alarms they had received in the past. 'The inhabitants of the islands hear it so many times they often don't take it seriously,' says David Guyer, president of Save the Children Federation, who has travelled extensively in Bangladesh. 'It becomes a bit like calling wolf.'

The victims were, in effect, served up to the storm on a platter, thanks to the table-flat terrain of the islands. Known locally as *chars*, the islands are highly fertile. But because they are little more than bars of silt, the chars generally have a maximum elevation of less than five feet and lack any natural shelter. And since the islands are constantly shifting in the delta, the farmers who flock there to graze their cattle and raise crops usually build only temporary lodgings out of flimsy materials. Despite the population of perhaps as many as 10,000, Urirchar, one of the hardest-hit islands, had only two concrete buildings.

Despite the advance warning, an evacuation of the islands was out of the question. Authorities had only eight large transport helicopters at their disposal to ferry the roughly one million people threatened by the storm. The country's tiny Navy has no large passenger carriers. And in any event, the draft around many of the islands is too shallow to accommodate anything but amphibious craft. Even if the country had suddenly been blessed with enough boats and choppers, a systematic evacuation would still have been difficult at best. Many of the islanders move from spot to spot, making it virtually impossible for authorities to keep track of their whereabouts.

There have been suggestions that the government should have banned squatters from inhabiting some of the more vulnerable islands altogether. But that, too, seemed unrealistic. In a country that is plagued by grinding poverty and a population that has doubled in thirty years to nearly 100 million, the fertile islands provide a rare opportunity for farmers to eke out at least a subsistence living.

In an attempt to offer some protection for the residents, the government embarked on a programme several years ago to build a series of concrete buildings on the islands that could serve as cyclone shelters. But the islands materialize and erode away without warning (Urirchar is so new it does not even appear on maps of Bangladesh), leaving officials unable to come up with a plan for a comprehensive network.

Newsweek

2: DROUGHT IN ETHIOPIA

This is an account by an Oxfam worker of what drought means to the people of Ethiopia.

We've all seen television pictures of people suffering from famine and drought in Africa. But what is it really like out there? What would you feel if you were to walk through one of those camps where people gather and wait for food? And why can't those people do more to help themselves?

This report is by someone working for the charity, Oxfam, and describes a visit to Ethiopia, a country in East Africa. The capital of Ethiopia is Addis Ababa.

We were only a few hours drive north out of the capital, Addis Ababa, when we saw the first unmistakeable signs of famine. Along the road whole families of hungry people were on the move, their few possessions in bundles on their backs.

On the road small children knelt down to beg in the face of oncoming traffic, forming a human chain roadblock at several points. By the side of the road women were in desperation offering their silver jewellery for any pittance they could get.

We hadn't left the central province of Shoa when we came across the first large roadside camp for displaced famine victims; the first of a string of emergency centres stretching along the tarmac as far as the much-visited Korem and beyond into Tigray. The camps, which provide sorely needed relief to many tens of thousands, are now familiar to millions worldwide thanks to television. But no amount of exposure to the TV pictures prepares you for the shock of the human reality.

How do you, how does anyone, cope with the experience of entering a camp shelter and finding literally thousands of starving children waiting patiently in lines for wet feeding? It was some comfort to see Oxfam energy biscuits much in evidence with even marasmic-looking children able to consume them while they waited for a proper meal.

In this one camp there were some 14,000 people at the time of our visit, but recent newspaper reports say the population has since climbed to well over 20,000. The daily death rate – eighteen deaths on the day before we visited – tragically has soared over the hundred mark.

We, however, were heading off the tarmac to see at first hand the conditions in the countryside from which the destitute people of the roadside had fled. I was accompanying Cathy Gibb who heads Oxfam's Nutrition Team in Ethiopia. Cathy had been asked by the Ethiopian Government's Relief and Rehabilitation Commission (RRC) to help relieve the mounting pressure on the established camps by developing feeding operations much closer to where the rural population live. So while Cathy was doing her homework on how feasible it was for Oxfam to set up shop off the beaten track, I was able to check on how far relief supplies were getting through.

Typically, farmers from each 'kebelle' (community association) affected come in by rotation on a set day to pick up their monthly rations from a central point and return home. At one distribution we chanced on at a place called Degan, it was the turn of a 'kebelle' with a population of 3,500 some six hours walk away. Here as elsewhere we were able to observe an efficiently run distribution providing a vital lifeline to many thousands of people with few if any other means of sustenance.

But this lifeline depends on an adequate supply of emergency food aid from Western donors through the Red Sea ports. We were told that at times supplies were intermittent. It is salutary when reading press controversies of the 'Western food aid goes astray' variety to keep firmly in mind the human beings whose very survival is dependent on a continuous aid flow.

One poor woman whose home I visited in a remote village had only her monthly grain ration and a few pathetic chickens to live on. She had ploughed her land but the rains had failed, so she had had to eat her seed. Sadly – but not surprisingly – in view of her meagre diet she had fallen ill some days before. Yet, despite the apparent hopelessness of her position, she invited us in offering hospitality from a proud tradition which has no experience of begging for charity.

We were later told by Fasil Asefa, the Chairman of the District Farmers Association in the town of Wegel Tena, that farmers on all sides were driven to eating their seed. 'It is a very hard drought,' he said, 'and people are desperate. They are selling livestock, farm tools (such as forks, ploughs and yokes) and household goods to buy food. They are even selling the thatch off their roofs before they move out.' The Chairman calculated that some 13,000 people had already fled from the district.

The hopes of those who stayed were pinned on the coming of the rains – the 'small rains' in February and the 'big rains' in July/August. But even if good rains return next year, problems of lack of seed and oxen to plough (almost all oxen had died or been sold) have to be overcome if any respite from famine is to be achieved.

The outlook for most of the inhabitants was bleak, the Deputy District Administrator Alem Seged Gezhain told us, 'most people have only RRC grain to survive on.' Unfortunately grain supplies had been irregular: 'We haven't been able to help all the drought victims, only the worst cases.' Lorry deliveries depended on the availability of foreign food aid and while in 'good' weeks in Wegel Tena they get three or four lorry loads of grain a week, sometimes they get only one or none at all. Gazing over a desolate panorama of barren hillsides and fields of stunted crops fit only for animal feed, Alem Seged warned: 'It's changing into desert.'

Yet only four to seven metres below the ground there are seemingly abundant groundwater supplies. These could be tapped to develop irrigation – if financial aid was only available for well drilling. The Deputy Administrator proudly showed us three modest water projects. I left in no doubt that, with substantial development aid for water and soil conservation programmes, much more could be done to alleviate the effects of drought even in this badly stricken area of Ethiopia.

Paddy Coulter

3: HOW MUCH IS A PACKET OF RICE?

This excerpt comes from Christian Aid News *and outlines the problems and the poverty of many rice farmers in the Philippines, the group of 7,000 islands in the south-west Pacific. It is a challenge to those in the west who sometimes think food grows on supermarket shelves.*

If you were asked, 'Where does rice come from?', your answer might be Tesco's or the Co-op. In this reading, we shall hear what life is like for the peasant-farmers who labour to grow rice in places such as the Philippines: a group of islands in the Pacific Ocean.

Next time you buy a small packet of rice in your local shop and have to pay around seventy pence, you might reflect how little of that gets back to the peasant farmer who grew it in Thailand, the Philippines or in India. For five pence is all the farmer gets. Sixty-five pence goes to the merchants, the transporters, the packagers and the shop.

It is not surprising, then, that millions of peasants who are the backbone of agriculture world-wide consider that they are being robbed. Now they want to change the system of trading and the system of land ownership which permits such injustice.

Half the world's population depends on rice. It is one of the great staple grain crops. For hundreds of millions of people in Asia it is life itself.

The colonial powers introduced the rice crop to West African coastal regions – the British in Sierra Leone and Gambia, the French in Senegal and along the inland valley of the Niger. It was meant to be a cash crop for export using the African villagers as cheap labour. But everywhere families who grew the rice suffered neglect and exploitation. It was very little different after independence.

One such peasant farmer is Rudolfo, who with his wife Zenaida, farm a one hectare plot in Central Luzon, one of the principal rice-growing zones of the Philippines. At the end of a good harvest Rudolfo had done his sums and reached the gloomy conclusion that they could not go on unless things changed. Yet what was the alternative? They knew no other way of life. They loved the land even though it was a harsh taskmaster. They had the same problems, they said, as millions of other peasant farmers.

First they had to buy the new miracle seed – the high yield hybrid variety developed by the International Rice Institute and enthusiastically promoted by the government to the exclusion of all traditional varieties.

Secondly, to succeed with this rice, they had to buy special fertilizer, insecticide and herbicide, otherwise it didn't mature. To obtain all these at the right time they had to go into debt. The unavoidable moneylender was the rice-merchant who also was going to buy the crop and in the meantime, levied an extortionate interest.

With the new rice, there was a much bigger harvest — a total of ninety sacks against thirty before, but when the bills were totted up they were worse off. From a gross income of £540, had to be deducted expenses of £344. This left £196 or approximately £3.75 a week for the household of five to live on for a year. It made no allowance for the labour in the fields of members of the family living at home or the buffalo they had managed to acquire in earlier years.

For Rudolfo and Zenaida that was the price of rice. Rudolfo would have to go off and look for labouring work for six months to try to balance the family budget. And even that was fraught with difficulties in a country with over thirty per cent unemployment.

It is easy to see the injustice of this but harder to find the solutions. For many it requires the radical transformation of society. But in the most impoverished countries the forces of order and privilege are so powerfully entrenched as to silence easily the voice of the poor.

The idea has taken firm hold in the churches that poverty is not part of God's plan and therefore it has to be fought.

The best chance of this happening without bloodshed is that the communities and people involved should understand the kind of society in which they live and show by their actions that it has to change.

Derrick Knight

4: HOME FOR THE DYING

One of Mother Teresa's best-known achievements is the establishment of her Home for the Dying in Calcutta; a place where the homeless of that city may be brought to die in dignity among loving people – or sometimes to recover. She talked about it in a television programme when she was interviewed by Malcolm Muggeridge.

In Calcutta in India there are many homeless people. As they get old or ill, they simply die on the streets. Mother Teresa of Calcutta is a Christian nun who decided to help these people when she found the hospitals would not accept them (as there was so little they could do for them). Mother Teresa started a Home for the Dying, where they could be brought to be comfortable and looked after by herself and her helpers – as she explained in this interview.

Mother Teresa: Yes, the first woman I saw I myself picked up from the street. She had been half eaten by the rats and ants. I took her to the hospital but they could not do anything for her. They only took her in because I refused to move until they accepted her. From there I went to the municipality and I asked them to give me a place where I could bring these people because on the same day I had found other people dying in the streets. The health officer of the municipality took me to the temple, the Kali Temple, and showed me the dormashalah where the people used to rest after they had done their worship of the goddess Kali. It was an empty building: he asked me if I would accept it. I was very happy to have that place for many reasons, but especially knowing that it was a centre of worship and devotion of the Hindus. Within twenty-four hours we had our patients there and we started the work of the home for the sick and dying who are destitutes. Since then we have picked up over 23,000 people from the streets of Calcutta of which about fifty per cent have died.

Interviewer: What exactly are you doing for these dying people? I know you bring them in to die there. What is it you are doing for them or seeking to do for them?

Mother Teresa: First of all we want to make them feel that they are wanted, we want them to know that there are people who really love them, who really want them, at least for the few hours that they have to live, to know human and divine love. That they too may know that they are the children of God, and that they are not forgotten and that they are loved and cared about and there are young lives ready to give themselves in their service.

Interviewer: What happens to the ones who don't die?

Mother Teresa: Those who are able to work we try to find some work for them, the others we try to send them to homes where they can spend at least a few years in happiness and comfort.

Interviewer: Who brings them to you, Mother? I mean who, as it were, delivers them to you?

Mother Teresa: At the beginning the Sisters used to find them in the streets and pick them up.

Interviewer: As you did this first woman.

Mother Teresa: Yes. But as the work became more and more known, more and more people came to hear that there was a place where these people could be cared for. They telephone for the municipal ambulance and it comes and picks them up and brings them to us. But under one condition, that they have first to take them to the nearest hospital.

Interviewer: You only want people who cannot get in anywhere else; for whom this is the last refuge, is that right?

Mother Teresa: Yes, the home is meant only for the street cases and cases that no hospital wants or for people who have absolutely no one to take care of them.

7

Human rights – and prisoners of conscience

1: TERROR IN IRAN

This is part of an Amnesty International report on the torture and ill-treatment of prisoners of conscience in Iran in 1983.

Thousands of men and women are in prison throughout the world simply because of their religious or political beliefs. Some are in prison because of their colour and race. Some are there simply because the government of that country doesn't like them – and where a government has no opposition, it can treat its prisoners as it likes. This is part of a report smuggled out of Iran. It tells of what went on in a prison called Evin in 1983. As you listen, remember that similar things are still going on in many countries around the world.

'The worst thing in Evin is being held blindfolded for days on end waiting for someone to tell you why you are there. Some people have been left blindfolded for months.

'One man has spent twenty-seven months like this. None of the prisoners appear to know what he is being held for. After twenty-seven months, he sits, largely in total silence, nodding his head from one side to the other.

'Obviously, they keep people blindfolded to add to the fear. But when they suddenly whip off the blindfold to question you, you are almost blinded; the light is painful and you feel dizzy.

'Many new arrivals are said to be thrown into windowless "isolation" cells designed for one person but because of the lack of space, sometimes holding up to twenty people.

'In Band-e Chah (Block 4) there is a special religious judge who deals out thrashing sentences to most who won't co-operate at interrogation sessions.

'The prisoners are held or tied down while the thrashing with a whip takes place. Most are hit repeatedly across the genital area.

'There is a rule in Evin . . . that men and women up to forty years of age can be lashed all over the body and those over forty can be lashed only on the feet.'

A long pole with a length of cord fastened at either end, like a bow, is used to hold the older victim's feet like a tourniquet. 'Then the soles of the feet are lashed, the punishment is carried out with such force that afterwards the victim's legs swell up like watermelons.'

Another block in Evin is the Zendane Zanan (Women's Prison), where the children of many young inmates are said to be held.

'There are around 40 chidren, aged from one to twelve. They are kept because they are an asset to the prison authority for gaining confessions: when the mother is lashed the child is made to watch.

'One such mother screamed that she was ready to confess when she could no longer stand the agony of her three-year-old daughter being made to watch in the grip of two guards.

'Often the guards slap the children about at the same time as the mother's lashing . . . Anyone who has seen the terror of such children cannot easily forget it.'

'The guards call the prison the "Hen House", probably because many of us have to squat for days on end on the balconies (encircling a central courtyard).

'When you are taken there, you are left blindfolded on one of the balconies. There is hardly room to sit, let alone lay down. All the cells behind are packed full too.

You are left blindfolded for days. No one will tell you what your fate is.

'At night the guards drag people in and out of the cells through the midst of the balcony people ... Sometimes those they dragged out did not come back.

'Every night until the early morning people were tortured, either in the open courtyard or in rooms off it. The screams were terrible.

'On the balconies we whispered to those inside the cells. Some gave us messages for their families in the hope that word could be got out. Some had been burned with irons; others said they had received electric shocks.

'Many times balcony people taken into the courtyard for whippings with wire cable kept on shouting obscenities against the regime ... often ... until they were beaten silent. They didn't return for hours.'

Amnesty International

2: PRISONER OF CONSCIENCE

These words are from an Amnesty International poster.

A political prisoner is someone who is arrested, put in prison and perhaps executed simply for what he or she believes. In many ways Jesus was a prisoner of conscience.

He was a political prisoner,
    imprisoned and tortured by the occupying forces
    of his country.
He was a prisoner of conscience,
    hated and persecuted.
He wasn't the first prisoner of conscience,
    and he certainly wasn't the last.

Today, about half a million
    political and religious prisoners
    are detained all over the world,

often in conditions no better than his back in the time of Tiberius.

Would you have done anything for him?

Will you do anything for them?

Amnesty International

3: IN BUCHENWALD

Paul Schneider was a pastor in Germany who refused to stop telling the truth. He ended up in Buchenwald concentration camp. In the prison camp, he was a source of great strength and encouragement to his fellow prisoners. One way in which he witnessed to the truth was by refusing to salute the Nazi flag.

Before and during World War Two, the Nazis in Germany set up concentration camps in which they imprisoned (and killed) millions of people – simply because they did not like them. Conditions were vicious. Even so, there were prisoners who were prepared to stick by their beliefs – even if this made them more likely to get in trouble with the guards. One such person was a Christian clergyman called Paul Schneider.

('Idolatry' means worshipping or giving too much praise to false people and objects.)

In the spring of 1938, there was an order that all prisoners passing by the Nazi flag on their march to work should greet it by taking off their caps. Schneider declared that this saluting of the Nazi flag was idolatry and he refused to obey the order.

At first, most of the prisoners did not think of refusing. None of them did it willingly; but, apart from Schneider, they all obeyed. One who envied him, or perhaps had a grudge against him, informed the authorities, and he was charged with refusal to obey a command.

Then began Paul Schneider's lone path of suffering. He was called to the SS and freely confessed his attitude. At first he received twenty-five lashes and was then put into the dark cell. This meant solitary confinement and he remained in this cell till his death. There he told the SS exactly what the Christian attitude to Nazism was. He spoke freely and without fear.

There was probably no other man in Germany who denounced the regime as fearlessly. He called the devil by his name: murderer, criminal, tyrant, monster. Because of this witness against Nazism — and he never failed to set against it the grace of Christ and call men to repentance — Schneider received in his body repeated and heavy tortures, humiliations and pains. All the ingenuity of Nazi sadism was used against him. Torture was alternated with good treatment and appeals to relax his strong opposition.

Schneider was unmoved and he was tireless in calling out words of Scripture to his fellow prisoners. Morning and evening, whenever his cell door was opened or he was taken out to fresh torment, his voice could be heard shouting aloud words of comfort and judgment from the Bible.

One January morning in 1939, when two escaped prisoners had been brought back and killed, Paul Schneider could be heard clearly denouncing the murder: 'In the name of Jesus Christ, I witness against the murder of prisoners . . .'

The worst time for Schneider was in the early summer of 1939. For several days he was hung up, with his hands behind him and his body permanently bent. This devilish device caused him continuous pain. His suffering was borne nobly, and he was greatly honoured in the camp.

E H Robertson

4: SPEAKING OUT

A short reading by a victim of the Nazis which reminds us that it is not always easy to speak out against evil. Pastor Niemöller became an active critic of the Nazi regime and was held in a concentration camp from 1937 till the end of the Second World War.

Suppose you're with a group of friends who start doing something cruel – perhaps bullying an animal or picking on someone who is weaker or different in some way. You know it is wrong, so do you speak out and say so? Firmly enough for them to stop? Suppose it was an even more serious wrongdoing. Would you have had the courage to speak out against the Nazis in Germany? This reading is a warning of what might happen if we don't speak out against what is wrong.

> First they came for the Jews
> and I did not speak out
> because I was not a Jew.
>
> Then they came for the communists
> and I did not speak out
> because I was not a communist.
>
> Then they came for the trade unionists
> and I did not speak out
> because I was not a trade unionist.
>
> Then they came for me –
> and there was no one left
> to speak out for me.
>
> *Pastor Martin Niemöller*

5: WE HAVE NEVER BEEN FREE

At the time of writing (one begins, optimistically), it is depressing to note how little has changed since this Newsweek *article was published in 1971. (Before beginning a reading of this passage, it is important to remind the assembly that in South Africa there are those who are classified as Blacks, Whites and Coloureds.)*

Hands up those of you whose surname begins with 'S'. Suppose you weren't allowed into the school dining hall [or other locally significant place] because your surname begins with that letter. How would you feel?

Hands up those of you who are left-handed. Suppose you weren't allowed into the school dining hall because you are left-handed. How would you feel?

Suppose you were not allowed into the school dining hall because you have fair hair or because your skin is a certain colour. Then how would you feel? This reading is about what it's like to be a Coloured person in South Africa.

I was born in South Africa. My early forefathers were born here. They were here long before there were any white-skinned people here. God put them here.

    Still, I cannot worship where I want to.
    I cannot learn where I want to.
    I cannot marry whom I want to.
    I cannot go where I want to or live where I want to.
    I cannot even be buried where I want to when I die.

I cannot do these things because in the mind of the white-skinned people of South Africa I am not a human being. I am not South African. I am 'Coloured'.

What is a 'Coloured'? We are an accident in history — the result of the passionate meeting of white-skinned rovers from Europe and the yellow-skinned Hottentot women they found at the southernmost tip of Africa. That was our beginning, and we were born into slavery. We are the only people who have never really been free. We are close to the whites because our 'culture' is white, but they discriminate against us because our skins are dark. We are told by the blacks that we belong with them because our skins are dark, but they distrust us because our 'culture' is white. Both need us.

I was visited last night by an agent for a life insurance company who is determined to sign me up. But I won't because he has told me that my premium will be higher than the premium of a white man who takes the same policy. Because I am 'Coloured'. Apparently 'statistics' show the insurance companies that whites live longer than 'Coloureds' and therefore they pay less.

I am stripped, in a sense, of my manhood. I sit in a bus in which some seats are 'reserved' for 'us' and most for 'them'. A woman, one of 'them', boards the bus. All 'their' seats are filled. And so are 'ours'. She is an old woman and none of 'them' gives her a seat. I want to but I cannot because she belongs to 'them'. So I sit and she stands. It is the law. *They* made it for me. But *they* suffer from it too, sometimes.

School: My son is impatient to go to school. But I cannot send him to school until he is seven-years-old. White children can go when they are six-years-old. Even earlier. But 'statistics' have proved that my son is mentally ready only when he is seven-years-old.

I am standing in the Caledon Square police station (Cape Town), waiting to pay a traffic fine. They bring in a white man. He is a hobo. He is drunk and covered with blood. He smells like a rotten fish and the spittle runs down his matted beard. He asks for a glass of water. The white sergeant turns to a 'Coloured' sergeant and commands, 'Bring the baas a glass of water'.

I walk out of the police station. My anger, resentment, chokes me. Is it hatred? I do not know, but it is getting worse. I know it is getting dangerous. For all of us. Them, and us. I would like to say, 'Please stop. This cannot go on.' But they will not allow me to warn them. If I do, I will be called an agitator, a Communist. So I do not say what is on my mind. But I scheme. And all my schemes are against them.

They have made me 'Coloured'. *They* make me live like a 'Coloured'. But there is a difference between my 'Coloured' and *their* 'Coloured'. I feel oppressed. I no longer feel that I am a part of *them*. They have forfeited their right to hold my hand in the journey into the future, for they have made it clear to me that they suppress every human desire and emotion in me because I am 'Coloured' in their eyes.

We have time on our side, time to find out that we do not need to rely on the white man for everything. We can do much ourselves. Each of us must become our brother's keeper until the white man feels that he is alone and that he cannot continue without us. He must learn to know that our heartbeats make this country of ours endure. He must learn that every law he makes which is designed to rob us of our destiny as human beings holds him back, too, and prevents him from growing from 'white man' to 'man'. And when the cost of it all gets home to the lowliest one of them, we will have won our struggle and I and my brown-skinned brothers will no longer be 'Coloured' men but men together with them and the blacks.

Howard Lawrence, Newsweek

6: HUMAN RIGHTS

These prayers were prepared by the British Council of Churches for a Human Rights Day service in 1980. It is appreciated that not every school will wish to involve its pupils in this sort of 'prayer'. In some cases it might be apt to paraphrase each paragraph so that it begins, 'We think of those who . . .' Simpler petitions and responses might be either:

'Lord, in thy mercy'
'Hear our prayer'

or:

'Let us not forget them'
'We shall remember them'.

(It will be necessary to devise a relevant 'local' introduction to this reading.)

Leader: We pray for those who have been exiled from their native land, who have been forced to leave behind their heritage and possessions, their families and their friends, and who have had to begin life anew in a foreign culture and among strangers.
  Lord, let justice run down like rivers

All: And righteousness as a mighty stream.

Leader: We pray for those who are discriminated against on the grounds of their race or sex, who offer the gifts of their presence, culture and personality, find them despised or rejected.
Lord, let justice run down like rivers

All: And righteousness as a mighty stream.

Leader: We pray for those who at this very moment are being tortured in their bodies or in their minds because of the convictions they hold so dear, that their pain may be eased and that the peace of God may bring them release even in the midst of suffering.
Lord, let justice run down like rivers

All: And righteousness as a mighty stream.

Leader: We pray for all rulers and those who hold positions of authority in the state and in all the powerful institutions of our society that they may use their power for good and not for evil, that the rights of men and women may no longer be abused.
Lord, let justice run down like rivers

All: And righteousness as a mighty stream.

Leader: We pray for all whose basic needs for food, shelter, clothing and healing are not met. Stir up the consciences of peoples and governments, speed the re-arranging of the world's economies, teach us all to live more simply, that others may simply live.
Lord, let justice run down like rivers

All: And righteousness as a mighty stream.

Leader: We pray for the nations of the earth that God in his mercy will save them from their folly and mankind from its sin, that men will be set free from vindictiveness and fear, that forgiveness will replace revenge, that none shall be in bondage to another and none shall hold another in contempt, that the cruel gods of Mammon and Caesar will be cast down,

and God alone will be worshipped over all the earth.
   Lord, let justice run down like rivers
All: And righteousness as a mighty stream.
All: [The Lord's Prayer.]

7: WE WILL NEVER DIE

In 1945, Alexander Solzhenitsyn was imprisoned for remarks he had made about Stalin. For the next eight years he was kept in labour camps including a 'special' camp for long-term prisoners. He has written many books and now lives in the West. In this short 'prose poem' he meditates about graveyards and what they have to teach us about death – and ourselves.

Today's reading is by a famous Russian writer, Alexander Solzhenitsyn. He was put in prison for what he wrote but was eventually set free by the Russians and now lives in the West. In it he thinks about graveyards (both in this country and in Russia) and about how it's important to remember those who have died. He tells us not to be afraid of talking about death and the dead.

Above all else we have grown to fear death and those who die.

If there is a death in a family we try to avoid writing or calling because we do not know what to say about death.

It is even considered shameful to mention a cemetery seriously. You would never say at work: 'Sorry, I can't come on Sunday, I've got to visit my relatives at the cemetery.' What is the point of bothering about people who are not going to invite you to a meal?

What an idea – moving a dead man from one town to another! No one would lend you a car for that. And nowadays, if you're a nonentity, you don't get a hearse and a funeral march – just a quick trip on a lorry.

Once people used to go to our cemeteries on Sundays and walk between the graves, singing beautiful hymns and spreading sweet-smelling incense. It set your heart at rest; it allayed the painful fears of inevitable death. It was almost as though the dead were smiling from under their grey mounds: 'It's all right . . . Don't be afraid.'

But nowadays, if a cemetery is kept up, there's a sign hanging there: 'Owners of graves! Keep this place tidy on penalty of a fine!' But more often they just roll them flat with bulldozers, to build sports grounds and parks.

Then there are those who died for their native land — it could still happen to you or me. There was a time when the church set aside a day of remembrance for those who fell on the battlefield. England does this on Poppy Day. All nations dedicate one day to remembering those who died for us all.

More men died for us Russians than for any other people, yet we have no such day. If you stop to think about the dead, who is to build the new world? In three wars we have lost so many husbands, sons and lovers — yet to think of them repels us. They're dead, buried under painted wooden posts — why should they interfere with our lives? For *we* will never die!

Alexander Solzhenitsyn

8: PEOPLE, NOT ENEMIES

An excerpt from the autobiography of the Russian poet, Yevgeny Yevtushenko. He was born in 1933 and his poems were first published in 1952. He is particularly noted for his poem, 'Babiy Yar', an attack on Soviet anti-semitism.

During World War Two, Russia (as well as the Western Allies) was at war with Germany. Germany made advances into Russia and, in October 1941, advanced on Moscow. The Russians and Germans developed a bitter hatred for each other. The Germans were forced to retreat by the larger Russian forces and the fierceness of the winter weather. Many Germans were taken prisoner and this is a description of what happened when some of these prisoners were marched through the streets of Moscow. They might have expected little mercy. The passage is written by a Russian poet who was eight at the time.

In '41 Mama took me back to Moscow. There I saw our enemies for the first time. If my memory is right, nearly 20,000 German war prisoners were to be marched in a single column through the streets of Moscow.

The pavements swarmed with onlookers, cordoned off by soldiers and police.

The crowd were mostly women — Russian women with hands roughened by hard work, lips untouched by lipstick and thin hunched shoulders which had borne half the burden of the war. Every one of them must have had a father or husband, a brother or a son killed by the Germans.

They gazed with hatred in the direction from which the column was to appear.

At last we saw it.

The generals marched at the head, massive chins stuck out, lips folded disdainfully, their whole demeanour meant to show superiority over their plebeian victors.

'They smell of eau-de-cologne, the bastards,' someone in the crowd said with hatred.

The women were clenching their fists. The soldiers and policemen had all they could do to hold them back.

All at once something happened to them.

They saw German soldiers, thin, unshaven, wearing dirty bloodstained bandages, hobbling on crutches or leaning on the shoulders of their comrades; the soldiers walked with their heads down.

The street became dead silent — the only sound was the shuffling of boots and the thumping of crutches.

Then I saw an elderly woman in broken-down boots push herself forward and touch a policeman's shoulder, saying: 'Let me through.' There must have been something about her that made him step aside.

She went up to the column, took from inside her coat something wrapped in a coloured handkerchief and unfolded it. It was a crust of black bread. She pushed it awkwardly into the pocket of a soldier, so exhausted that he was tottering on his feet. And now suddenly from every side women were running towards the soldiers, pushing into their hands bread, cigarettes, whatever they had.

The soldiers were no longer enemies.

They were people.

Yevgeny Yevtushenko

8
Lessons from the past

1: THE GREAT FIRE OF LONDON
(2 September 1666)

The Great Fire of London began on 2 September 1666. Part of Samuel Pepys' description of it (taken from his Diary) is included here partly for its intrinsic interest, but also for its illustration of life in that period and as a warning of the power and danger of fire.

Before beginning a reading, it might be helpful to alert listeners to the differences between a modern city and London in Pepys' time: e.g. the number of wooden buildings, narrower streets, lack of adequate fire brigades, no telecommunications, less effective water mains, etc.

The fire began on Sunday, 2 September 1666. In those days, one of the main ways of getting about London was by boat on the River Thames. The fire was on the north side of the river. It began where the Monument now stands, not far from the Tower of London. This description is taken from the diary of Samuel Pepys, an important government official.

The fire takes hold

(NB Jane is one of Samuel Pepys' maids.)

Jane called us up about three in the morning, to tell us of a great fire they saw in the City. So I rose, and slipped on my nightgown and went to her window; and thought it to be on the back side of Marke Lane at the farthest; but, being unused to such fires as followed, I thought it far enough off; and so went to bed again, and to sleep. About seven rose again to dress myself, and there looked out at the window, and saw the fire not so much as it was, and further off. So to my closet to set things to rights, after yesterday's cleaning. By and by Jane comes and tells me that she hears that above 300 houses have been burned down tonight by the fire we saw, and that it is now burning down all Fish Street, by London Bridge. So I made myself ready presently, and walked to the Tower; and there got upon one of the high places, Sir J Robinson's little son going up with me; and there I did see the houses at the end of the bridge all on fire, and an infinite great fire on this and the other side the end of the bridge; which, among other people, did trouble me for poor little Michell and our Sarah on the bridge. So down, with my heart full of trouble, to the Lieutenant of the Tower, who tells me that it begun this morning in the King's baker's house in Pudding Lane, and that it hath burned down St Magnus's Church and most part of Fish Street already. So I down to the waterside, and there got a boat and through bridge, and there saw a lamentable fire. Poor Michell's house, as far as the Old Swan, already burned that way, and the fire running further, that, in a very little time, it got as far as the Steele Yard, while I was there. Everybody endeavouring to remove their goods, and flinging into the river, or bringing them into lighters that lay off; poor people staying in their houses as long as till the very fire touched them, and then running into boats, or clambering from one pair of stairs, by the waterside, to another. And, among other things, the poor pigeons, I perceive, were loth to leave their houses, but hovered about the windows and balconys, till they burned their wings and fell down. Having staid, and in an hour's time seen the fire rage every way; and nobody, to my sight, endeavouring to quench it, but to remove their goods, and leave all to the fire; and having seen it get as far as the Steele Yard, and the wind mighty high, and driving it into the City; and everything, after so long a drought, proving combustible, even the very stones of churches; and among other things, the poor steeple by which pretty Mrs — lives, and whereof my old school fellow Elborough is parson, taken fire in the very top, and there burned till it fell down; I to White Hall, with a gentleman with me, who desired to go off from the Tower, to see the fire, in my boat; and there up to the King's closet in the Chapel, where people come about me, and I did give them an account dismayed them all, and word was carried in to the King. So I was called for, and did tell the King and Duke of York what I saw; and that, unless his Majesty did command houses to be pulled down, nothing could stop the fire.

Fighting the fire

The fire was by now so strong and so big that the only way to fight it (as Samuel Pepys suggested) was to pull down a wide circle of the houses around the fire to make a gap so that it would not go on spreading from house to house.

The King commanded me to go to my Lord Mayor from him, and command him to spare no houses, but to pull down before the fire every way. The Duke of York bid me tell him, that if he would have any more soldiers, he shall; and so did my Lord Arlington afterwards, as a great secret. Here meeting with Captain Cocke, I in his coach, which he lent me, and Creed with me to Paul's; and there walked along Watling Street, as well as I could, every creature coming away loaden with goods to save, and, here and there, sick people carried away in beds. Extraordinary good goods carried in carts and on backs. At last met my Lord Mayor in Canning Street, like a man spent, with a handkercher about his neck. To the King's message, he cried, like a fainting woman, 'Lord! what can I do? I am spent: people will not obey me. I have been pulling down houses; but the fire overtakes us faster than we can do it.' That he needed no more soldiers; and that, for himself, he must go and refresh himself, having been up all night. So he left me, and I him, and walked home; seeing people all almost distracted, and no manner of means used to quench the fire. The houses, too, so very thick thereabouts, and full of matter for burning, as pitch and tar, in Thames Street; and warehouses of oyle, and wines, and brandy, and other things. Here I saw Mr Isaac Houblon, the handsome man, prettily dressed and dirty at his door at Dowgate, receiving some of his brother's things, whose houses were on fire; and, as he says, have been removed twice already; and he doubts, as it soon proved, that they must be, in a little time, removed from his house also, which was a sad consideration. And to see the churches all filling with goods by people who themselves should have been quietly there at this time. By this time, it was about twelve o'clock; and so home, and there find my guests, who were Mr Wood and his wife Barbary Shelden, and also Mr Moone.

We were in great trouble and disturbance at this fire, not knowing what to think of it. However, we had an extraordinary good dinner, and as merry as at this time we could be. While at dinner, Mrs Batelier come to enquire after Mr Woolfe and Stanes, who, it seems, are related to them, whose houses in Fish Street are all burned, and they in a sad condition. She would not stay in the fright. Soon as dined, I and Moone away, and walked through the City, the streets full of nothing but people; and horses and carts loaden with goods, ready to run over one another, and removing goods from one burned house to another.

The fire continues to rage

The fire raged all day. In the evening, Pepys, his wife and some friends went on a boat on the River Thames to see the fire.

So near the fire as we could for smoke; and all over the Thames with one's faces in the wind, you were almost burned with a shower of fire drops. This is very true: so as houses were burned by these drops and flakes of fire, three or four, nay, five or six houses, one from another. When we could endure no more upon the water, we to a little alehouse on the Bankside, over against the Three Cranes, and there staid till it was dark almost, and saw the fire grow; and, as it grew darker, appeared more and more; and in corners and upon steeples, and between churches and houses, as far as we could see up the hill of the City, in a most horrid, malicious, bloody flame, not like the fine flame of an ordinary fire.

We staid till, it being darkish, we saw the fire as only one entire arch of fire from this to the other side the bridge, and in a bow up the hill for an arch of above a mile long: it made me weep to see it. The churches, houses, and all on fire, and flaming at once; and a horrid noise the flames made, and the cracking of houses at their ruine. So home with a sad heart, and there find every body discoursing and lamenting the fire; and poor Tom Hater come with some few of his goods saved out of his house, which was burned upon Fish Street Hill. I invited him to lie at my house, and did receive his goods; but was deceived in his lying there, the news coming every moment of the growth of the fire; so as we were forced to begin to pack up our own goods, and prepare for their removal; and did by moonshine, it being brave, dry, and moonshine and warm weather, carry much of my goods into the garden; and Mr Hater and I did remove my money and iron chests into my cellar, as thinking that the safest place. And got my bags of gold into my office, ready to carry away, and my chief papers of accounts also there, and my tallies into a box by themselves. So great was our fear, as Sir W Batten hath carts come out of the country to fetch away his goods this night. We did put Mr Hater, poor man! to bed a little; but he got but very little rest, so much noise being in my house, taking down of goods.

About four o'clock in the morning, my Lady Batten

sent me a cart to carry away all my money, and plate, and best things, to Sir W Rider's at Bednall Greene, which I did, riding myself in my nightgown, in the cart; and, Lord! to see how the streets and the highways are crowded with people running and riding, and getting of carts at any rate to fetch away things. I find Sir W Rider tired with being called up all night, and receiving things from several friends. His house full of goods, and much of Sir W Batten's and Sir W Pen's. I am eased at my heart to have my treasure so well secured.

Samuel Pepys

2: USEFUL WORK

A passage that suggests the importance of thinking positively and one that reminds us that there is a dignity and value in the routine and mundane.

One of the buildings destroyed in the Great Fire of London was the old St Paul's Cathedral. The new, present one was designed by Sir Christopher Wren.

There is a story told about something that was supposed to have happened when St. Paul's Cathedral was being built. Sir Christopher Wren was walking round (so the story says) watching the men at work. None of them realized, as Sir Christopher Wren walked round, that this was the great architect himself, the master mind whose plans they were all busy working on. As he walked round Wren stopped for a while to watch a stonemason shaping a piece of masonry and he asked him what he was doing. 'I'm chipping this block of stone', said the man – rather crossly. Presently Wren stopped again opposite a wood carver who was working on one of the panels of the choir screen. 'What are you doing?' he asked. 'Who me?' said the man. 'I'm earning my living, that's what I'm doing.' Then Sir Christopher Wren came upon another man, just an ordinary unskilled labourer, sweeping up the dirt and chips from the pavement, and again he asked him what he was doing; and this man answered – 'I'm helping Sir Christopher Wren build this Cathedral.' This man had got something. It wasn't much of a job, but it was a job that somebody had got to do. Any useful job of work is something to take just that kind of pride in, because it is helping God to carry out a very important plan that he has made.

John G. Williams

3: A WESLEYAN CHILDHOOD

John Wesley (1703-1791) is generally said to be the founder of Methodism. At first a movement within the Church of England, it later became an independent church. John Wesley wrote an extensive Journal *and arranged for excerpts to be published. He included two letters from his mother. This is part of one of them.*

How strictly will you bring up your children? What rules will you insist they follow? And how were children brought up two or three hundred years ago? Someone who grew up in those days was John Wesley, the man who, with others, started the Methodist Church – there's a Methodist church . . . (refer to local one). When he was famous, he arranged for his diaries to be published and asked his mother to write him a letter describing how he was brought up when he was very young. This is part of her letter.

24 July 1732

Dear Son,
 According to your desire, I have collected the principal rules I observed in educating my family. The children were always put into a regular method of living, in such things as they were capable of, from their birth: as in dressing, undressing, changing their linen, etc.
 When turned a year old (and some before), they were taught to fear the rod, and to cry softly: by which

means they escaped the abundance of correction they might otherwise have had, and that most odious noise of the crying of children was rarely heard in the house.

As soon as they were grown pretty strong, they were confined to three meals a day. At dinner their little table and chairs were set by ours, where they could be overlooked; and they were suffered [i.e. allowed] to eat and drink (small [i.e. weak] beer), as much as they would; but not to call for anything. If they wanted aught they used to whisper to the maid which attended them, who came and spoke to me; and as soon as they could handle a knife and fork, they were set to our table. They were never suffered to choose their meat, but always made [to] eat such things as were provided for the family.

Drinking or eating between meals was never allowed, unless in case of sickness, which seldom happened. Nor were they suffered to go into the kitchen to ask anything of the servants when they were at meat; if it was known they did, they were certainly beat, and the servants severely reprimanded.

At six, as soon as family prayers were over, they had their supper; at seven the maid washed them; and, beginning at the youngest, she undressed and got them all to bed by eight; at which time she left them in their several rooms awake — for there was no such thing allowed of in our house as sitting by a child till it fell asleep.

In order to form the minds of children, the first thing to be done is to conquer their will, and bring them to an obedient temper. To inform the understanding is a work of time, and must with children proceed by slow degrees as they are able to bear it; but the subjecting the will is a thing that must be done at once, and the sooner the better.

The children were taught, as soon as they could speak, the Lord's Prayer, which they were made to say at rising and at bed time constantly; to which, as they grew bigger, were added a short prayer for their parents, and some collects: a short catechism, and some portions of Scripture, as their memories could bear.

They were very early made to distinguish the Sabbath from other days, to understand they might have nothing they cried for, and to speak handsomely for what they wanted.

Every one was kept close to their business, for the six hours of school; and it is almost incredible what a child may be taught in a quarter of a year, by a vigorous application, if it have but tolerable capacity and good health...

There were several by-laws observed. That no girl be taught to work till she can read very well, for the putting children to learn sewing before they can read perfectly is the very reason why so few women can read fit to be heard, and never to be well understood.

Susannah Wesley

4: ENGLAND'S FIRST WOMAN DOCTOR

Elizabeth Garrett (1836-1917) was the first woman in this country to overcome the prejudice that prevented women from becoming doctors of medicine. (She subsequently became the first woman mayor in England – of Aldeburgh in Suffolk.)

In the last century women were allowed to do very few jobs. Indeed, if you were a 'respectable' woman, a 'lady', you did not work at all. One young lady, Elizabeth Garrett, wanted to change this – and to become a doctor.

As a teenager, Elizabeth was sent to boarding school. The headmistress expressed the view that women should be able to lead a fuller life than that which was spent entirely in the home. The idea of greater opportunities for women appealed to Elizabeth, but she could not see how this could come about. After leaving school, she lived at home in the conventional way until she was about twenty-two years old. During this time, she tried to improve her own education, studying Latin and mathematics among other subjects.

While visiting an old school friend, Elizabeth met Elizabeth Blackwell, who was the only woman doctor in the world. After a fight to overcome enormous difficulties, Dr Blackwell had qualified in America. Elizabeth Garrett resolved that she would become the first woman doctor in England.

Mr and Mrs Garrett were very much against the idea, but once her father realized how determined Elizabeth was he supported and helped her all he could.

Since there were no facilities for women to be trained as doctors, Elizabeth began by becoming a nurse at the Middlesex Hospital. She picked up as much medical knowledge as she could and arranged to have private tuition from some of the hospital's doctors.

Difficulties and obstacles were placed in Elizabeth's way, not because she was unable to do the work or pass the examinations, but because she was a woman. Gradually, with the help of her father (who even threatened legal action against the medical authorities), Elizabeth completed the necessary training. She sat the examinations and passed, gaining the Licentiate of the Society of Apothecaries. At the age of twenty-nine, she became the first woman medical practitioner in Britain.

Elizabeth was not content to make her successful medical practice the whole of her work. Many of her patients were women, who were glad to discuss their ailments with another woman. There was no National Health Service at this time. Treatment had to be paid for. Elizabeth was aware that many poor women were unable to afford a doctor's fee. In order to help them, she opened St Mary's Dispensary, and here women and children were treated by Elizabeth Garrett, who charged very little for her services.

Another thing Elizabeth was not content with was her qualification. The Licentiate of the Society of

Apothecaries permitted her to dispense and practise medicine. Most male practitioners held a degree enabling them to use the title 'Doctor'. With her usual determination, Elizabeth found out how she could become Doctor Garrett. Since women were not admitted to courses in Britain, she enrolled at the University of the Sorbonne in Paris, where, not long before, it had been agreed to admit women.

In 1870, Elizabeth Garrett was examined by the University. She passed each of the six required subjects with distinction, even though the whole of the proceedings were in French.

She was now Doctor Elizabeth Garrett. No longer could the British medical profession regard her as inferior.

Shortly afterwards, Elizabeth married James Anderson, a shipowner. It was agreed that Elizabeth should continue her work, and she became known as Dr Elizabeth Garrett Anderson.

Eva Bailey

5: GEORGE AND THE CHOCOLATE FACTORY

This presentation outlines the work of the Quaker philanthropist, George Cadbury (1839-1922). Besides expanding his father's chocolate business, he planned and developed the first 'model' village.

CHARACTERS:

Storyteller

F. Ward, a hosier

J. G. Palmer, a sinister dentist

Miss Fisher, a corsetière

John Cadbury, a blunt man

Richard Cadbury, 25, his enthusiastic nephew

George Cadbury, 21-60, a logical man

Lessons from the past

A girl from Bristol (Bristol lass)
Reader
House Agent

N.B. Strict Quakers, at this time, still used the forms 'Thee' and 'Thou' for the singular 'you'.

Storyteller: Bull Street in Birmingham is one of those streets where they allow buses but no other traffic; and there are lots of different shops. But what was it like back in 1835? Well, there were shops then. Let's hear how some of them were advertising themselves in those days.

Each of the traders enters and advertises his or her business.

F. Ward: F. Ward, hosier and glover; silk and gingham umbrellas for ladies and gentlemen; 48 Bull Street, Birmingham.

Dentist: J. G. Palmer announces that he replaces decaying teeth either with natural ones no longer required by their owners, or with artificial substitutes; children's teeth carefully attended to, and straightened.

Miss Fisher: Miss Fisher most respectfully requests the attention of ladies in general to her splendid collection of corsets entirely of her own manufacture; Fisher of 96 Bull Street, Birmingham.

Storyteller: And just across the road from Miss Fisher was the first shop ever to have a modern plate glass window.

John: John Cadbury's of 93 Bull Street, Birmingham. Tea and coffee dealer. Also cocoa; prepared by myself; a most nutritious breakfast beverage; no chemicals used; absolutely pure; Cadbury of Bull Street.

Storyteller: That was John Cadbury who made and sold cocoa, a new breakfast 'beverage' or drink. It became very popular which pleased John, partly because he thought alcoholic drinks were wrong. Until then, for breakfast, most people drank – beer! But this isn't the story of John Cadbury, because after a few years, by when he had also built a separate factory to make the cocoa powder, he retired. His nephew took over the shop and his two sons, Richard (who was 25) and George (who was 21) took over the chocolate factory.

Enter George and Richard Cadbury.

George: These accounts . . . I thought that father's business had been more successful . . . Richard when he opened the factory as well as the shop, wasn't he –

Richard: Sales of cocoa, George, are not what they were. People have stopped buying –

George: We must improve its quality. I have heard of a new machine in Holland. It is said to improve the cocoa powder. I shall go and inspect it.

Richard: But thou knowst no word of Dutch!

George: I shall speak by signs and by the dictionary.

Richard: And when we have improved the cocoa, we must advertise.

George: On omnibuses. That would be . . . sensible.

Storyteller: People did buy the new cocoa, and the chocolate they started making. Richard and George employed more workers. But what was it like, actually working in a chocolate factory? This is how one young woman described her work in another chocolate factory, in Bristol.

Bristol lass: When I started, I had to cover little creams with chocolate. We had to cover 120 creams to earn three farthings. After you been there a couple of weeks they put it up to one penny. We daren't talk and we daren't laugh. If we laughed or talked we had to leave off. She'd tell you, 'Leave off and sit.' And we had to sit on our stools and wait half an hour till we could start earning again.

Storyteller: But was it like that in Richard and George's factory?

Richard: Ours is the first firm in Birmingham to introduce a Saturday half holiday for all our workers –

George: And when it is frosty, we give the men time off for skating –

Richard: Or soccer at other times.

George: Sport is good for a man. As is fresh air.

Richard: We must arrange outings to the countryside!

George: The countryside! Brother Richard –

Richard: Thou has a new idea?

George: The countryside. A garden! Why not a factory in a garden?

Richard: A factory in a garden? That would be . . . pleasant.

George: It is sensible. Sensible.

Richard: Explain thy reasons, Brother George.

George: One, manufacturing food in a city is . . . the smoke, the grime . . . it is not –

Richard: Sensible?

George: Precisely. And two, I know just the place. Four miles south of the city. By the Worcester Canal –

Richard: So the barges can bring the cocoa direct from where it is unloaded from the ships at Bristol –

George: And three, it is beside the new railway line from Birmingham –

Richard: So our workers can reach the factory.

George: And we shall arrange special cheap fares for the men and girls. Workmen's returns! And I shall design a new, sensible factory. Where the sun shines in the south, there will be no windows.

Richard (*admiring the genius*): To keep the chocolate cool. To stop it from melting.

George: And we shall build a canteen. There'll be a cricket field. And there is a little stream there. Called Bourne Brook.

Richard: It will be called Bourne Factory. No, it will be like a town. Bourne Town.

George: A French name would be more sensible.

Richard: It would?

George: People believe French chocolate is best.

Richard: So we'll call it (*French pronunciation*) Bourne Ville!

George (*very English pronunciation*): Bourneville, more like!

Richard exits.

Storyteller: The factory in the garden was a great success. When the Cadburys moved there in 1879, they had 230 workers. Twenty years later, there were nearly three thousand — all making drinking cocoa and chocolate: a new kind of chocolate, lighter in colour, made with milk. The Cadburys were getting richer and richer; but there was one sadness: Richard died of a disease called diptheria while he was on holiday abroad. George carried on running his factory. But something still worried him: the houses his work-people had to live in, in the poorer parts of the city.

Reader: They are so clustered in upon each other, long terraces of them, built back to back and facing onto a tiny narrow street. This is unpaved. Down its middle, a gutter forces its way . . . Women throw household slops of every description into that gutter . . . The houses are tiny, and very dark inside; the window panes being many of them broken and stuffed with rags. The smell everywhere is terrible. And in two small rooms, there live nine people. In the rooms upstairs, two other families . . .

Storyteller: Not every factory owner worried about where and how his workers lived. George Cadbury did. He was also worried that more and more of these slums were being built, spreading outwards from the centre of Birmingham. So, with his own money, he bought a lot of land near the factory and began to plan Bourneville Village.

George: People need *gardens*. Gardens will prevent all the evils which arise from the insanitary houses in the city. I must secure for workers in factories some of the advantages of the outdoor life; the opportunity for the healthful occupation of cultivating the soil. It is *sensible* for each house to have a garden.

House Agent: . . . and as you can see, the garden is three times the area of the house. Each house, again as you can see, is the shape of a country cottage; some being of brick, some of black and white timber construction. The typical house contains a parlour, living room and kitchen downstairs and three bedrooms up. Great care has been taken to preserve all trees on the site and others have been planted along the exceptionally wide and attractive avenues.

George: . . . and though I've paid for the houses, I won't make a penny out of land or homes. The rent will go to a charity; the Bourneville Village Trust. For the improvement of the estate.

Storyteller: And George Cadbury arranged for much more to be done at Bourneville. He had schools built; museums, a hospital and parks. He himself taught in a school for grown-ups who'd had to leave school when they were only eleven or twelve. And he arranged holidays for poor children from Birmingham, even if they were nothing to do with his firm. But *why*? Why did he do this? Did he perhaps feel guilty or embarrassed because he'd become so very rich?

George: When those city children come on a holiday here and are given proper meals, they put on two and three-quarter pounds weight in a fortnight. It's sensible for them to be given a holiday.

Storyteller: 'Sensible', yes. But why did George Cadbury spend his money like this? Well, he was a Quaker. Quakers are Christians who are members of the 'Society of Friends'. For them, religion isn't just something you do one day a week, when you go to church. Religion is what you do all the time. And listen to a question that Quakers are meant to ask themselves:

Reader: Are you working towards the removal of social injustice? Do you, as followers of Jesus Christ, take a living interest in the social conditions of the district in which you live? Do you seek to promote the welfare of those in any kind of need?

Storyteller: George Cadbury could answer 'Yes'. For him, his Christian faith meant building proper houses for his workers, giving them a good place to live; *and* helping all the people in the area in which he lived.

David Self

6: JESSE BOOT, CHEMIST

Jesse Boot (1850–1931) was born in Nottingham, the son of John Boot, a herbalist and Methodist lay preacher. When Jesse was ten, his father died and Jesse left school to help his mother gather herbs and sell them in their small shop which provided natural remedies for the poor in the working-class district in which they lived. But the working classes were now transferring their allegiance to the new 'patent' medicines (many of which were of little value). The quick-witted (and honest) Jesse Boot realized how he could help the people around him and build up a thriving retail business (which later expanded into drug manufacturing as well).

In almost every big shopping centre, you'll see one particular chemist's shop: Boots the Chemists. But how did this chain of shops get started?

CHARACTERS:

Presenter

Reader

Jesse Boot, a herbalist's son

Elliott, one of Boot's employees

Presenter: Until just over a hundred years ago people relied on herbal medicines: medicines made mainly from plants and flowers. Then, what were called 'patent medicines' began to be sold: bottles of sweet syrup and boxes of pills. This is how one writer described them.

Reader: These pills sell at a penny a box. Any doubts about how good they are are taken away by the picture of their maker smiling from the lid. He has cause to smile. Nearly all the pills appear to do two things. 'For the head and stomach' says one box. 'For the blood and stomach' says another. But whatever their aim, all the pills contain the *same* ingredients. Soap and a mild laxative. That is all. But they *do* differ in colour. Some are red, some green, others pink. And people buy them all.

Presenter: There were some good new medicines on the market though, and Jesse Boot decided to sell these — but at much less than they were being sold in other shops. He was determined to be fair to his customers — and to help himself. The shop's weekly takings went up from £20 to £100. As the bluntly spoken Jesse Boot said:

Boot: There was nothing remarkable about my methods. It was simply the application of common sense. I found that everywhere articles, especially medicines, were being sold at ridiculously high prices. And sold without any regard at all for neatness – or attractiveness. My idea was simply to buy tons of the stuff where others bought 'undredweights – so I could buy more cheaply *and* sell more cheaply. Some of these medicines, you know, I found I could knock two pence off the price other shops charged, and still make a nice little profit!

Presenter: And so Jesse Boot's business grew and grew. He opened more and more shops and took on staff to help. One of them, a man called Elliott, who worked for the firm all his life, remembered how Jesse ran the business.

Elliott: One of the earliest examples I remember was the case of the Epsom Salts. The usual price was a halfpenny for an ounce. Suddenly Mr Boot offered it at a penny for a full pound and made an advertisement about it. Well, the people came to buy. They did that . . . Then there was the soft soap. The ordinary price was four pence a pound. Suddenly Mr Boot offered it at four pence halfpenny for two pounds! All packed in a nicely shaped parcel, tied up neatly with string *and* labelled. Then there were the tins of salmon. Mr Boot must 'ave 'ad the opportunity of buying an 'uge quantity. Now, the price at that time was eightpence a tin. Mr Boot's price was . . . four pence halfpenny!!! Well, as the news went round, the sales were . . . sensational! You know, we sold 120 dozen tins in a single day from one shop. And many of the orders were, 'A tin of salmon, please, and will you open it?' You see, tin openers weren't to be found in every house in them times. Oh no, people weren't well off them times.

Presenter: So 'Boots the Chemists' as the shops were becoming known, sold different things at low prices, which helped the poor – and it all made Jesse Boot very rich. But he also worked very hard. He worked sixteen hours every day except Sundays (when he went to church and took exercise in the country). Jesse Boot once looked back on his life.

Boot: They all said I might be honest, but I wouldn't make money. Well, I've made money.

Presenter: He had too. He was very, very rich. But was he honest? Was he a 'good' man? Well, he looked after his young staff. He arranged parties and outings for them. When the girls left to get married, Mrs Boot gave every one a present. A Bible. And Jesse thought of the customers. He wanted even the poorest to be able to afford the new medicines. But, as we've heard, all this made him very rich. So how did he use his money?

Boot: Any man can give five pounds to a good cause. I'll support the bigger schemes.

Presenter: Jesse Boot gave away over two million pounds. Half of it, he gave so that Nottingham University could be built. He paid for new chapels in the poorer parts of Nottingham. He gave a quarter of a million pounds to pay for a new park; £50,000 for Nottingham General Hospital.

Jesse Boot became Sir Jesse Boot; later, Lord Trent of Nottingham.

So, what do you think of Jesse Boot? Not everyone liked this rather grumpy business man who seemed to think only about work and his factory and opening more shops. But others knew he was a religious man, an honest man, a good man. What do you think?

David Self

7: ONE HUNDRED YEARS AGO

A presentation, arranged for five readers (though the number could be altered) intended to show what it was like running a home one hundred years ago.

You may sometimes dislike being asked to help about the house: washing up, tidying up, or maybe being sent on an errand. But what would doing the housework have been like a hundred years ago?

Reader 1: A hundred years ago housework was a much harder and more time-consuming job than today. All the cleaning was done by hand, which meant hours of scrubbing and heavy lifting. All food and all cleaning materials had to be made in the home – there were no ready-made frozen meals and no bottles of instant cleaner. All this work was done by women. A man might garden or clean the shoes, but housework was women's work. For working men had to put in a very long and hard day's work to support their families. Therefore they didn't expect to have to work when they got home as well.

Reader 2: Running a home was a different matter if you were rich enough to employ servants, but here again it was the women servants who did the housework. Male servants looked after the horses, drove the carriage and opened the front door, but they didn't cook, wash or clean. Even modest, middle-class homes usually had one female servant – a 'maid of all work' as they were called.

Victorian houses were hard to clean. The fashion was to have lots of shelves and ledges, mantelpieces, skirting boards, moulded ceilings – all places where dust could collect easily. Furniture was very large and heavy to move.

Reader 1: A prosperous, working-class family might have a small house to themselves, but poorer families were often crowded into one or two rooms. Housework must have been particularly inconvenient when there was no space to store things, when beds had to be made up in the living room and people were running in and out. In some houses there were mice, rats and bugs to contend with too.

Reader 3: 'The question of vermin is a very pressing one in all the small houses. No woman, however clean, can cope with it. The mothers accept the pest as part of their dreadful lives but they do not grow reconciled to it. Repapering and fumigation are as far as any landlord goes in dealing with the difficulty.'
[Maud Pember Reeves, *Round About a Pound a Week*]

Reader 2: A large percentage of the population lived in bad housing and there was no alternative – no council flats, no housing advice centres and no laws to protect tenants. To buy a house was completely beyond the reach of working people, so most families rented rooms. This cost about 3 to 6 shillings a week (15-30p) – about a quarter to a third of the average working-class family's income.

Reader 1: Most working-class houses had only cold running water from one tap in the kitchen or yard which meant carrying buckets of water up and down stairs to wash. Sharing a house often meant going down to a neighbour's kitchen or walking through their rooms to get to the yard. Few homes had bathrooms, or the newly-invested gas 'geyser' to heat water. Working people had to boil their water in pots and kettles, and a bath was a weekly event when they sqeezed into a tin tub in front of the fire, sharing the water with the rest of the family.

Reader 3: 'A woman with six children under thirteen gives them all a bath with two waters between them on Saturday morning in the wash tub. She generally has a bath herself on Sunday evening when her husband is out. All the water has to be carried upstairs, heated in her kettle, and carried down again when dirty. Her husband baths when he can afford two pence, at the public baths.'
[Maud Pember Reeves, *Round About a Pound a Week*]

Reader 2: If you had an out-house or scullery for doing the washing, you could bath inside the 'copper'. This was a big copper-lined stove for boiling water, heated by lighting a pile of wood underneath it. Mrs Murray, a Derbyshire housewife, explained:

Reader 4: 'I used to bath all my brothers and sisters in the copper. I would boil it up, then leave it so that the bottom wasn't too hot. I'd sit them on the side and soap them all over with pieces cut off from a big bar of Sunlight soap, then dip them in the copper.'

Reader 1: Everyday washing meant a wash-down with carbolic soap or soda from an enamel bowl on the kitchen table or a wash stand. Before the invention of toothpaste, people used tins of tooth powder, or just salt.

Reader 2: The toilet was outside, often at the end of the garden, so it was common to keep a chamber pot under the bed. A Lancashire man remembered:

Reader 5: 'In the middle of winter you weren't going to risk pneumonia by running out in the night, so it was just the normal thing to do. The first job my mother did every morning was to go round with a pail and empty all the pots and clean them with carbolic.'

Reader 1: Heating was by coal fires which had to be cleared out and lit every morning. This was no easy job in a cold draughty house, first thing in the morning.

Coal fires also meant carting heavy coals up flights of stairs, and they gave off thick black dust which settled all around the house.

Reader 2: The carpet sweeper had just been invented a hundred years ago but the vacuum cleaner was still a thing of the future. Most working people had rugs made at home out of rags. Carpets had to be brushed by hand – the best method was one using tea leaves. A London woman explains this method of carpet cleaning:

Reader 3: 'You sprinkled your old tea leaves over the mat and they absorbed the bits of dust — then it's easier to sweep up. But you weren't considered a good housewife unless you took your mats down to the yard, put them on the washing line and beat the life out of them.'

Reader 1: Jobs done outside did at least provide the chance to chat to neighbours:

Reader 4: 'The morning cleaning proceeded to the accompaniment of neighbourly greetings and shouting across garden and fence; for the first sound of the banging of mats was a signal for others to bring out theirs, and it would be "Have 'ee heard of this?" and "War d'ye think of that?" '

[Flora Thompson, *Lark Rise to Candleford*]

Reader 5: Even so, is everything better nowadays?

Reader 2: In theory, labour-saving machines have made housework much easier. It doesn't take all of Monday to do the washing, but several small washes a week may be necessary because the family expect clean clothes every day. A living room that was once cleaned weekly may now get hoovered daily. Freezers and blenders are an encouragement to do more and better cooking. In other words, there are new pressures on the housewife.

Reader 1: Another recent development is high-powered advertising aimed at housewives to encourage them to buy certain products by playing on their conscience: Is your wash white enough? Is your family getting the best of food? Should they eat butter or margarine? Are you getting the best value for money?

Reader 2: Many people brought up eighty or a hundred years ago recognize that things have changed, but not always for the best. Mrs Halls, a London woman, explains:

Reader 3:   'We were more contented then . . . we had nothing and everyone else had nothing . . . now we are all on each other's backs. Our spirit is gone . . . Then if you didn't see the woman next door you knocked on her door . . . now she could die.

'I wouldn't want to go back to all that housework, but we are no happier . . . a modern house doesn't make you happy or contented. We got as much pleasure out of going shopping with a few bob as out of anything we've got today.'

Carol Adams

9
Stories from the faiths

1: IN THE BEGINNING

'How did the world begin?' This question has been asked in almost every society or culture. It is one that continues to fascinate the modern scientist. The religions of the world have always attempted to provide their own answers. The Judaic-Christian answer is in the first chapter of the Book of Genesis. Many would say its details are not to be taken literally but that the story is to be seen as an affirmation that there was a divine inspiration behind the creation.

A   The Chinese creation story

Chinese tradition teaches that the world is kept in balance by two forces: 'yin' and 'yang'.

How do you think the world began? Some sort of chemical accident that brought everything into being by mistake? Or did something we call God carefully plan it all?

This is how Chinese people have traditionally told the story of the creation.

O listener, let it be told of a time when there was nothing but chaos, and that chaos was like a mist and full of emptiness. Suddenly, into the midst of this mist, into this chaos of emptiness, came a great, colourful light. From this light all things that exist came to be. The mist shook and separated. That which was light rose up to form heaven, and that which was heavy sank, and formed the earth.

Now from heaven and earth came forth strong forces. These two forces combined to produce yin and yang. Picture, O listener, this yang like a dragon – hot, fiery, male, full of energy. Imagine, O listener, this yin as a cloud – moist, cool, female, drifting slowly. Each of these forces is full of great power. Left alone, they would destroy the world with their might, and chaos would return. Together, they balance each other, and keep the world in harmony.

This then is yin and yang, and from them came forth everything. The sun is of yang, and the moon, yin. The four seasons and the five elements – water, earth, metal, fire and wood – sprang from them. So did all kinds of living creatures.

So now there was the earth, floating like a jellyfish on water. But the earth was just a ball, without features. Then the forces of yin and yang created the giant figure P'an Ku, the Ancient One. P'an Ku, who never stopped growing every year of his great, long life, set to work to put the earth in order. He dug the river valleys and piled up the mountains. Over many thousands of years he shaped and created the flow and folds of our earth.

But such work took its toll. Even mighty P'an Ku could not escape death, and worn out by his struggle he collapsed and died. His body was now so vast that when he fell to the ground, dead, his body became the five sacred mountains. His flesh became the soil, his bones the rocks, his hair the plants and his blood the rivers. From his sweat came the rain, and from the parasites – the tiny creatures living on his body – came forth human beings.

The people at first lived in caves, but soon Heavenly Emperors came to teach them how to make tools and houses. The people also learned how to build boats, to fish, to plough and plant, and to prepare food. O listener, this is how it all began.

The meaning behind the story

The story opens with chaos, which is felt to be threatening and confusing. Into this murky chaos falls the brilliant light – the opposite of the murky, vague mist. When these two meet, chaos begins to separate, and heaven and earth are created. It is at this point that the two great forces of yin and yang appear.

Life only begins with the two forces of yin and yang. This is the heart of Chinese belief: that everything, from trees and water to animals and people, is composed of yin and yang. They are seen as the male and female forces of the universe. So the sun, hot and forceful, is yang, while the cool, quiet, but powerful moon is yin. But even yin and yang, these great forces that come from the shattering of chaos, are only able to work because the destructive power of each is balanced by the other. Each carries part of the other, and each needs the other to become whole.

To help understand this, the Chinese point to the four seasons. Winter is yin, summer is yang. But winter gives birth to spring – it has to, so summer arises. You cannot have one without the other. They need each other, for without that balance, chaos would reappear.

Looking at the world, the Chinese saw that it was usually people who upset the balance. If, for instance, people mistreat the environment, then the balance is thrown out. The Chinese believe that this can lead to disasters such as great floods, fires, famines, earthquakes or wars. So it can be seen how important it is that yin and yang are balanced.

Martin Palmer and Esther Bisset

B The Greek creation story

This is a re-telling of the Greek myth that provides an explanation of how Earth and Sky began.

To begin with, there were no shapes. Nothing existed; there were no forms of things. All the elements and atoms that would one day make matter, swirled and seethed in endless, meaningless movement. If a mortal had existed and been able to watch the dance of the elements, it would have seemed as beautiful as dust dancing in a sunshaft. But there was no dust, no sun, no mortal: only the endless dance. The name of the swirling elements was Chaos.

From time to time as things seethed and whirled in Chaos, in the dance of the elements, patterns were formed. For a fleeting moment, in one place or another, shapes appeared: circles, ridges, humps and hollows in the elemental flow. Most of them vanished as quickly as a mirage; but some repeated themselves, growing ever stronger and more permanent. The heavy atoms began to make patterns separately from the light atoms, gradually the patterns of each grew fixed and purposeful, until the first shapes of things were formed. The heavy atoms made the shape called Gaia (Earth): a living organism with clefts, folds and hills like gigantic limbs. The light atoms made Ouranos (Sky): quick-moving, always changing, as restless as breath itself.

Turning and twisting in the swirl of Chaos, Gaia and Ouranos danced a slow dance of love. Sky embraced Earth; Earth opened herself to Sky and grew fertile. Life-giving rain from Sky sought out Earth's cracks and crevices; streams, rivers and oceans formed; the ground produced trees, green plants and flowers, and soon there were birds, animals and insects of every kind. These were the first children of Earth and Sky.

So they floated peacefully in the space made by their own creation. Earth was like a huge flat dish, hillocked and humped by mountain ranges, river-valleys, lakes and seas; Sky soared above like an umbrella of clouds and light. All round, at Earth's circumference, they touched. The touching point, the horizon, was marked by a fast flowing river called Ocean; it whirled round in an endless circle and held everything in place. At the eastern edge of Earth, the Sun rose each morning to begin its journey across the dome of Sky; each evening it plunged into Ocean at the western edge and began its night's voyage to the east, ready to emerge again next morning. Below Earth lay the Underworld, so far below that a dropped object would take nine days to reach it. The entrances to the Underworld were at the edge of the circle of Ocean; there were also cracks and openings in Earth's floor itself. The shortest distance between Earth and Sky was at Ocean's edge, the dome of Sky at the centre, its highest point, rose above Earth to the height of three great mountains piled on top of one another, Mount Olympus, Mount Pelion and Mount Ossa.

Kenneth Macleish

C The Christian view of creation

The Judaic-Christian account of creation continues with a description of the Garden of Eden (Genesis 2, verses 8, 9 and 15). This is a Christian explanation of that account.

We do not think that there ever was a beautiful garden called 'the Garden of Eden' and that two people called Adam and Eve lived in it, but we do believe that this picture gives a true idea of the place of man in the world. Man does have power over God's world, and he does change and alter it just as a gardener changes and alters a garden by digging new flowerbeds, planting new trees and so on. There is a story told of an old man who begged a farmer for the corner of a field which the plough did not reach. This bit of the field was growing wild with brambles and thistles, and the old man got to work and turned it into an allotment. He was looking after his bit of ground with his beans and his peas looking neat and tidy in their rows when the parish priest came by. The clergyman leant on the gate and exchanged a few words, and then he looked at the man's work and said, 'Well, George, you and the Almighty have made a good job of that, haven't you?'

The old man looked up, spat on the ground and said,
'You should have seen it when the Almighty had it to
himself.' This story brings out very well the fact that
man has a part to play in God's world: God did not
make the world to run itself, he made man in the world
to run it.

David Cox

D The creation

A poem which is both a re-telling of, and a commentary on, the Genesis creation story.

And God stepped out on space,
And he looked around and said:
I'm lonely —
I'll make me a world.

As far as the eye of God could see
Darkness covered everything,
Blacker than a hundred midnights
Down in a cypress swamp.

Then God smiled,
And the light broke,
And the darkness rolled up on one side,
And the light stood shining on the other,
And God said: That's good!

Then God reached out and took the light in his hands,
And God rolled the light around in his hands
Until he made the sun;
And he set that sun a-blazing in the heavens.
And the light that was left from making the sun
God gathered it up in a shining ball
And flung it against the darkness,
Spangling the night with the moon and stars.

Then down between
The darkness and the light
He hurled the world;
And God said: That's good!

Then God himself stepped down —
And the sun was on his right hand,
And the moon was on his left;

The stars were clustered about his head,
And the earth was under his feet.
And God walked, and where he trod
His footsteps hollowed the valleys out
And bulged the mountains up.

Then he stopped and looked and saw
That the earth was hot and barren.
So God stepped over to the edge of the world
And he spat out the seven seas —
He batted his eyes, and the lightnings flashed —
He clapped his hands, and the thunders rolled —
And the waters above the earth came down,
The cooling waters came down.

Then the green grass sprouted,
And the little red flowers blossomed,
The pine tree pointed his finger to the sky,
And the oak spread out his arms,
The lakes cuddled down in the hollows of the ground,
And the rivers ran down to the sea;
And God smiled again,
And the rainbow appeared
And curled itself around his shoulder.

Then God raised his arm and he waved his hand
Over the sea and over the land,
And he said: Bring forth! Bring forth!
And quicker than God could drop his hand,

Fishes and fowls
And beasts and birds
Swam the rivers and the seas,
Roamed the forests and the woods,

And split the air with their wings.
And God said: That's good!

Then God walked around,
And God looked around
On all that he had made.
He looked at his sun,
And he looked at his moon,
And he looked at his little stars;
He looked on his world
With all its living things,
And God said: I'm lonely still.

Then God sat down —
On the side of a hill where he could think;
By a deep, wide river he sat down;
With his head in his hands,
God thought and thought,
Till he thought, I'll make me a man!

Up from the bed of the river
God scooped the clay;
And by the bank of the river
He kneeled him down;
And there the great God Almighty
Who lit the sun and fixed it in the sky,
Who flung the stars to the most far corner of the night,
Who rounded the earth in the middle of his hand;
This great God,
Like a mammy bending over her baby,
Kneeled down in the dust
Toiling over a lump of clay

Till he shaped it in his own image;
Then into it he blew the breath of life,
And man became a living soul.
Amen. Amen.

James Weldon Johnson

2: THE BLIND MEN AND THE ELEPHANT

A traditional Hindu tale about the importance of not being satisfied with a part of the truth.

Most of us find it very difficult to look at familiar things, places and words in a new light. Children who were born and brought up in Newcastle may be surprised and even irritated if a new child at school, coming from the south of England, invites them home to tea and his mother doesn't produce anything more substantial than a pot of tea and some cakes. What tea *means* partly depends on where we come from, and each meaning is, in a sense, a true meaning of the word. Yet each of us would like to think that our own meaning is the only true one. We hold to our own opinions and often remain blind to other people's ways of looking at things. 'I don't quite see what you're getting at', and 'Why can't you see things from my point of view?' are frequent everyday sentences.

Wise men in India have often argued about the meaning of truth without arriving at an agreed answer. In ancient India, a king who was interested in studying the meaning of truth collected together many stupid men who happened to have been blind from birth, and divided them into groups. He then brought forward an elephant, and allowing each group to feel just one part of the animal, asked them all to describe what an elephant was like.

The first group, after feeling the elephant's head, said that an elephant was like a pot. The second group, however, had felt an ear, and said that an elephant was like a winnowing basket. This is a large, flat basket used for winnowing the harvested whole grain, which is tossed up and down in the basket, the wind blowing the chaff away from the eventually husked grain. But those men who had felt a tusk insisted that an elephant was like the cutting part of a plough. These people were angrily interrupted by those who were convinced that an elephant was like a broom because they were at that very moment firmly clutching the elephant's tail. Finally, the blind men started fighting with each other while the king stood back and laughed, since he could see that each group had got hold of a bit of the truth but nobody was prepared to find out the whole truth.

In real life, of course, we often meet blind people who are more sensitive to the world about them than many sighted people.

3: CONFUCIUS AND FRIENDS

Confucius is the Latinized version of K'ung Fu-tzu (551-479 BCE). Little is known for certain about this great Chinese philosopher, but after some years of manual labour he became an accountant or court official and then a teacher. During a period of civil war, he fled to a neighbouring province and his fame began to spread. While Confuciusism has always been regarded as the major Chinese religion, he was not a religious leader but a teacher of ethics and morals.

Many hundreds of years ago, there lived in China a man called K'ung Fu-tzu. We know him as Confucius, but we don't know what he *looked* like. Some people say he was tall and very dignified. Others say that he had big ears and big sticking-out front teeth. And some people say he was a fussy, niggling, old-fashioned sort of person. But that is unlikely to be true because his friends wrote down a lot of the things that Confucius said, and from these sayings we can tell that he was kind and generous; he liked making jokes, going swimming and playing other sports. And he liked music.

But Confucius was not always popular. At first all went well when Confucius's job was to look after some sheep and cattle. As he said, 'All I have to do is to see that the sheep and cattle grow up to be strong and healthy.' And because he was good at his job, they did.

In fact, he soon became a special adviser to Duke Ai, who was ruler of that part of China, which was called Lu. Confucius planned the building of new roads and bridges, started schools and established a fair system of justice. One day, Duke Ai asked him, 'What must I do before the people will respect me?'

'If you promote the good people over the bad, you will be respected. If you let the bad take advantage of the good, then you will not be respected.'

And this is where the trouble began. In those days, the nobles and powerful people in China were not always good. They loved showing off, strutting about in embroidered garments. In winter they wore lambswool and fox furs and the skins of rare animals. They collected jewels and pieces of jade, which is a precious, bluish-green stone. They rode in expensive carriages, decorated with bronze and brass and pulled by fine horses. And the poor people had to work to provide for all this extravagance. Confucius said, 'If you can stand these people, who can you not stand?!' So when they heard him saying this and advising the Duke (and remember Confucius had once just been an ordinary shepherd and cowherd), they became jealous. 'Confucius,' they said, 'Confucius must go.' And Confucius, who was of course very wise, knew what they were thinking. So Confucius went. He went before anybody could do anything to harm him. But he didn't go alone. With a few friends he set off, travelling in a small procession of very simple carriages. Confucius was hoping to find a ruler wise enough to listen to his teachings.

At last he and his friends came to part of the country called Wei, which was rulled by Duke Ling. There,

Confucius started teaching. He taught ordinary, everyday things. 'Do not eat food that has not been properly prepared or which has gone bad. Do not eat except at the proper times. Eat wisely, eat slowly,' he said. And he taught other things. 'What you do not like when it is done to you, do not do it to others.'

But Duke Ling of Wei was a cunning man. He'd been wanting to attack a neighbouring city and knew that Confucius was wise and clever. So Duke Ling asked Confucius about the best ways of leading an attack.

'I have never studied the matter of commanding troops,' said Confucius; and the next day, he and his friends decided it would be a good idea to leave.

They travelled on. The rulers that Confucius had annoyed were looking for him, so he and his friends travelled in disguise, riding in simple farm carts. But Confucius was still hoping to find a ruler who would listen to what he had to say about being good and kind to others.

One day, he met a hermit; a man who wants nothing to do with other people and who hides away, keeping himself to himelf.

The hermit listened to Confucius. 'Huh,' he said. 'You're wasting your time. People are mean. People are cruel. You're wasting your time, trying to teach them to be good. You're stupid.' Sadly, Confucius and his friends went on their way. 'Why did you not say anything more to him?' asked his friends.

'To have people be rude to you and not to mind, that is the wise way,' said Confucius.

In the next village, they met a woman who was crying bitterly. 'What is the matter?' asked Confucius. She told him how her husband, uncle and son had all been killed by a tiger (for tigers lived in that part of China in those days). 'Why do you not move away, to a safe district?' 'Ah,' she said, 'but we have a good ruler. I would not move to where there is a bad government.' 'You see,' said Confucius to his friends, 'Bad government is worse than a tiger.' Soon after this, men came looking for Confucius, bringing presents. Duke Ai of Lu had realized how wrong he had been and how wise Confucius was and now he wanted Confucius to return home. Confucius thought for a minute and then said, 'Let us go home.' And so, happily, they went back to Lu and there his friends wrote down the sayings of the wise old Confucius. And one of them, Tseng Tzu, wrote down what he had learned about being a good friend:

'Every night, I ask myself three things. Have I done my best in what I have done for others today? To my friends, have I been loyal and true? And have I told others to do only what I would do myself? If so, I've been a good friend.'

David Self

4: DAVID AND GOLIATH

This must be one of the best known Old Testament stories. It is told in Samuel I verse 17. The two passages that follow are offered as possible illumination of the original story and to suggest that there might be more to stories which are sometimes dismissed with the remark, 'We did that in primary school.' See also page 200.

You perhaps know the story of how David killed the giant, Goliath. David, of course, was a shepherd boy, an Israelite. Goliath was a Philistine. David was too young to be in the Israelite army but visited the army, bringing food for his elder brothers who were soldiers.

So what was the situation? The Israelites were trying to defend their Promised Land, land which they had only comparatively recently conquered and which was now being attacked by the invading Philistines. So how might a pro-Israelite journalist have reported the situation?

Our army is encamped in the Valley of the River Elah, some fifteen miles west of Bethlehem. And facing our boys on the other side of the valley (between the towns of Socoh and Azekah) is the mighty Philistine army, which has invaded, with no right whatsoever, our promised land. And every morning, one of their soldiers, Goliath, said to be a giant several metres tall, has been issuing a challenge to our troops.

With no one accepting the challenge, there have been accusations of cowardice, and it must be admitted that some of our soldiers have been speaking quite openly of their fear of Goliath: no one seems to want to take up the challenge — despite losing face in front of our new young king, the recently annointed King Saul, who is with the army here in the Valley of Elah.

David Self

This is a less one-sided report, researched and written by a BBC Defence Correspondent:

From my position between the two armies the difference between them is obvious.

The Israelites are mostly farmers, making their living from the land the Philistines want to take. They're small people, mostly on foot — the Israelites don't have many cavalry. Most have swords and shields and either a battle-axe or a mace — a wooden club with a heavy stone to break the skull even of a man wearing a helmet. Some of the shepherds who've joined this volunteer army are even carrying sling-shots. These are leather cups with two thongs. You put a stone in the cup, whirl it round your head, then let go of one end. They say the best men can kill a wolf at fifty metres.

The Israelites are dug in on one side of the valley, so any Philistine attack will be up the slope. And that will offset the Philistines' greater weight in horsemen and war chariots. It looks as if the fighting will be hand-to-hand, so both sides will suffer heavy casualties. The Philistines in their kilts and with their long spears remind me of the Greeks. They're heavily armoured and it's said their iron swords are better than those of the Israelites.

But the most impressive thing is their size. They're big men anyway, made to look even taller by their plumed helmets. But even they are dwarfed by Goliath of Gath, a giant of a man who's challenged any Israelite to fight by single combat to determine the outcome of the war. King Saul's offered a reward to anyone who will take on Goliath, but so far there haven't been any takers. As one Israelite said to me just now: 'I prefer to be poor and alive.'

Christopher Wain

5: AMRITSAR

The Sikh holy city of Amritsar has often been in the news in recent years for a number of mainly tragic reasons. This passage explains its origin and importance for Sikhs.

One of the early teachers or leaders of the Sikh religion was a man called Guru Amar Das. He was the third of the Sikh gurus and lived at a place called Goindwal. This is the story of how he chose the next guru to teach after him and how that guru built the Sikh holy city which is called Amritsar.

Many Sikhs used to visit Goindwal to see the third Guru, Amar Das. One day young Jetha also joined a group of people coming to see the Guru. He liked the Guru's teachings and found the place so attractive that he stayed there. He served the Guru with love and respect and stayed for a long time. As time went on, he grew into a saintly young man. The Guru was very pleased with his work, manners, talk and behaviour. The Guru made up his mind to offer his gentle and kind daughter to Bhai Jetha in marriage. Very soon, the Guru's daughter, Bibi Bhani, and Jetha were married. They lived happily in the Guru's company and served him as much as they could. In 1574, at the time of his death, the Guru made Bhai Jetha the fourth Guru of the Sikhs. His name had now been changed from Jetha (first born) to Ram Das (God's slave).

The Guru now planned to build a city at the place where the famous city of Amritsar stands today. First he chose a suitable site and bought it from the *zamindars* (landlords) of Tung for 700 rupees, which was a big sum in those days. Later, he moved his home to this place and asked the Sikhs to come and live there.

First of all, the Guru and his Sikhs dug two pools, which can still be seen there. Then they built small huts in which the Guru and his followers lived and worked, both in the morning and evening. They remembered God all day and sang praises to His Name. A few more huts were later built for the daily visitors. Hundreds of Sikhs visited the Guru every day. They would come to see the Guru and assist in the great work. A free common kitchen (*langar*) was run there. People of different castes and creeds sat together and ate the simple food from the Guru's *langar*. All worked hard and enjoyed the Guru's company. As time went on, a small town grew up there and it began to be called *Chak Guru Ram Das*. The Guru wanted the town to be famous, so he invited men of fifty-two different trades to come there, settle down and open business in the Guru's market, which was called the *Guru Ka Bazar*. The Guru lived there with many faithful Sikhs like Bhai Budha and Bhai Gur Das. The Guru always lived, worked and sang hymns among his Sikhs. He taught his Sikhs to keep their hands busy in work and their hearts fixed on God's Name. This made the common people gather round him from all sides. The town grew up very fast and the Guru's fame spread all over the country.

Later, the city was named Amritsar (pool of nectar) after the sacred pool which was completed in 1589. Even today, Sikhs going there on a visit, out of respect for the Guru say, 'Great is the city of Guru Ram Das.' Thus, in a very short time, this new city became the great central place of the Sikhs. The Sikhs living there started trade and other kinds of work. They made the city famous all over the world.

Today, Amritsar has become a great centre of trade and learning. The city is full of famous buildings, such as the Tower of *Baba Attal*, the Golden Temple, the *Akal Takhat*, the Castle of Maharaja Ranjit Singh, the great Khalsa College and the famous *Durgiana Mandir* of the Hindus. There is also a Sikh museum which contains paintings, pictures, old books, old weapons and the things which the Gurus used during their life time. On the 500th birthday of Guru Nanak (the first of the Sikh gurus), celebrated in 1969, the Sikhs started the 'Guru Nanak University' in this city. These days, the people call Amritsar, 'The City of All Praise.'

G. S. Sidhu, G. S. Sivia and Kirpal Singh

6: HANNAH SENESH

In the national military cemetery, situated on top of the highest of the Judean Hills overlooking Jerusalem, there is a small circle set apart; within it are seven graves in the shape of a 'V', the outline of a parachute carved on each headstone. Buried in that circle are seven of the thirty-two Palestinian-Jewish parachutists, members of the British Armed Forces, who were dropped into Nazi-occupied Balkan countries during World War 2 in an effort to save their people from the Nazi holocaust. Of the thirty-two sent, seven fell. One of the seven was Hannah Senesh, aged twenty-three and the only one of the seven about whom there is a clear, definite testimony regarding her fate from the time of her capture until her execution.

Hannah Senesh has been called the Joan of Arc of Israel; she is a national heroine who has inspired books and plays. There are few in Israel who had not read her diary and poems, which have been translated into many languages.

Marta Cohn

The Plan

One of the most important things in the world for Jews is their homeland, Israel. The modern state of Israel came into being only in 1948. But before then many Jews had moved to that area, then called Palestine, to work for the time when they would have their own country. One of those Jews was a girl called Hannah Senesh. Her home was in Hungary. She left there in 1939 when she was eighteen. Soon afterwards the war started. Jews in all the countries under Nazi influence were in danger. In January 1943, Hannah Senesh wrote in her diary:

I've had a shattering week. I was suddenly struck by the idea of going to Hungary. I feel I must be there during these days in order to help organize youth emigration, and also to get my mother out. Although I'm quite aware how absurd the idea is, it still seems both feasible and necessary to me, so I'll get to work on it and carry it through. For the time being this is but a sudden enthusiasm, a hopeful plan to get Mother out and bring her here, at any cost. I spent three days in Tel Aviv and Jerusalem trying to arrange the matter. At the moment chances are slim, but who knows . . . ?

Well, she did manage to get her plan to work. Two months later, thirty-two Jewish parachutists (who were also members of the British Armed Forces) were ready to fly, not to Hungary, but to the next-door country of Yugoslavia to help the Partisans, the Resistance workers. Hannah was the only woman in the group. This account was written by one of the men on the dangerous mission.

We sat inside the crowded plane, parcels all around us, some for the partisans, some for our own needs. We felt weighed down. What with the harness on our backs, the weapons, and our heavy winter clothes, we had almost no freedom of movement at all.

The thunderous roaring of the engines killed conversation. I studied the faces of my comrades, all deep in thought, and felt our hearts must be pounding in fateful unison. My eyes rested on Hannah. Her face was aglow, and she exuded happiness and excitement. She winked at me, waved her hand encouragingly, and a delightful, impish smile enveloped her features. Below her paratrooper's helmet her face seemed smaller, her expression almost elfin, and her luminous smile reminded me of a little girl on her first merry-go-round ride. Her excitement was contagious; we were all infected by it. Gradually tension relaxed, and the air seemed lighter. Fears and black thoughts receded, finally disappeared, and we began feeling peacefully confident.

Time ticked by. Fatigue and tension had taken their toll; blessed sleep embraced us, one by one.

We awoke to find the crew tossing parcels out of the hatch, and the plane circling its target. I'll never forget the moment I made that jump, Hannah standing by, so slim, her face wreathed in a huge smile, her expression calm, happy, thumbs up – her favourite victory sign.

I jumped . . . and she was right behind me. A few moments later we were on the soil of Yugoslavia, land of the partisans.

For months we wandered across that land together, witnessing the cruel yet wonderful, ferocious partisan battle for victory and liberty. We saw incredible heroism, victory, tragic defeat. We saw destruction – entire towns and villages in total ruin, flames consuming the labour of generations. We encountered attacking as well as retreating forces, joined up with caravans of brave, simple people escaping from the relentless enemy, or returning to repossess their hills, fields, villages. Everything we saw touched us deeply: the cruelty, the terror, the humanity and tenderness. Our goal lay further on . . . our mission was to try to save at least some of our brothers.

A great number of people – partisans and civilians – were fascinated by Hannah, the young British officer smart in her army uniform, pistol strapped to her waist. She fascinated them. They had heard about her before our arrival, and she became something of a legend.

When she encountered members of the high command she aroused their respect, and although the Yugoslavs had taken women into the army on an equal footing, and partisan women marched into battle alongside the men, there was a special, mysterious quality about Hannah which excited their wonder and respect.

Hannah was to continue on into Hungary, the neighbouring country, but we encountered a wall of reality at the very outset. We had to reach the Hungarian border on foot, and the partisans informed us that there was no possibility of crossing the border because the Germans had recaptured the entire region. 'You'll just have to wait,' they said.

A few days later we were sitting at the partisan headquarters when the news reached us that the Germans had occupied Hungary as well. It was catastrophic news for all of us – and it was the first time I saw Hannah cry.

Reuven Dafne

Into Hungary

This account of a subsequent stage of Hannah Senesh's mission is by another of the parachutists.

With the Nazis in full control of her home country, Hungary, it was now even more dangerous for Hannah Senesh to attempt to go back there. Already the Nazis were rounding up the Jews in the cities (and especially in her home town, the capital, Budapest), and sending them off to prison or to concentration camps. Hannah and the other parachutists (who of course were still in Yugoslavia) did not yet know this.

One day, Hannah came across a group of refugees who had escaped from Hungary. Among them were three young men who were willing to join the rescue mission – a non-Jewish Frenchman and two Jews who had been planning to reach Palestine. All three agreed to go back into Hungary with Hannah.

The four set out, and although the area was unknown to them they nevertheless decided to cross into thickly patrolled enemy territory, a map and a compass as their only guide. I still don't understand how, in the circumstances, they managed to reach their goal – a Hungarian village – without encountering German patrols. But somehow they did. It was decided that Hannah and the Frenchman would hide among some bushes on the outskirts while the other two went into the village to contact friends who were to provide them with permits to travel to the capital. However, on the way the two men were stopped by Hungarian police. What took place in the mind of one of the boys we'll never know. What we do know is that instead of trying to bluff his way through, or even use his guns against the few policemen, he shot himself instead. Farmers then came forward and told the police that the men had been accompanied by another two partisans who they had seen hiding in the bushes. Hannah and her companion suddenly found themselves surrounded by soldiers, with no chance of escaping. That was how she was caught, only a little while after she finally reached Hungary.

She suffered dreadful tortures, and she didn't want to talk about them. The tooth missing from her mouth testified to this. I heard from others how they had tied her; how they had whipped her palms and the soles of her feet; bound her and forced her to sit motionless for hours on end; beaten her all over the body until she was black and blue. They asked her one thing, only one thing: what is your radio code? Yes, the code was important to them, for they had found the transmitter she hid just before she was caught – and now they wanted to use it to send out false information, to mislead bomber squadrons so that they could be greeted by fighters and anti-aircraft guns. Hannah was perfectly aware of the value of her code, and she didn't reveal it. When she was being transferred by train to Budapest she tried to kill herself by jumping from the window, because she didn't know how long she could hold out. But she was caught in the act and beaten even more. 'You don't have the right to destroy yourself,' her guard told her. 'You are state property; we'll do away with you when we no longer need you, not before.'

But her most awful test was yet to come. They brought her to the gaol – to Budapest. But it was not the meeting with her hometown that Hannah had dreamed of. Upon arrival they threw her into a room and there, to her horror, she found her beloved mother. She hugged her and could find only the words: 'Forgive me, Mother, I had to do what I did.'

The Germans knew their business. They threatened that if she did not reveal her secret, they would torture her mother before her eyes and kill her. Still Hannah would not yield.

But the Germans didn't give up. They kept Hannah and her mother in the same prison, believing that prison, hunger and the fear of death would humble her. Friends in the prison – there were some prisoners who had known the family before the war, or had heard of them – did what they could to make things easier for them, and even managed to have mother and daughter transferred from their separate, distant cells to nearer ones, thus making it possible for them to meet. Once or twice a week prisoners were allowed to stroll in pairs in the tiny prison yard, the eyes of the SS guards fixed firmly upon them. Every snatch of conversation was firmly punished.

Yoel Palgi

The execution

The last passage was written by one of the men who parachuted into Yugoslavia with Hannah Senesh. His name was Yoel Palgi. Later, he made his way into Hungary where he had arranged to meet Hannah Senesh outside the synagogue in Budapest. She of course was not there: she had been caught and imprisoned. He himself was caught and thrown in jail; the same one as Hannah. Although they had some contact they were later kept separate. The weeks went by. Hannah's mother was released but Hannah was put on trial.

By now the Russians were not far from Budapest and the Americans were also bombing the city. Soon it might be freed from the Nazis and Hannah's judges might themselves be later put on trial if they condemned Hannah. The judges talked among themselves.

In the corridor outside stood a black-clothed mother awaiting news of her daughter's sentence. Those were times when Jews were not allowed on the street; but she, the mother, had come.

While the court was in consultation the defendants had been taken out into the corridor. The Hungarian sergeant assigned to Hannah turned a blind eye as mother and daughter embraced. Hannah had noted the consternation she had caused her judges, and was confident of victory. 'Why worry about a sentence when we'll all soon be free,' she encouraged her mother.

The news spread like wildfire. Before the defendants had reached the prison corridor we all knew of the strange decision and had understood its significance. They did not dare to execute her, and they did not have the courage to pronounce any other sentence.

That was November 4. Three days later, Yoel Palgi was still in his own prison cell with some other prisoners including a Frenchman.

November 7 was a dark, cloudy day. We sat around quietly, leaning against the wall, huddled together in an effort to conserve the little body heat we had. Suddenly we heard shots. We looked at each other, frightened and bewildered. What had happened? Had someone been executed? Impossible! This was not their method. Last respects were always paid. There was always the marching of the firing squad, the reading of the sentence, prayer and a bugle call accompanying the dark moment of execution in the grey courtyard beneath our cell window. Someone climbed up to the high window, and looking down informed us that he could see a table with a crucifix on it, but no sign of an execution. At the same moment we heard voices in the courtyard — an order to rearrange the straw. Apparently a guard had fired a bullet by accident and the reverberation had amplified the sound.

That afternoon one of our cellmates went to the doctor. Every day one of us would go for treatment or a pill because the clinic served as a centre of information and communication. The return of that 'patient' was the most important event of our day. That afternoon we waited even more eagerly than usual for our cellmate's return. He was back within half an hour, pale and shaken, as if he really were ill. He leaned against the wall for support, removed his hat, and announced in a faint voice, 'They've executed Hannah. That was the firing we heard.'

We were stunned. Hannah? Executed? No! Impossible! Why Hannah? Why not us? 'It's a mistake . . . a mistake . . .'

After the first wave of shock I became sure it was an error, that my cellmate had misunderstood, and I mumbled over and over again, 'It's a mistake . . . a mistake . . . a mistake . . .' until the Frenchman, imprisoned with me at the time, gripped my hand and whispered, 'Calm down, control yourself.'

We pounded on the door until the guard came and asked what we wanted.

'We want to know who was just executed.'

'What do you care? Shut up!' he roared.

We pleaded with him and for the first time since we had come under his protection he heard from us the official formula prisoners were ordered to use when addressing a guard: 'We respectfully request . . .' The guard sensed that something had undermined our self-confidence, that we were frightened, and he consoled us: 'Don't worry. She wasn't one of yours. Just some young girl . . . a partisan, they say . . . a British parachutist. But that's surely a lie. Whoever heard of a young girl being a British officer?'

So it was Hannah after all. Wonderful, sparkling Hannah, who had encouraged us with her upraised thumb when we had last parted. She was the first to go. She, who had been so sure we would return to tell our comrades of our exploits, to spin tall tales. I felt I had to speak. But the words strangled in my throat, left me stuttering. I saw them all staring at me, and I managed to utter, 'She was the most wonderful person I ever knew.' And they repeated after me, as in prayer, 'She was the most . . .'

Yoel Palgi

Blessed is the Match

The parachutists, among them Hannah, took off on their mission from Brindisi, Italy, on March 13, 1944, and were dropped into Yugoslavia. Reuven Dafne, a fellow parachutist part of whose account appears on page 164, said during a conversation: 'We parachutists were not supermen – nor superwomen. Supermen exist only on television. We were small, frail, inexperienced, romantic people with all the shortcomings of the average person. None of us was unique – excepting perhaps Hannah. She was different . . . a spiritual girl guided almost by mysticism. Perhaps one can say she had *charisma* . . . She was fearless, dauntless, stubborn. Despite her extraordinary intelligence and prescience, she was a kind of tomboy – a poet-tomboy – which sounds rather odd, I know. A girl who dreamed of being a heroine – and who was a heroine.'

Dafne parted from Hannah on June 9, 1944, at a village near the Hungarian border, just before she crossed into Nazi-occupied territory. 'When we said goodbye she pressed a piece of paper into my hand saying,

"If I don't return, give this to our people." I was amazed by her attitude. It was so unlike her. I looked at the piece of paper and was even more surprised. At a time like that she had written a poem. I had had no idea she even wrote poetry. I almost threw it away. It was *Blessed is the Match*, the poem every Israeli, young or old, can now recite from memory.'

>Blessed is the match consumed
>>in kindling flame.
>
>Blessed is the flame that burns
>>in the secret fastness of the heart.
>
>Blessed is the heart with strength to stop
>>its beating for honour's sake.
>
>Blessed is the match consumed
>>in kindling flame.

>>>>Sardice, Yugoslavia, May 2 1944
>>>>*Hannah Senesh*,
>>>>translated from the Hebrew
>>>>by Marte Syrkin

10
The Christian way

1: THE MAGIC PICNIC

An 'investigation' of the Miracle of the Feeding of the Five Thousand, the only miracle recorded in all four gospels. (Matthew chapter 14, verses 15–21; Mark 6, 35–44; Luke 9, 10–17; and John 6, 5–14.)

During his life, Jesus performed many miracles; events which seem to go against the rules of science. One of them was when five thousand people had followed him into a desert place to hear him talk and preach. They became hungry. How were they to be fed? (This is what the Bible tells us happened . . .)

But is that what happened? What would it have been like to be there? Suppose a reporter had been able to cover the event and interview some of those who were there.

CHARACTERS:
Presenter
Reporter
Philip, a disciple
Woman
Man
Professor
Newsreader

Presenter: Yes, we've had this report of a so-called 'magic picnic' which took place a few days ago. Apparently five thousand people were given a sur-

Themes

prise meal in the middle of the desert. Our reporter, who we sent along to find out what happened, began by interviewing this woman.

Woman: Yes, that's right, we was filled. We had plenty to eat. More than enough. Bread and sardines they were.

Reporter: Bread and sardines?

Woman: Yeh. We were given chunks of bread — black, barley bread — and some sort of fish. Sardines I think.

Reporter: Who gave it to you? Where did it come from?

Woman: Dunno. People just brought it round. We was all sitting down in groups, and people brought it round.

Presenter: Just one of the five thousand people who claim to have been given a free meal in the middle of the wilderness when apparently no one there had any food at all. Or almost no one.
 But first, exactly who were the people there and what did happen?

Man: Well you see, I'd been following the teacher along with my mates. He'd crossed the lake and some of us followed him in boats, and some of us come round the shore, you know, round the north end of the lake.

Reporter: This 'preacher', as you call him, where does he come from?

Man: Teacher. Well, he come from Bethsaida that night.

Reporter: Originally, though?

Man: Oh, Nazareth I think. Some folk say he was born down south or somewhere. But I think he's a northerner, you can tell by the accent.

Reporter: And what was he doing in Bethsaida?

Man: Well I don't know, but he and his disciples, his

The Christian way

immediate followers, they'd come there, and so, as I told you, we followed.

Reporter: Then what happened?

Man: Well we all come out of the town, 'cause we'd heard he'd gone into the desert. And then when we'd found him, he seemed glad to see us 'cause he welcomed us and talked to us and healed them as needed it. And then in the evening, just about when the sun was going down, some of us was beginning to feel really hungry, (*laughs*) famished I was, anyway we were all told to sit down and they brought round these sandwiches, well rolls more like. With fish.

Presenter: But was in fact this evening's distribution of food a miracle? Was it perhaps not just a sharing out of food that people had with them?

Man: (*positive*): Oh no, no. No it wasn't like that. We didn't know what we were going to do, how long we were going to be, not when we set out, so we didn't bring any food with us. No, no one had any food with them.

Woman: Well, of course some people had some food at the start, but I mean this was evening. They'd nothing left, see. It wasn't a matter of sharing, there was nothing to share.

Presenter: It seems that the actual distribution of the food was carried out by the preacher's group of immediate followers, or disciples as they're known. Our reporter asked one of them, a man who gave his name as Philip, whether the Feeding of the Five Thousand, as this picnic is becoming known, was in fact a miracle.

Philip: Definitely. Definitely. I didn't think such a thing was possible, not until I saw it happen.

Reporter: Tell me, how did it happen?

Philip: Well, the crowd had been following the Master all day you see, and by then it was evening, and we were miles from anywhere, right out in the desert, and we said that he should make all the people go back to the towns or villages so they could buy food for themselves – I mean, they'd all starve if they stayed where they were.

Reporter: So what did he say?

Philip: Well he asked me where we could buy food for them.

Reporter: What, in the desert?

Philip: Exactly. And anyway, I mean, even to give them each just a little, it'd have cost a fortune. They were hungry. Anyway, just then Andrew comes along –

Reporter: Andrew?

Philip: One of us. Anyway he came along with a young lad who was about to get mobbed because the crowd had found he'd got a little food. Just five loaves of bread and two small fishes. Well, the Master asked for the food and I don't think the boy wanted to hand them over – well, I mean, obviously he was hungry like everyone else and wanted to keep them for himself, but anyway he handed them over and the Master asked the twelve of us to make the crowd sit down in groups of fifty or a hundred and when they were all sitting down, the Master said a prayer and then gave us each a loaf to give to one of the groups and then we came back for more and gave that out to another group and then more and more and then the fish . . .

Reporter: But how exactly did it happen? I mean, there were only five loaves. Was it like a sliced loaf that never ran out?

Philip: It wasn't wrapped bread. They were just rough buns. Barley bread.

Reporter: Could he have had a hidden supply that you didn't know about?

Philip: You can't hide enough bread for five thousand people up your sleeve.

Reporter: But you're saying there was enough to go round?

Philip: There were five loaves to start with and there were enough for us to give to each group and there was enough to go round each group. And afterwards, when we cleared up, we filled a dozen baskets with crusts.

Presenter: Our reporter tried to find the preacher, to ask him about what appeared to be a miracle, a 'happening' for which science has no known explanation. But he seems to have disappeared, apparently to avoid publicity. Likewise there was no trace of the boy who brought the original loaves and fishes. However, those I talked to had no doubt that they'd seen a miracle.

Woman: We were hungry and he fed us – surely that's all there is to it. I tell you, he's a good, kind man and for that and what he's taught me, I'm grateful. I am.

Presenter: Our reporter there was . . . And now a news report from . . .

Newsreader: Further to this extraordinary event, there's a report that the National Union of Bakers is threatening industrial action; that unless the government intervenes, they say, and outlaws such means of bread production, they'll go on strike from midnight; and there's been a similar outcry from the bosses, from the Federation of Industrial Managers, that such methods of production will mean the end of the manufacturing industry and retail trade system as we know it.

Presenter: And now with me in the studio to comment on this 'magic picnic' I have Professor Welkin. Professor, was this a miracle?

Professor: It isn't easy to answer. You've got to understand, this wasn't just a picnic. The people were following a man they believe is a great teacher. They believe they were fed. So they were fed.

Presenter: The man himself didn't claim it was a miracle.

Professor: There is no record of his having done so. Except of course the baskets that remained. We have seen them. Genuine crusts.

Presenter: The people could have had the food with them all the time?

Professor: If everybody shared all they had with everybody else, fair shares for all! Now that would be a miracle! You sound as though you don't believe it? Just as God provided manna in the wilderness in the time of Moses, so He might do again. We have a tradition, you know, that when the saviour comes, there will be a great banquet.

Presenter: More than bread and fish?

Professor: They are good foods.

Presenter: Professor, in a word, was it a miracle?

Professor: In a word, maybe.

Presenter: Professor, thank you. So that means it's up to *you* to decide just what did happen out there in the desert. Thank You.

David Self

2: ONE MAN

A description of Jesus of Nazareth, written from a Christian viewpoint but one that might be accepted by many non-believers. Indeed, one of the topics it raises for discussion is how true it is objectively (as well as being a statement of faith).

This reading is a description of one man. You will probably recognize who it is. But how true do you think it is?

Here is a man who was born in an obscure village, the child of a peasant woman. He worked in a carpenter's shop until he was thirty, and then for three years he was an itinerant preacher. He had no credentials but himself. While still a young man, the tide of popular opinion turned against him. His friends — the twelve men who had learned so much from him, and had promised him their enduring loyalty — ran away, and left him. He went through a mockery of a trial; he was nailed upon a cross between two thieves; when he was dead, he was taken down and laid in a borrowed grave through the pity of a friend.

Yet I am well within the mark when I say that all the armies that ever marched, and all the parliaments that ever sat, and all the kings that ever reigned, put together, have not affected the life of man upon this earth as has this one solitary life.

Anon

3: PRAYER

An anecdote to explain, in part, the nature of prayer.

This story points out that Christians and indeed followers of all religions should say their prayers regularly. Praying is not something you do only when you are in trouble.

He was a very simple old sailor, the skipper of the small boat that was taking them to the Shetlands, and they were a young, lively party, actors and actresses from London on tour, going to do a night or two on the Islands. They were not above 'taking the mickey' a bit, and they thought his way of saying grace before meals very quaint and old fashioned. However, before long a storm blew up, a really severe north-easter, and as the little ship began to pitch more and more violently, morale among the visitors got lower and lower.

A small deputation went up to ask the Captain's opinion. 'Well,' he said, 'maybe we'll get through, and maybe we won't. I never remember such a storm.' The news was greeted with dismay down below, and finally another deputation went up to the bridge to ask whether perhaps the Captain would be so good as to come and say a prayer with his terrified passengers. His reply was simple: 'I say my prayers when it's calm; and when it's rough, I attend to my ship.'

Anon

4: FOOTPRINTS

A parable that teaches the Christian belief that 'the Lord' (i.e. God or Jesus) cares for us at all times.

Christians believe that God cares for them at all times. This is a story which illustrates that idea.

One night a man had a dream. He dreamed he was walking along the beach with the Lord. Across the sky flashed scenes from his life. For each scene, he noticed two sets of footprints in the sand: one belonging to him, and the other to the Lord.

When the last scene of his life flashed before him, he looked back at the footprints in the sand. He noticed that many times along the path of his life there was only one set of footprints. He also noticed that it happened at the very lowest and saddest times in his life.

This really bothered him and he questioned the Lord about it.

'Lord, you said that once I decided to follow you, you'd walk with me all the way. But I have noticed that during the most troublesome times in my life, there is only one set of footprints. I don't understand why, when I needed you most, you would leave me.'

The Lord replied, 'My son, my precious child, I love you and would never leave you. During your times of trial and suffering, when you see only one set of footprints, it was then that I carried you.'

Anon

The Christian way

5: ARMY WITHOUT GUNS

The story of the start of the Salvation Army and of its founder, William Booth.

You may have seen a Salvation Army band playing in the town. Or seen members of this 'Army without guns' collecting money for the poor and homeless. The Salvation Army is a Christian organization. This is how it was started by a man called William Booth.

When public hangings were still attracting curious crowds, London sewage was being emptied straight into the Thames, and many people living in back streets had 'lost everything but the mere outside appearance of humanity', William Booth took the gospel to the English capital's East End.

On Sunday 2 July 1865, he conducted a service in an old tent on a disused Quaker burial ground between Vallance Street and Fulbourne Street, Whitechapel. A few days earlier he had spoken in a missioners' open-air meeting outside the 'Blind Beggar' public house, by Mile End Gate. From that small beginning grew the work of the Salvation Army – a Christian organization now at work in over eighty countries.

In 1829 William Booth was born in Nottingham. As a young man he worked in a pawnbroker's shop, where he saw poverty in the raw. At twenty he was unemployed and moved to London, there finding work only by remaining in the pawnbroking trade.

All William's spare time was given to preaching and in 1852 he became a minister in Methodism. Three years later he married Catherine Mumford, born in Ashbourne, Derbyshire, also in 1829.

From 1854 to 1862 he served with the Methodist new Connexion Church, until he became a travelling revivalist. Despite current opposition to women in any position of authority, Catherine herself had become a dynamic preacher and together they won hundreds of people to the Christian faith.

Early days

It was after they had settled in London that their real life's work began — the founding of The Salvation Army, or The Christian Mission as it was known until 1878.

Their earliest 'places of worship' included a dancing academy, a skittle alley, a stable, a loft, a penny gaff (low theatre), a disused public house, and an old wool store.

William Booth had no intention of starting a new organization. He wanted to see people saved from sin and then join the churches, but some would not go, others felt they were not wanted and he soon found that he needed his converts to help him win more.

By mid-1878 his work had spread throughout England and Wales. He had fifty stations with eighty-eight evangelists.

Early one morning in May of that year he, with his son Bramwell and George Railton, the Mission's secretary, was reading the proofs of the 1878 report. It read that 'The Christian Mission . . . is a volunteer army.' 'No!' said William Booth, 'we are not volunteers, for we feel we *must* do what we do, and we are always on duty.' He took a pen and changed the word 'volunteer' to 'salvation'. The idea 'Salvation Army' gripped his followers' interest and, with this new name, the work increased even more rapidly.

As early as 1879 The Salvation Army began to spread beyond the boundaries of England and Wales, when Scotland was 'invaded'. The following year saw the first contingent of officers land in the United States of America, and work was commenced in Ireland. Women officers were predominant in these pioneering enterprises. From earliest days women have had equality with men in all positions, and William Booth's own daughter, Evangeline, was General from 1934 to 1939.

Cyril Barnes

6: IN THE STREET

Written as a prayer, this passage is a warning against judging by appearances and always thinking the worst of people.

When we see people in the street, we very often judge them just by their appearance. We also often think the worst of them. Sometimes we are right to do so and we do need to be on our guard against strangers – but that doesn't mean getting into the habit of thinking all *people are up to no good – as this reading makes clear.*

She was pretty and she smiled at the men approaching.
I could see her in profile. A sweet thing, and cheeky, too.
    Embarrassed males turned away.
    Quickened their pace; looked guilty, some blushed.
But undaunted, she met with an expectant smile the next.
    Only again to be refused.
Soliciting, I thought; a prostitute; in broad daylight;
Until she turned.
And I saw she was selling buttons for a charity.

He staggered down the steps and fell, Lord,
    A crumpled mass on the footpath.
His bottle broke and liquid spilled across the walk.
    He's drunk. I thought. Disgust. Disdain. Until . . .
Two girls rushed from a nearby car and cried:
'It's Daddy. Please help. He's ill.'

He caught my gaze. This greedy-eyed young man.
    He too had seen the open handbag on the aged arm,
With the few dollars exposed to view.
    He stalked his prey, and the old woman just window shopped.
He'll grab and run, I thought. But no.
Quietly he tapped her shoulder, pointed to the bag.
    exchanged smiles.
They went their way.

Roger Bush

11
Stories from the world of Islam

1: YOUNG MUHAMMAD

The author of this story became a Muslim when she and her husband were living in Indonesia. It tells of how the orphaned young Muhammad came to work for (and marry) the wealthy widow, Khadija. (See also page 187.)

Muhammad, who later became the great Prophet of Islam, the Muslim religion, was brought up by relatives after his parents died. One of these relatives was his uncle, Abu Talib. When Muhammad grew up, he worked as a trader, or merchant, helping his uncle in his business.

Muhammad, in his early twenties, had become a successful merchant; not so much because he liked his work, but because he was honest in his dealings and could be trusted. He never overpriced his goods, nor skimped on weights, and usually gave other merchants the benefit of the doubt. Because of this, they called him 'Al-Amin' which means 'The Trustworthy', and this became his nickname.

On that morning, Muhammad was on his way to meet someone. His uncle had sent him to see the wealthy widow Khadija who was requesting an overseer for her caravans. Abu Talib had said that morning: 'Now Muhammad I would love you to stay with me but, as you know, my business is not going too well. Khadija needs someone to look after her trade and has asked if I could spare you.' So Muhammad presented himself to the widow.

Khadija looked up from her account books and was pleased with what she saw. The handsome young man in front of her with his high dark eyes and neat appearance impressed her.

'I am looking for an honest man who will take charge of my caravans on their various journeys. Abu Talib, your uncle, has recommended you to me. Would you be interested in such a position?'

Muhammad, who was never hasty, remained silent for a while and then accepted the job. Together they sat and discussed the responsibilities he would undertake: the number of beasts required for each caravan, the quantities of food and water to be stored, the kinds of merchandise and the prices they might fetch; and finally, the routes most favourable and the time of year of the departures. When all this had been gone over, Muhammad took leave of his new employer, and as he turned to go, Khadija called after him:

'I hear they call you "Al-Amin", "The Trustworthy".' Her kind face broke into a smile. 'I hope that while you are in my employment you will live up to your name!'

Muhammad blushed slightly and assured her that he would.

Muhammad did indeed live up to his name. He worked very hard, as Khadija had given him the management of all her caravans. His time was spent travelling across deserts and through oases to distant lands and foreign cities – to Damascus, to Jerusalem, and Aleppo. Khadija, each time he left, waited more and more eagerly for his return.

One day a surprising thing happened. Khadija's personal maid came to see Muhammad privately. She came with a marriage proposal from Khadija! Muhammad was astounded. He had never even had a girlfriend. He had never thought much about women, nor had he even been close to one since the death of his mother. Some time back, when he was tending sheep, some shepherds passing by had called to him:

'Come to town with us tonight, Muhammad – we'll have a little fun with the girls!'

Muhammad, who liked the idea well enough, agreed to join them later. But he never turned up at the rendezvous. The following day the shepherds asked him:

'What happened to you last night?'

'Well', Muhammad confessed, 'when the time came, I fell asleep.' Of course they all burst out laughing and he joined in with them.

But Khadija, in the eyes of Muhammad, was a very special lady. She was warm and kind, and still quite beautiful despite the fact that she was older than he. This time, Muhammad did not take long to accept. The marriage between Muhammad and Khadija took place, and turned out to be a very happy one.

Mardijah Aldrich Tarantino

2: THE CALL OF THE PROPHET

For Muslims, the greatest prophet, the Prophet, is Muhammad. He was born in the city of Makka in what is now Saudi Arabia in the year 570 CE. Such religion as there was in the area at that time was primitive. It was also a fairly lawless period with much feuding between family clans. NB When mentioning the Prophet Muhammad, Muslims usually say 'Peace be upon him' as a mark of respect.

This is a story about how Muhammad came to be a messenger of God and the greatest prophet of the Muslim religion, known as Islam. Muhammad lived some five or six hundred years after Jesus and lived in the city of Makka. His father died before he was born and his mother soon after. He was brought up by relatives, and especially by his grandfather. Like many Arabs of his time, he worked as a trader. With a long train, or caravan of camels, he trekked across the desert, taking goods made in one place to be sold in another. He became known for his honesty and, perhaps because of this, was noticed by a wealthy widow called Khadija. She gave him a job as manager of her trading business. After some time they married. Muhammad treated her with honour and respect; the marriage was happy, the business prospered. All went well — except for one thing.

Now there were many times when Muhammad, peace be upon him, felt tired and almost suffocated with work. Yes, he knew he was fortunate; he knew he was lucky — and he was ashamed he wasn't more grateful. But spending all his life buying and selling things did not make him . . . well, satisfied. And at times when he felt like this, then he wanted to feel close to God.

In the city of Makka there was a religious place called the Ka'ba but the Arabs who lived in Makka in those days misused it, and filled it with strange idols and statues that were supposed to be magic. One was said to have the power to make you rich, another to cure you of the plague and a third to have the power to grant you a son or to bring you the princess of your dreams.

So when Muhammad *did* feel the need to be near God, he didn't go to the Ka'ba but walked out of the city, north to the hills of Hira; and especially to one particular cave, high in the mountains. There he could be alone; and there he could think. And from the mouth of that cave at dusk he could watch the beauty of the twilight; and at night, the stars and the moon. And there, in the cave of Hira, Muhammad knew the greatness of God.

He began to spend more and more of his time at the cave, praying and wondering and thinking. Sometimes he even stayed for several days and his wife, Khadija, would send him food so that he didn't starve. Now one particular time, during the last ten days of the month the Arabs called Ramadan, Muhammad was again in his cave, spending a night in prayer and thought.

Perhaps he slept, but just before dawn, when the night is at its darkest, he heard a voice. He was now wide awake. The voice seemed to come from all directions — and then, there appeared an angel. Muhammad sat in silence, his eyes staring, wide in amazement.

'Recite!' said the angel.

'What shall I recite?' asked Muhammad. This happened three times. Then the angel spoke again.

'Recite!' said the angel. 'In the name of God who made mankind from a drop of blood. Recite in the name of Almighty God who taught man the use of the pen and taught him what he did not know before.'

Trembling, Muhammad repeated these words until he knew them by heart and could repeat them perfectly. Suddenly, he was alone. The angel had gone but the words remained in his memory. He was lonely now and, although it was still dark, he made his way down the mountain path, back to Makka and to his wife, Khadija, wondering as he half-walked, half-ran, whether the cave had been haunted or whether he was losing his senses.

When he did reach home, still trembling with cold and shock, he told her about the sudden appearance of the angel and recited the words he had learned. 'Praise God,' she said — for she did not doubt that Muhammad had been chosen to be God's messenger. But he was still doubtful. She told the story to her wise old cousin, Waraqa, who knew much about the religion of the One True God. 'Muhammad has indeed heard the word of God,' he said and when Muhammad heard this he was reassured because he trusted Waraqa.

Months passed. Muhammad went again to the cave — but nothing happened. Then, ten months later, the angel appeared again. 'Arise,' said the angel. 'Warn the people. Praise the Lord and turn away from all that is wrong . . .' And after that the angel appeared often to Muhammad, giving him many more messages which he was to repeat to his family, his friends and his followers; and from then on Muhammad was called the Prophet, or God's messenger, peace be upon him.

David Self

3: RAMADAN

Ramadan is the ninth month of the Muslim year and is held in special regard as it was the month in which the Prophet Muhammad first received God's message. Muslims are supposed to fast each day in Ramadan from dawn until sunset. This means that they must not eat or drink anything at all during those hours, nor smoke nor have sexual relations. They also say additional prayers and try to be especially kind and helpful. Pregnant women, nursing mothers and the sick are excused from the fast. Fasting ('saum') is one of the Five Pillars of Islam.

What is the longest you have gone without food? Imagine what it's like to go without anything to eat for twelve hours or more! Members of the Muslim religion go without food all day during each of the thirty days of their month of Ramadan. That is, they neither eat nor drink anything from the moment there is any daylight at all until after sunset. The month of Ramadan can occur during any of the Western months. If it occurs during a summer month, it means going without food for much longer than when it occurs in a winter one! (In Britain, when it occurs in Summer, the fast can be for more than eighteen hours.) In our reading today however, we hear what a day in Ramadan is like in one of the Middle Eastern Countries.

No, it is not a gloomy month, nor a time to dread. It is, yes, different, almost . . . exciting. Especially that last Friday before Ramadan. Then the markets are full of all the things we shall need for *suhoor* and *iftar*.

Iftar? This is the ending of each day's fast immediately after sunset when we eat a few dates and drink a little water. And *suhoor*, that is the meal we eat before dawn the next morning. So yes, you can see from the market that Ramadan is to begin. The stalls are laden with dates. Laden! Other fruit too. Especially water melons. You see, the farms around the cities rival each other in sending lorry loads of the very best water melons to the markets in time for Ramadan.

Life *is* different during Ramadan. As our Holy Prophet (peace be upon him) said, 'Anyone who does not, without illness or any other valid excuse, keep fast on a single day during Ramadan will not succeed in making amends even were he to fast daily for the rest of his life.' Of course, the very young children do not fast but there is a tradition. Yes, a tradition that children should be persuaded and encouraged to fast for as many of the days as possible.

But fasting is not easy for anyone so life has to be different during Ramadan. In the towns, all the offices close early and by mid-afternoon taxi drivers look in vain for passengers in the deserted streets – for if you are fasting through a long hot day, then you will want to rest in the afternoon. But, when the long day draws to an end and there is shade in even the wider streets, then the city comes to life again in a special way. The shops open. People come out to buy spicy and salty snacks and fresh lettuce to eat after *iftar*.

The young children come out to play in the streets – but they only half-think about their games. They are listening for the *adhan*, the prayer call from the minaret of the mosque that will announce the end of the day's fast. And as that time approaches, the stalls in the side streets open up. Little, tempting snacks are arranged on display. One stallholder pours a little oil into a frying pan and it begins to simmer on a tiny stove, ready for the samosas to be put in. The smell is delicious. But everyone must wait. And wait!

Then, the cannon booms out over the city to say it is *iftar* and then, from all the minarets comes the call of the muezzin. People eat their dates, drink a little water and enjoy the other snacks. And the children rush back indoors for a glass of cold milk or sherbet.

And even after night prayers, the children still play out in the warm night air. Some play football while their parents go to the coffee houses where they sit outside on wooden benches and share memories of Ramadans of long ago.

You see, in Ramadan there is *time*. Time for the family, time to be together and to remember that this is the month of the year in which the Holy Book, the Holy Quran, was revealed to the Blessed Prophet, and this is the month in which we once again re-dedicate ourselves to do the will of God. It is the holiest of months.

David Self

4: THE HIJRA

The hijra *(or 'departure') marks the beginning of the Muslim calendar and the departure of the Prophet and his companions from Makka (where they were facing increasing unpopularity) for Medina (July 16 622 CE).*

When Muhammad started preaching the message he had been given by God (considering what life was like in Makka in those days), it was not surprising that he became unpopular. He had his followers of course – but he also had his enemies.

'He's not a dreamer and a mad-man! He's dangerous!' So shouted one of the Prophet's enemies to the crowd which was listening eagerly. 'Don't you see what'll happen? If he convinces the people that their idols are worthless and has them destroyed, who'll ever visit our city? We'll soon become poor.'

'He should be slain,' shouted one of the crowd.

'Let him and his family be starved to death in his own house,' said another.

'That's it,' said the first speaker. 'We'll impose a ban that'll cut off all his sources of food.'

'And no one shall trade with any of his family!'

But despite the many people who hated him, the Prophet (peace be upon him) had his loyal followers. He had even more in another city called Yathrib and indeed some of his followers in Makka had already left that city to go and live in safety in Yathrib.

For two years, the leaders of Makka tried to impose their ban on the Prophet and his family — all to no effect. Eventually the leaders of the city decided it was not enough. 'What if he should escape to Yathrib? With all his followers there, he could return and attack us?' So they took a vote and decided to plan to kill him.

But as his true followers prayed that the Prophet would be saved, he himself was calm. God had warned him in a dream of what would happen.

That night, the men who were supposed to be watching his house to see that he did not escape, began to feel weary. Soon, they were in a deep sleep.

The Prophet and his faithful servant, Abu Bakr, watched. When they saw the men were asleep, they crept out of the house and the Prophet took some sand and sprinkled it over the men. They slept on. They did not see Muhammad and Abu Bakr leave the city and walk in the direction of a cave called Thur. They were woken some time later by a passing goatherd. 'What are you doing here?' he asked them.

'Waiting to kill Muhammad,' they muttered.

'But he's gone. I saw him go. He sprinkled some sand on you as he went. Look.'

The enemies of the Prophet were furious. They sent out search parties. They employed men skilled in following tracks across the desert. A reward was offered. One hundred camels for the man who captured Muhammad. It was all to no avail. For three or four days, the Prophet and Abu Bakr hid in the cave until Abu Bakr's son brought them camels to ride, and so they set off for Yathrib.

For years, the people in the country around Yathrib had been at war. Now they heard a man was coming who would bring them peace and they were eager to welcome the Prophet. But the journey was a slow and difficult one of three hundred miles. But, at last, lookouts in Yathrib spied the two men approaching, and some of the crowds went to welcome him at a nearby oasis called Quba. 'Our Prophet is here,' shouted the people. The Prophet returned their welcome and for three days he rested in Quba, accepting gifts of dates and honey. There he laid the foundation stone for the very first mosque, the Muslim place of worship. He preached a sermon, the first he had given in safety and in the open air.

And then, in a joyful procession he went on into the city of Yathrib. Amidst all the celebration, the Prophet called the procession to a halt. He dismounted and spread a cloth on the ground. Then he stood up and called aloud, 'God is most great'. And then he bowed his head to the ground and completed his prayer of thanksgiving.

In Makka he might have been killed. In Yathrib he was loved. The name of that city was changed in honour of his arrival. It became Medinaten Nabi, which means 'the City of the Prophet', a name which was soon shortened to Medina.

And since then, those events have been remembered as Al Hijrah, the first day of the Muslim year.

David Self

5: SULEMAN THE HUMBLE

A Muslim story which teaches the importance of humility and the dangers of pride.

I wonder if you've ever met anyone who thinks they're very important. Even if they're not. They say things like, 'I should have first go, 'cause I'm older than you.' Or, 'You've got to do what I say, because I'm bigger than you.' And they don't like doing ordinary things for themselves. 'Carry this for me,' they say. 'I'm important, I don't have to carry things for myself.'

Well, this is a story about someone who really was *important. He was called Suleman (and God be pleased with him) and he lived a long, long time ago in the time of Muhammad who was the great prophet of the Islam religion.*

Muhammad's home was in an Arab city called Makka. And Muhammad had been telling the people of Makka about God and how God wanted them to live good lives and to be kind to the people around them – but the people of Makka didn't like what Muhammad was saying and they became very angry with him. In the end, Muhammad (and his few friends) had to leave Makka. They crossed the desert and came to a place called Medina. Which is where Suleman lived.

And Suleman (as I said) was important – in fact he was the ruler of Medina. Now although Medina was called a city, in those days it wasn't at all like a modern city. Remember, I said Muhammad had to cross the desert to get there? Well, Medina was just a place in the middle of the desert; but it did have a spring which meant there was water, and trees grew there, so there was shade. An oasis. An important place for travellers who could stay and rest there; and also for all the people who lived there – whose ruler was Suleman.

Well, when Muhammad came to Medina, Suleman listened to the message that Muhammad brought from God. He listened. And listened. And he knew that what Muhammad was saying was true, and he believed and became one of Muhammad's friends, or companions. And he also went on being ruler of Medina. But you'd never have thought so. He lived in a simple house. He had servants, yes, but no more than he needed and he treated them very fairly. He never said, 'I'm important, you must do what I say.'

And if you'd met him in the street, you'd never have guessed who he was.

And that's what happened one day.

Just as Muhammad had come travelling across the desert to Medina, so another traveller came to the city. He was a merchant. He travelled across the desert from town to town with many camels, and his camels carried all the things he bought and sold. And so, as I said, he came to Medina (with his camels) and the first person he met was Suleman. Suleman was walking along, all on his own because he hadn't liked to bother a servant to saddle up one of *his* camels just so that he could take a look round his city. And of course the merchant had no idea who he was. He called to him. 'You! Come here!'

Now Suleman might have gone on his way or he might have said, 'Don't you know who I am?' But he didn't. He came over to the merchant.

'Assalam-o-Alaikum,' he said, which was the greeting they said in that place. 'Peace be with you', it means. But all the merchant said was, 'Look, I've got a bale of hay. That big bundle there. On the first camel. It's for someone who lives in this place and it needs delivering, so *you* can carry it! I'm far too important to start carrying bundles of hay around. I'm a merchant.'

Suleman said nothing.

'Tell you what,' said the merchant. 'You stand with your back to the camel. I'll untie the bundle, lower it onto your shoulders and then you can carry it the rest of the way. Look sharp.'

And that's what he did. Without a word, Suleman took the weight of all the hay onto his shoulders – and struggled off down the street, with the merchant walking proudly behind him. It was a very heavy bundle.

'Hurry up. You're dawdling,' said the merchant as Suleman began to go more slowly. So Suleman hurried up as best he could. And then, coming towards them came another man (who lived in Medina). As this man approached them, he recognized Suleman and greeted him. 'Assalam-o-Alaikum,' he said (which, as I told you, means 'Peace be with you'). And he bowed very low and very respectfully to Suleman. And from under the bale of hay and a bit out of breath, Suleman said, 'Wa Alaikum salam!' which means 'And peace be with you, too'.

Well, the man was about to go on his way but the merchant stopped him.

'Aren't you going to greet *me*?' he said, very pompously.

'Oh, yes. Assalam-o-Alaikum,' said the man and started to go on his way again. 'Wait a minute,' said the merchant.

'Yes?' said the man.

'Aren't you going to bow to me? Why don't you bow to me, as you did to this, this . . . person?'

'Oh!' said the man. 'Well, no. No. I bow only to the ruler of the city of Medina.'

'Very well,' said the merchant, rather crossly. 'Off you – You what? You bow only to . . . You mean this man who is carrying my bale of hay is the . . . ruler of this city?'

'Yes, that is Suleman, who we call Suleman the Humble.'

'But he said nothing . . . I asked him if he would mind carrying . . . Well, I suppose I did actually rather *tell* him . . . Look, my dear sir,' he said to Suleman. 'I apologise. And I must carry my own bale of hay.'

'No,' said Suleman. 'You are a visitor. I will honour a visitor to our city and I will not put the bale down till we have reached the house where you're going.'

'But you're an important person.'

'An important person can do things for other people. Just as we can all think of other people. You see, my friend – I may call you my friend? Yes, my friend . . . some people happen to be rulers of cities. Some happen to be very strong. Or very clever. Or very patient. Or humble. Or . . . whatever. That is the will of God. It is no reason to boast. And no reason not to care for those they meet.' And as you can guess, everyone liked Suleman because he followed the way of God and his Prophet Muhammad — and because he was good and kind — and not proud, even though he was important.

David Self

6: BE MY GUEST

A story originally published by the Islamic Foundation. Be My Guest *is a reminder of the need to help the poor, to offer hospitality (and honour a guest) and to keep one's word.*

Suppose you made a promise (say, to help someone you didn't really know) and later you discovered that if you were to keep your word, it would cause you to suffer. Would you keep your promise?

In the days when the Prophet Muhammad (peace and blessings be upon him) lived in Medina, there were many poor people in the city. They did not have enough money to buy food and often lived in broken-down houses.

One day, a poor man came to see the Blessed Prophet, hoping to get some food. But that day it so happened that there was no food in the Blessed Prophet's house — there were many times when the Blessed Prophet and his family went without eating for several days.

The Blessed Prophet was not alone when the poor man came to his house. He was sitting with a group of other Muslims. The Blessed Prophet decided to ask one of these Muslims to take this poor man home with him and give him something to eat.

'Who will invite this man to dinner?' the Blessed Prophet asked.

No one replied. Everyone kept silent. So, the Blessed Prophet asked the question again. But again, no one responded.

Then, one man from the group stepped forward. His name was Abu Talha.

'I will invite him to dinner, O Prophet,' he said. 'I will take care of him.'

Then, Abu Talha turned to the poor man and welcomed him: 'Be my guest tonight, oh my brother!'

The poor man, very pleased and happy, accepted Abu Talha's kind invitation.

The two men left Muhammad's house and walked together through the streets until they arrived at Abu Talha's house. Abu Talha's wife met them and learned from her husband that the poor man was to be a guest at their table that night.

Abu Talha expected her to smile and greet the man. But instead she looked worried. Taking her husband aside, she said 'What am I to do?'

Abu Talha was puzzled. 'What is the matter, dear wife?' he asked her. 'Is anything wrong?'

Abu Talha's wife took her husband to a quiet corner of the room where the guest could not hear what they were saying.

'Oh my husband,' she told him. 'This is terrible. I would gladly give food to this man you have brought with you, but I have only enough food in the house for our children! This puts us in great difficulty!'

'It certainly does,' agreed Abu Talha. 'What are we going to do? I have given my promise to be a host to this man.'

Abu Talha thought for a while, and then he had an idea. It was rather a clever one, as you will see. 'Send the children to bed,' he told his wife. 'Send them to bed now.'

'But what about their meal?' she replied. 'They haven't eaten.'

'Never mind about that, send them to bed,' her husband insisted. 'They can go without food for one night.'

Then, Abu Talha told her what she was to do with the meal they were going to give the guest.

Abu Talha's wife did as her husband told her. She

sent the children to bed and then set about preparing what little food she had. Then, Abu Talha called his guest to the table and they all sat down to eat. Or at least, so thought the guest.

As Abu Talha's wife sat down, she said 'I don't think we need to have the lamp on this table burning so brightly. I'll turn it down. Isn't it more pleasant to eat when the light is dim?'

Abu Talha smiled to himself. His wife was giving a very good performance. She was doing exactly as he had instructed her. She turned the lamp down so low, in fact, that the flame was almost out and it was rather difficult for the guest to see his host at all. But this is just what Abu Talha wanted.

Abu Talha's wife served food to the guest, and then fussed about with a plate for her husband and then one for herself. But when the meal began, only one of the three people at the table was actually eating! Can you guess who this was? It was the guest. Abu Talha's wife had given him all the food she had in the house. There was nothing for her husband or herself. Instead, the two of them sat in the dim room and moved their hands from their plates to their mouths, pretending to be eating. But the guest did not realize what was happening, because it was too dark in the room for him to see properly. If he had known what was going on, the guest might have felt embarrassed – and Abu Talha did not want a guest in his house to feel that way.

This had been Abu Talha's plan and it worked perfectly. The guest finished his meal and for the first time in many days he did not feel hungry. He was a very happy man when he left Abu Talha's house and blessed his host for his kindness and his wife's good cooking.

The day after this happened, Abu Talha visited the Blessed Prophet's house. The Blessed Prophet greeted him warmly.

'Talha', said the Blessed Prophet, 'Allah is very pleased with your good deed last night and has described you as being one of those who prefers to sacrifice his own needs for the sake of others.'

Khurram Murad

7: DAUD CONQUERS JALUD

Muslims honour many of the Jewish prophets, and of course Jesus. This passage is an Islamic version of the story of David (Daud) and Goliath (Jalud). Talut is King Saul. The Jewish account can be found in Samuel 1:17. Assembly leaders might devise their own introductions to this reading to take account of whether listeners know the Judaic-Christian version of the story. See also page 159.

Talut and his soldiers had crossed the river Urdun. They were going to fight the army led by Jalud. This would be an important battle in the struggle of the Israelites for their homeland. But Talut was worried. He knew that Jalud's soldiers were well-armed and his army was huge.

The two armies came nearer. Talut's men began whispering in fear to each other, 'We cannot defeat Jalud. Look at the size of his army!' The sound of horses' hooves grew louder and the cries of the soldiers mingled with the flying dust.

Daud, a young shepherd boy, was among Talut's men with his father, Isya. Isya was in charge of the army's supplies. Daud wanted to see the battle and begged his father to let him take the soldiers' food to the front. His father was unwilling to let him go, but Daud argued so much, and someone had to take the food, so in the end Isya agreed.

Daud ran between the ranks of men towards Talut. He could hear the clash of battle already. The soldiers' faces were white with fear as they marched grimly on. The cries of Jalud's men filled the air, *'Allaahu Akbar! Attack! Attack!'*

The ground was strewn with the bodies of Talut's men; it was red with their blood. As Daud came up to

Talut, Jalud shouted from the battlefield, 'Send me your champion! I will fight him! If he wins, I will admit defeat. If I win, I will rule your kingdom!'

Talut was white with worry. His soldiers were trembling. Daud did not hesitate. 'Let me go and fight Jalud!' he cried.

'No', said Talut. 'You're too young, Daud. You're still a child.'

'Strength and courage do not depend on age or size,' said Daud. 'What matters is a strong will and faith.' He told Talut how he had fought and defeated both a wild bear and a lion that attacked his sheep.

'Talut! What are you waiting for? If your champion doesn't come forward, we will attack and you will all die!' shouted Jalud. Then he roared with laughter as Daud came forward. Both armies were amazed too, to see this young boy prepare to fight the mighty Jalud.

As Jalud put an arrow in his bow, Daud prepared his shepherd's sling. Remembering the names of Allah, Ibrahim and Ishaq, he let the stones fly. A stone hit Jalud's head and the mighty warrior fell face forward to the ground. As fast as lightning Daud took Jalud's sword and killed him. His soldiers ran away in fear.

Daud and Talut and his men gave thanks for their victory, repeating *Al-Hamdulillah*' over and over again.

Abdul Rahman Rukaini

12
Looking ahead

1: OPTIONS

As pupils approach the time they must make their 'options', they need to think ahead about their lives.

How often do you think ahead to what your life will be like? What sort of career or job will you have? Will you have a job? Listen to the story of Prince Charming...

'Prince Charming' had a good life and great expectations. Wasn't he going to be King? There were no career worries — he knew he would take over Dad's business. Of course, one day he would have to think seriously about ruling his own little corner of the world, but for now there were maidens to rescue, dragons to slay, and servants to meet his every need. Life could be good when one's home really was one's castle!

Occasionally the young prince had a nagging feeling that the kingdom was changing. And, indeed it was. Many Sleeping Beauties were beginning to wake up on their own. Snow White had just been appointed manager of the Seven Dwarfs Diamond Mine plc, and rumour had it that Cinderella was opening her own slipper factory.

His future as King was starting to look a bit shaky too. Would there be a revolution? People were saying that kings were old-fashioned and that knights in shining armour could easily be replaced by robots. Since the prince hadn't counted on anything changing, he hadn't thought about what he would do if he didn't become king. He had studied 'nation administration' at school, so how could he switch to teaching or urban planning? Would he have to re-train in a new skill or trade? Somehow it seemed easier to fight dragons than to face these challenges.

Maybe you are worried too. While finding the *right* job has always been difficult, today, finding *any* job is becoming increasingly more challenging. Many jobs and trades are being eliminated by new technology. And while this technology is creating many new and exciting occupations, most people have not trained for them.

And what about 'Princess Charming'? For wives, slaving all day in a hot kitchen is almost a thing of the past. What if the future wife wants to work, or the family needs her income to make ends meet? Traditionally, men have been the 'breadwinners', while women have taken care of the home. But today nearly 46% of married women work outside the home. If the wife works, will the man be ready to take more responsibility for the children and the home?

Now here is the good news: Men are beginning to realize that with the sharing of the responsibility for the economic support of the family, there is more free time to explore other interests and have more career flexibility. They are finding a working wife is an exciting partner and the added income helps them avoid the financial treadmill. With marriage becoming a more equal economic partnership, both lives are becoming more significant.

Look around you. Besides the traditional family life pattern, there are a number of other options. Many men are spending more time bringing up their own children. There are single-parent families, families in which the woman has an outside job, while the man has an office in the home allowing him to take the major responsibility for child care, and childless marriages. Others have decided not to marry at all. Of the many choices, which appeals to you the most?

Mindy Bingham, Judy Edmondson and Sandy Stryker

2: EQUALITY FOR ALL

Many of us look forward to an ideal future in which everyone is equal. But would we really like a world of complete equality and complete equality of opportunity? This extract from a short story by Kurt Vonnegut Jnr is a nightmarish vision of a future in which intelligent, athletic and beautiful people are handicapped.

As you know, there seems to be a lot of unfairness in the world. Some people are rich, others poor. Some are clever, some are slow. Some are handsome or beautiful, others less so. But would you like it if everyone was equal and people who were gifted in some way were given a handicap?

The year was 2081, and everybody was finally equal. Nobody was smarter than anybody else. Nobody was better looking than anybody else. Nobody was stronger or quicker than anybody else. All this equality was due to the unceasing vigilance of agents of the United States Handicapper General — the H-G men.

It was in April that the H-G men took George and Hazel Bergeron's fourteen-year-old son, Harrison, away.

It was tragic, all right, but George and Hazel couldn't think about it very hard. Hazel had a perfectly average intelligence, which meant she couldn't think about anything except in short bursts. And George, while his intelligence was way above normal, had a little mental handicap radio in his ear. He was required by law to wear it at all times. It was tuned to a government transmitter. Every twenty seconds or so, the transmitter would send out some sharp noise to keep people like George from taking unfair advantage of their brains.

George and Hazel were watching television. There

were tears on Hazel's cheeks, but she'd forgotten for the moment what they were about.

On the television screen were ballerinas.

A buzzer sounded in George's head. His thoughts fled in panic, like bandits from a burglar alarm.

'That was a real pretty dance, that dance they just did,' said Hazel.

'Huh?' said George.

'That dance — it was nice,' said Hazel.

'Yup,' said George. He tried to think a little about the ballerinas. They weren't really very good — no better than anybody else would have been, anyway. They were burdened with sashweights and bags of birdshot, and their faces were masked, so that no one seeing a free and graceful gesture and a pretty face would feel like something the cat dragged in. George was toying with the vague notion that maybe dancers shouldn't be handicapped. But he didn't get very far with it before another noise in his ear radio scattered his thoughts.

George winced. So did two out of the eight ballerinas.

Hazel bore a strong resemblance to the Handicapper General, a woman named Diana Moon Glampers.

'I think I'd make a good Handicapper General,' said Hazel.

'Good as anybody else,' said George.

He began to think glimmeringly about his abnormal son who was now in jail, about Harrison, but a twenty-one gun salute in his head stopped that.

'Boy!' said Hazel, 'that was a doozy, wasn't it?'

It was such a doozy that George was white and trembling, and tears stood on the rims of his red eyes. Two of the eight ballerinas had collapsed to the studio floor, and were holding their temples.

'All of a sudden you look so tired,' said Hazel. 'Why don't you stretch out on the sofa, so's you can rest your handicap bag on the pillows, honeybunch.' She was referring to the forty-seven pounds of birdshot in a canvas bag, which was padlocked around George's neck. 'Go on and rest the bag for a little,' she said. 'I don't care if you're not equal to me for a while.'

George weighed the bag with his hands. 'I don't mind it,' he said. 'I don't notice it any more. It's just a part of me.'

'You been so tired lately – kind of wore out,' said Hazel. 'If there was just some way we could make a little hole in the bottom of the bag, and just take out a few of them lead balls. Just a few.'

'If I tried to get away with it then other people'd get away with it – and pretty soon we'd be right back to the dark ages again, with everybody competing against everybody else. You wouldn't like that would you?'

Kurt Vonnegut Jnr

3: IN THE DOCK

This script, by a twelve-year-old, was an award winning entry in the 1985 W. H. Smith Young Writers' Competition. It raises the profound question of how optimistic we can (or indeed must) be about the future. The witnesses might wear or carry placards bearing their name to reinforce their impact. The script might also encourage the writing of similar scripts for presentation in assembly.

Today you are going to see a court room trial. On trial is not a person but 'Tomorrow' or the future. Will the future or 'Tomorrow' be a good thing, a good time; or is it something evil, something to dread? Is Tomorrow innocent or guilty? You will have to pass your verdict after you have heard the evidence . . .

The Trial of Tomorrow

Witness for the Prosecution

Judge: Call Despair.

Despair: My Lord, you must surely understand that this

Looking ahead

   Tomorrow is but a
figment of the imagination,
an illusion, nay, a delusion
on which the souls of weak worms feast
but grow no fatter, and starve, and die,
That tepid mass in one's stomach
when reality breaks, as a wave,
and you know, yes my lord, you know
that despite all your strivings
you cannot change the world in which you live.
Therefore surely Tomorrow is cause for worry,
cause for uncertainty,
cause for jealousy?
Cause, no less, for misgivings, for useless
      preparations,
cause even for Hope?
And for the belief that tomorrow brings more and
better than today?
All the trees bear fair fruit tomorrow,
But in reality – they are bitter.
Great flowers bloom tomorrow –
But in reality, they wither.
My lord, I rest my case.

Judge: Call Typical.

Typical: My Lord, I represent all the ordinary
      thousands.
My case is one of false pretences,
of an inexplicable urge not to differ,
Not to break new ground,
but to tread the same mill until we drop.
My witnesses are smog, old warehouses
now abandoned, and patched with plastic,
And the knowledge that day after day
Is the same.
If a life consists, M'Lud, of days alike,
then surely Tomorrow is no novelty?
Tomorrow must give way to Today.
My Lord, I rest my case.

Judge: Witness for the prosecution, do you call any more speakers?

WftP: But one, M'Lud. Call Reality.

Reality: My Lord, the populace is under the impression
that all one's worries will vanish
should one but wait.
This, My Lord, is untrue.
Left unattended, worrying matters grow
as a canker. Surely then,
with the abolition of Tomorrow
All these aspects will be attended to today?
My Lord, look around you. See the threats,
Pollution, the slow death of the environment
That increase tomorrow?
See the extinction of species, the imminent danger
of Nuclear War, that could break out tomorrow?
That tomorrow, we may be no more?
My Lord, I rest my case.

Witness for the Defence

Judge: Call Tomorrow.

Clerk: Absent, M'Lud. The trial is to be conducted in his absence.

WftD: Call Hope.

Hope: Gentlemen of the jury, Tomorrow is wonderful.
Sometimes there is the happy knowledge that
Tomorrow is a day of rest.
Sometimes you may have Tomorrow to finish
that which you have begun.
Tomorrow is a day to start anew, to start afresh.
To forget what is done today and just to live.
Tomorrow is a comfort, a refuge.
'It will all be all right tomorrow,' people say,
and they are right.
For what, M'Lud, could be worse than today?

Tomorrow is for seeing flowers, for hearing birds,
For not caring, for loving.
Tomorrow is an aid to help us through now.
We all need Tomorrow.
M'Lud, I rest my case.

Judge: Are there any more witnesses for the defence?

WftD: Only Hope, My Lord. Only Hope.

Judge: Then let the jury consider their verdict.

Guy Burt

4: AFTER THE BOMB

Robert Swindells' novel, Brother in the Land, *is a powerful and moving novel for teenagers about life after a nuclear bomb has been dropped on a northern city.*

This reading makes us think about what we might prefer to ignore: what life would be like after a nuclear bomb has been dropped on this country. It wouldn't kill everyone; there would be survivors. What would it be like for them? The storyteller in this passage is a teenage boy called Danny. Ben is his much younger brother.

It sounds daft now, but we lived in hope those first few days. We kept expecting somebody to come. Dad's booklet said the dead would be collected and feeding centres set up. It said to listen to the radio; there'd be news, and instructions.

We knew there were people up at Kershaw Farm with fallout gear and weapons. People in authority. We assumed they were soldiers, and that they'd come down and start sorting things out like the soldiers in Turkey when there was that earthquake. In the meantime, we had to shift for ourselves.

A lot of people went mad. Not raving mad, but wandering aimlessly about in the ruins, muttering; or sitting absolutely still, staring at the ground.

You'd think people would've got together to organize tents and cooking and first-aid, and that, but they didn't. They were stunned, I suppose. They'd be outside and it'd start to rain and they'd just stand or sit getting wet with places all round they could shelter in.

I think it was the ones who thought too much who went mad. I mean, if you went round thinking about how it was before and how you used to take it all for granted and that, I guess it could drive you daft. I think Dad realized that. He was always doing something, keeping himself busy so he hadn't time to brood about Mum and the shop and that.

What kept me going was Ben. You know how it is with little kids, some big change comes into their lives, a new school or moving house or something, and they're upset for maybe a couple of days. After that, they pick up their lives and carry on and it's like nothing's happened. They adjust to new situations with fantastic speed.

Ben was like that. I mean, one day he was this ordinary little lad, going off to school with his reading book and pencil case, coming home to watch telly and eat toffees and go to sleep in a warm bed; and the next he was a little survivor with no mum, living amongst ruins and sleeping on the floor. And he just did it. His mum wasn't buried three days before he was racing about in the rubble, playing soldiers. It was incredible. It kept me sane, watching him.

Nobody came, and there was only crackling on the radio, so Dad and me dug a hole in a garden opposite the shop and put Mum in it. It was raining. Dad said something he remembered from the Bible and rain ran down his face so you could only tell he was crying by his voice and you couldn't tell about me at all. It was evening, and Ben was asleep. We'd have shown him where she was later, only he never asked.

Robert Swindells

SEASONAL READINGS

Autumn term

1: ROSH HASHANAH

Rosh Hashanah is the Jewish New Year's Day and occurs in late September. Its exact date can be found in many diaries. It commemorates God's creation of the world and the 'shofar' (a long horn) is blown to commemorate Abraham's obedience in being prepared to sacrifice his son Isaac.

New Year's Day in the Jewish calendar occurs this year on . . .

For Jews, New Year's Day (or Rosh Hashanah) is a time to think of the things they have done wrong in the past year and to remember that God judges each person. It is also a time to look ahead and wish each other a lucky and happy new year. At Rosh Hashanah, Jews eat apple dipped in honey: the apple is a sign of the sharpness of wrong-doing, the honey a sign of sweetness for the new year. And at this time, 'a shofar', a kind of long ram's horn, is blown – as this passage (by a Jewish rabbi) explains.

If you live in a middle-class Jewish suburb, and it is late summer, you might be woken up before breakfast by a braying sound from your neighbour's garden. It is so shrill and so insistent, you might think it is the end of the world.

Well, for your Jewish neighbour it is – sort of. He has been practising on the ram's horn – 'an ill wind that no one blows good', in the words of the comedian Danny Kaye. No one blows it good because the horn is so ancient – it has no modern innards, no reed or whistle. I myself have never been able to coax a note out of it. But then I can't whistle either.

Although the liturgy for the Jewish New Year says, 'Happy the people, who hear this joyous sound', it sounds really more like an air raid alarm or an early warning system. Judgement, it says, is coming to everyone. All that you tried to hide in the last year from your neighbours, from your nearest and dearest, and especially from yourself, is coming under review. You have a last chance to put everything right in the ten days after the New Year. Then comes the great Day of Atonement and the foretaste of your own last judgement.

Now this is not a cosy thought, and though there are a lot of sweet things to eat on the Jewish New Year, you can't help eating them rather thoughtfully . . .

And all this goes through my mind on the Jewish New Year which celebrates the birthday of the world, as I meet my friends in their best clothes, and we eat honey cake together. That's the flavour of Jewish life and Jewish festivals, bitter-sweet, holding together happiness and insecurity, pride and shame, triumph and tragedy.

[My grandfather – may he rest in peace – on the New Year used to wish everyone Gentile luck, – because Jewish luck, he said, isn't up to much. So, like him, I wish you Gentile luck and Happy New Year, Jewish-style.]

Rabbi Lionel Blue

2: THERESE OF LISIEUX

(3 October)

Therese Martin was born in northern France in 1873, the daughter of a watchmaker. Five of his daughters became nuns. In 1888 she entered the Carmelite convent of Lisieux in Normandy where two of her sisters were already nuns. Her remaining nine years of life were uneventful and 'ordinary'. She died of tuberculosis in 1897. After her death her 'little way', a book called **The Story of a Soul,** *had a sensational success and she was made a saint in 1925. Her life story* has been an example and comfort to millions of (especially) Catholic Christians in that it shows that everyone can serve God by doing 'small', everyday things in a spirit of love and kindness.

This reading is about quite an ordinary person: Therese of Lisieux, in France. For a start, she did not live very long. She died when she was only twenty-four. But what did she do?

Not a lot. In fact, not very much at all. So why was she special? Why was she 'picked out' as a very holy person? Why did she become Saint Therese?

Therese Martin was born over a hundred years ago in a town in northern France called Lisieux. Her mother died when she was quite young and she lived with her father and her four older sisters.

Marie, the oldest of the sisters, became a kind of mother to the family. Except to little Therese. She turned instead to her next oldest sister, Pauline.

'You're my mother now,' she said.

And Pauline did take special care of Therese. In fact, perhaps because Therese was the youngest, they all rather spoilt her.

Once, Leonie (who was the middle sister) came along with a basket of dolls and sewing things she no longer wanted. 'Here,' she said to the two youngest sisters. 'Choose which of these you'd like.'

When it was Therese's turn to choose, she thought for a moment and then said, 'I choose the lot.'

She got them all, as well.

If things didn't go as she wanted, Therese would burst into tears. There were times when she deliberately 'cried', just to get her own way.

But when she was eight, something happened that really did upset her. Pauline decided to become a nun and to go and live in a nearby convent.

These particular nuns believed (indeed they still do believe) that by staying in 'Carmel' as they call it, they can do more for people by praying for them than by doing anything else.

The years went by. Therese was getting used to life without Pauline. Then, her oldest sister Marie said that she too was going into Carmel. There were more tears. Lots more tears.

But at the next Christmas (by which time Therese was thirteen), things changed.

When they had been little, all the Martin sisters had had their Christmas presents after they got back from church. They would come home and find them, tucked inside a pair of their boots, in a special corner of the house. All of them had grown out of this – except Therese. This year, just as they got into the house, she overheard her father saying, 'Oh this is far too babyish for a girl like Therese. I hope it is the last time we have to do it.' He did not mean her to hear him – but she did!

She started to cry. Then something stopped her. At that moment, she knew she must stop thinking just of herself, of what *she* wanted. Soon, she made another decision. She too would enter Carmel.

At first there were problems. People said she was too young. But that Autumn, her father took her on a visit to Rome. She was allowed to see the Pope, to be blessed by him. When she was kneeling in front of him, although she was not meant to say anything, Therese spoke up. 'Holy father, allow me to enter Carmel.'

The Pope seemed unsure what to say. At last he said, 'If it be God's will.'

So, in the year 1888, at the age of fifteen, Therese entered Carmel and became a nun.

Even though she was near her older sisters again, not everything was easy. One of the much older nuns often used to criticise her. 'This child does absolutely nothing. She's no good at anything.'

Gradually, Therese learned to say nothing to all this, but just to keep quiet. One of the first times she managed this was when someone else had left a jar by a window and it had got broken. One of the nuns supposed it was Therese's fault. Therese said she was sorry.

And so, in little ways like this, she learned to be patient.

After five years, Pauline became prioress, or leader, of the nuns. One evening she and Marie were talking with Therese about when they were children. Pauline told Therese to write down her memories.

So Therese wrote about her childhood and about her 'little way'; that is, her way of pleasing God by doing little things for other people, and for putting up with things and not complaining.

She finished her writing in July 1897. But by now she had an illness called tuberculosis. In those days there was no cure and, two months later, Therese died.

Since then, the book has sold millions of copies all around the world and Therese has become Saint Therese of Lisieux.

And why?

Because she showed that ordinary people can become saints by following her 'little way'.

David Self

3: DIVALI

(late October/early November)

Divali can be compared with the Jewish festival Hanukah, the Christian celebration of Christmas and Epiphany and, more especially, the bonfire festivities throughout Europe in the dark days of late autumn. Flames and fireworks are the first things that the visitor to India is aware of at the time of Divali.

At this time of year, members of the Hindu religion hold their festival of Divali. 'Divali' means 'row of lights'. Hindus celebrate the festival in various ways (just as Christians celebrate Christmas in different ways) but this is one account of what happens on the first three days of the festival.

Day 1

Divali starts on the thirteenth day of the dark half of the Hindu month of Ashwin. In India, as in many other places, there are thirteen months in the year. Each month is exactly twenty-eight days, from one new moon to the next. This is called a lunar month. The dark half of the month is the second half, when the moon is getting smaller and smaller. By the thirteenth day of the second half there is hardly any moon at all and the nights are very dark.

Divali is of great importance to the traders and merchants of India. On this first day a model of Lakshmi, the goddess of wealth and wife of Vishnu, is brought out and thoroughly washed – often in milk. This is because, according to legend, she was created from a churning sea of milk. In similar fashion the women take a bath and put on perfume. The family has special food, especially sweets made from thickened milk and sugar, or coconut and sugar.

Day 2

Now it is the turn of the men. Before sunrise on this second day they bathe after rubbing perfumed oil over their heads and bodies. Then they sit down while the young girls of the family dance around them, often with flickering lamps containing rice flour and oil. Each man is handed a small piece of fruit called chirat. This he squashes with his left foot, and then, with the same foot, he snuffs out the flame of the lamp. The men then take a second bath, put on fresh clothes and share a meal of cakes and sweetmeats with their friends. Firecrackers are often let off both morning and evening.

Day 3

This is the last day of the old year. Hindus believe that Vishnu gave four main holidays, one for each caste. To the Vaishyas, or traders, he gave Divali.

Because it is the end of the year all accounts have to be settled. The books which show the trading of the past year have to be balanced and traders know exactly how much money they have made – or lost! This is why

Autumn term

Lakshmi, the goddess of wealth, is so important to the festival. Every effort is made to make sure that Lakshmi sees into every home. Everything is a blaze of light and all doors and windows are left open so that Lakshmi can visit. Shops and offices as well as homes are decorated. This is to thank Lakshmi for past help and to ask her for a 'prosperous new year'.

During the month of Ashwin, the sun passes through the zodiac sign of Libra, the scales. It is easy to see a link between the scales of Libra and the end of the trading year. Shopkeepers and traders balance their books; farmers weigh the fruits of the harvest. It is the time for working out what we have and for planning the future.

It is a time for new beginnings, for buying new clothes and giving old ones away to the poor. Other presents, especially food and sweets, are given to friends and relatives.

Howard Marsh

4: REMEMBRANCE SUNDAY

(The Sunday nearest 11 November)

Remembrance Sunday can seem an awkward occasion to young people. It can either appear to glorify war or to be something that involves only old people. This passage was originally written as an introduction to the Two Minutes' Silence.

This . . . (coming/last Sunday) is Remembrance Sunday. On it we remember all those who lost their lives in the two World Wars. Many people wear a poppy as a sign of remembrance. The money from the poppies goes to help those who were wounded in the wars and their families. Many people keep silence for two minutes on the Sunday morning at eleven o'clock as a sign of respect. But why should we bother to think about what happened long ago?

We want to live. We did not ask to be born into a world of guns and bombs. We do not want to fight. Leave us alone, you statesmen and rulers, let us live our lives in peace. We want to live.

So did they, the boys, girls, men and women who lived, suffered and died in the wars. Of course they wanted to go on living; and yet, for some strange, inscrutable reason that God alone knows, they were destined for wounds and slaughter. God let them be killed. Before they died, many of them had to endure hell on earth. Somehow they struggled on. Where did they find the strength? Some, in the people they loved, or the country they loved, or the sheer animal will to survive; some, in their faith in God.

There were those who believed that they were giving themselves to build a world for us. They died for the future, for an ideal world that we could live in, an earth at peace. Now it is our turn to strive for peace on earth. War is not only made by statesmen. It is made by us, ordinary people who strive to achieve our own selfish ends, quarrelling and hating as we pursue our petty, sordid, self-seeking quest. We *can* make peace, with God's help, if we have faith, and hope, and love for one another. *We* are responsible for peace. Let us begin here, to build what the dead of the wars left unfinished. Perhaps we were not worth dying for: but without their sacrifice we would not be alive today.

Let us thank God for them, and let us honour them, in silence.

Michael Davis

5: ST MARTIN

(11 November)

St Martin was born in what is now Hungary about 315 CE, and brought up in Italy, the son of an officer in the Roman army. He himself joined the army and also became a Christian. Later, on becoming a pacifist, he left the army to live the life of a monk. In 371, by popular demand, he became Bishop of Tours in France.

It is not easy to do something that may make others think you are stupid or (perhaps worse) a coward – even when you are certain that what you are doing is right. This is the story of a young man who lived at the time of the Roman Empire and who had the courage to do what he thought he should, even when those around him thought differently. And he was also a man who cared for those in need.

By the time he was fifteen, Martin was strong, fit and tall; tall enough to join the Roman Army. And that is where this story begins – in a small town in Italy, not far from where he lived.

The army doctor had examined him and all the other young men who were hoping to become soldiers. Next, an officer interrogated them, hoping to make sure they were not runaway criminals or slaves who ought to be at home serving their masters. Each of the young men had brought with him a letter from someone recommending him as likely to be a good soldier. Martin handed over his letter. The officer read it. 'Most impressive,' he said. 'From your father, isn't it?'

'Yes, sir,' said Martin.

'Met him once. In Macedonia. Very brave soldier. And you're going to be just like him. Excellent.'

Martin took the army oath, saying he would be a soldier loyal to the Roman Empire and he was given, as was usual, four months pay in advance. The only trouble was he didn't want to be a soldier.

Martin's family worshipped the Roman gods, especially Mars the god of war. And in their home (or villa) in Italy there were many statues of Mars – which of course was not surprising seeing that Martin's father was a brave and famous army officer, who wanted his son, Martin, to be like him.

But Martin had other ideas. As a young boy, he'd heard about what was then known as the 'new' religion: people who followed the teachings of a man called Jesus. Many of these people (called Christians) thought it wrong to go to war, to fight and kill – and Martin thought so too. Secretly, he wanted to become a Christian himself and to spend his life praying and helping people, but he was obedient and did what his father wanted – which was why he was now a soldier.

In fact, Martin proved to be a very good soldier. He was reliable and popular. Soon, he was promoted. He became an officer – only a junior officer, but still, an officer. Now he no longer marched on foot with all the other soldiers as they tramped the long miles along the straight Roman roads. Martin rode on a silver-white horse. He wore a sword and a warm red cloak over his armour. Then, in the winter when Martin was eighteen, he and his soldiers were posted to another part of the Roman empire. They were sent to guard the town of Amiens in the north of what's now called France but was then called Gaul.

Martin and his soldiers were not too pleased about this: winter in northern France can seem quite damp and cold to someone used to the warmth of Italy and the sunny Mediterranean countries.

One raw, damp evening, Martin was riding slowly through the town, his soldiers marching behind him, when he saw a beggar. There was nothing unusual in that, there were many beggars in those days. But Martin couldn't help noticing this man. He was wearing just a few damp, torn rags and shivering with the cold.

Martin pulled up his horse, drew his sword and with one swift movement, cut his warm red cloak in two – and gave half to the beggar who could hardly believe his luck. Martin's soldiers were amazed. They began to giggle. Had their officer gone mad? Ruining his cloak for a beggar? They tried not to laugh out loud. They couldn't help it. But Martin wasn't angry or embarrassed.

He simply said, 'That man was cold. I'd got a cloak. It was right to share it.'

In silence, they marched back to their barracks.

That night, Martin had a dream. He thought he saw Jesus, wearing half a Roman soldier's cloak. 'Look,' said Jesus in the dream. 'This is the cloak which Martin has shared.'

This dream made Martin more and more determined to become a Christian and indeed that's what happened. He was baptised and so became a follower of Jesus. Now he wanted to leave the army even more but a war was beginning against a fierce tribe called the Goths. Martin was immediately accused of being a coward, of wanting to run away from danger. When he continued to refuse to fight, this was thought to be mutiny and so he was put in prison. At the end of the war, he was released and allowed to leave the army.

He decided to give up everything. He became a monk, sharing everything with the other monks and helping the poor people of that part of France. He became so popular with the people that, when they needed a new bishop, they insisted that he should be their bishop.

Now he could live in luxury in a palace. But no, he shared out all the wealth that he could have had and lived in a simple wooden hut with his friends, the other monks. And from there he taught that we should love one another, help those in need and share what we have.

David Self

6: HUGH OF LINCOLN

(17 November)

As part of his penance for his part in the murder of Thomas à Becket, Henry II founded a 'Charter House' (or Carthusian monastery) in Somerset. As its prior, Henry chose a French monk, Hugh of Avalon, the youngest son of a noble Burgundian family. As prior and later as Bishop of Lincoln (a diocese which then stretched from the Thames to the Humber and included nine counties), Hugh

proved himself a brilliant administrator – yet remained always sympathetic to the needs of ordinary people.
   The story may be read in two parts, if required.

Eight hundred years ago, the city of Lincoln was one of the biggest in the country. Not so big as it is now, but for those days, a great city. And eight hundred years ago, as now, high upon Lincoln Hill, there stood a cathedral – except that then, in the year 1186, it was in ruins. The roof, other parts too, had come crashing down during an earthquake the year before. And something else was wrong at Lincoln. There was no bishop; no man to be in charge of all the churches and priests in the area all around. Today's story is about a man who was good at organizing; good at getting things done.

Part One

The story doesn't begin in Lincoln or even in the year 1186. It begins forty years before that, in part of what's now called France. There, in the castle of Avalon, there lived a knight. A storybook knight in shining armour! He had three sons: Peter, William – and Hugh.

   When their father was at home, Peter and William had him teach them how to fight. Hugh was different but, in his way, equally brave. His mother looked after people who were ill or deformed and especially people who suffered from the disease of leprosy. Most folk wouldn't go anywhere near them but Hugh's mother did – and young Hugh had the courage to go and hold the towels while she washed their sores and their damaged hands and feet.

   Peter and William grew up to become brave knights, like their father. But Hugh decided he would become a monk. That is, he would never marry but spend his whole life praying and studying, with other monks, in a building called a monastery; in fact in a particular kind of monastery called a Charter House.

   Hugh loved this peaceful, quiet life and, as the years went by, he became one of the older and most respected monks. A holy man – kind and gentle.

Meanwhile, in England, the king, King Henry II was in trouble. The Archbishop of Canterbury had been murdered and Henry had been partly to blame. To prove his sorrow, he'd arranged for a monastery to be built at a place called Witham in Somerset. It, too, was to be a 'Charter House' and now he needed a monk from another Charter House to be in charge. He'd heard about quiet, gentle Hugh of Avalon and decided that he needed Hugh. He sent for him.

Gentle Hugh came to Witham. And what did he find? Just a few huts, nothing else. He got back on his horse and rode straight off to see the king.

'My dear King,' he said, 'do you call that a monastery? A few huts made out of branches? There's no church! And what about the people who were living on the land before? What about them? No, don't interrupt – ' (yes, he was quite outspoken) ' – I'll tell you what you'll do. You'll give them land and pay for new homes for them. And you must pay stonemasons and carpenters to build a proper Charter House. And then – ' (he added tactfully) ' – everyone will know how generous you are. But if you don't, I won't stay in England. All right?'

'I'll pay,' said the King.

'To the last penny, mind!' said Hugh and off he went, back to Witham.

Everyone was very surprised, not least the king. Was this the same, quiet Hugh of Avalon that they'd heard about? But in the end, the monastery was built and Henry realized Hugh was nowhere near as soft as some people had thought. So later, when Henry had another problem, again he thought of Hugh.

This problem was Lincoln. For some years, the diocese of Lincoln had been without a bishop. It really needed one: to get the ruined cathedral re-built and the diocese properly organized. So a message was sent to Hugh telling him he was now Bishop of Lincoln; he'd be in charge of the Church through nine counties and one of the most powerful men in the country.

'But I'm happy as a monk,' he said. 'I don't want to go to Lincoln.' In the end though, he agreed and, eight hundred years ago, Hugh of Avalon became Bishop of Lincoln. And when he got there of course he found his cathedral was in ruins.

Straight away he arranged for it to be re-built. 'It must be bigger. It's God's house and the bigger it is and the more beautiful it is, the more it'll remind the people that there's nothing more important in life than God.'

Bishop Hugh got everyone organized. Stone was quarried and brought to Lincoln. Stonemasons were found who cut and carved the stones. Carpenters carved the woodwork. Other men made beautiful stained glass windows and the silversmiths got to work. Hugh got them all organized. Indeed, that was one of the things he was best at, organizing people. And when he'd time, Bishop Hugh joined in himself, carrying wood and stone up to where it was needed. Yes, the most important man in the diocese doing one of the most ordinary jobs. It may have been unusual but it was a good example and had its desired effect. No one skived!

Part 2

While he was Bishop of Lincoln, Hugh lived near a place called Stow, not far from the city of Lincoln. Round his house at Stow, there was a moat and, on the moat, there lived a fierce swan. When Hugh arrived, his servants warned him about it.

'Leave the door ajar,' he said. 'P'raps it'll come in and see me.'

'Be careful, my Lord,' they said.

But they left the door open and . . . in walked the swan. Hugh held out a piece of bread. With a little flap of its wings, it stretched out its neck and took the bread. From then on, Hugh and the swan became friends. But Hugh often had to travel away from Stow. And the

Autumn term

swan *always* seemed to know when he was coming back. Just before he arrived, it would get terribly excited and swim up and down, making an enormous fuss. And then when Hugh came through the gate, it would come quietly up to him. He began to hide bread for it up his sleeve, and the swan would push its beak gently up the sleeve looking for the bread.

Meanwhile, the re-building of Lincoln cathedral went on. And Hugh was also busy organizing the building of hospitals and helping anyone in trouble. Once, he was in a town called Stamford. A group of Jewish people who lived there had been accused of doing something against the law although they were quite innocent. Bishop Hugh saw that a crowd of people were attacking them with sticks and stones. Without hesitating, he strode straight into the middle of the riot. He spoke firmly to them all. He calmed them down, even made a few jokes (which made them laugh and lose their anger) and then made sure everyone was treated fairly.

Each Autumn, Hugh went back to Charter House at Witham to spend some time in peace and quiet with his friends the monks who still lived there. Even though he was one of the most important men in the country and there were people prepared to do all his jobs for him, he did all his own cooking. There was something else that he really loved doing. After every meal, he did the washing-up. Bishop Hugh had a passion for washing-up. Not only did he do his own pots but everyone else's as well.

One time, when Hugh was away from Stow, everyone noticed that the swan had suddenly become dejected, sad. Its wings floated limply in the water, its head drooped. 'Perhaps it's dying,' the people said.

It wasn't though. As they found out later, just at that moment, far away in London, *Hugh* was dying.

His body was brought back to Lincoln cathedral and thousands of people (including the Kings of England

and Scotland) came to his funeral, not to be sad or sorrowful but to give thanks for the man who had given Lincoln such a wonderful building in which to worship God; a man who had done so much to help the sick and to see that ordinary people were treated fairly and who'd been so ready to do ordinary jobs himself; clever, kind, fierce but friendly, Bishop Hugh of Lincoln, a man who got things done.

David Self

CHRISTMAS

7: THE CHRISTMAS TREE

Research into customs, traditions, myths, legends and superstitions associated with trees reveals a seemingly endless list of fascinating stories and beliefs. Indeed, the power of trees seems to have made a very special impact on people's spiritual lives throughout many centuries. As a religious symbol, the tree is well-known. Early tribes worshipped trees of various kinds, a 'Tree of Life' features in a number of religions, and various legends are associated with trees mentioned in the Bible – for example, the tree whose wood was used for the crucifixion of Jesus Christ and the tree upon which Judas hanged himself.

Some people are superstitious about different trees. Some used to believe that a birch tree would keep demons away and others thought that an ash tree in your garden would protect you from witches. Holly growing near your house was said to protect it from thunder and lightning. And then there are trees connected with different religious festivals...

Probably the best-known tree associated with a major religious festival is, of course, the Christmas tree. Some believe that the tradition of Christmas trees may be linked to the ancient custom of tree worshipping. It seems that Germany was the first country to establish the annual tradition of decorating trees at Christmas time. There, the custom may date from as early as the eighth century when it is said that one Christmas Eve, St Boniface substituted a fir tree as a symbol of the Christian faith instead of the pagan oak which he chopped down. Trees established in people's homes were traditionally fir, and decorated with apples, sweets, candles and coloured paper flowers.

The popular use of the Christmas tree in our own country is usually linked to the name of Prince Albert. It is said that, in the German tradition, he decorated a conifer tree as part of the Royal Family's Christmas decorations of 1841. By the late nineteenth century Christmas trees were common in homes in our country, a tradition that has survived to the present day, when a great variety of trees (both real conifers and artificial ones) are used. Other Christmas decorations also involve the use of evergreen trees, particularly holly, a well-known symbol on Christmas cards and trimmings. The use of evergreens to decorate homes and temples on festive occasions dates from way back in history: the Romans and Norsemen used such plants as symbols of perpetual life.

Joy Palmer

8: FATHER AND SON

Edmund Gosse's mother died in 1855 when he was six. He was brought up by his father, a strict and serious Plymouth Brother, first in London and later in Devon. His father refused to take any notice of Christmas celebrations as he held them to be either pagan or 'Popish'.

Oddly, not all Christians have celebrated Christmas. This is the story of one boy who lived in the last century. His father was a very strict Christian who refused to have in the house anything he thought was originally 'pagan' and had nothing to do with the Christmas story, such as holly or Christmas puddings. The boy, who tells the story, was called Edmund Gosse. At this time he was about eight and lived with his father and two servants in a big house in Devon, his mother having died two years earlier.

He would describe the antiquity of the so-called feast, adapted from horrible heathen rites, and itself a soiled relic of the abominable Yule Tide. He would denounce the horrors of Christmas until it almost made me blush to look at a holly berry.

On Christmas Day of this year 1857 our villa saw a very unusual sight. My father had given strictest charge that no difference whatever was to be made in our meals on that day; the dinner was to be neither more copious than usual nor less so. He was obeyed, but the servants, secretly rebellious, made a small plum pudding for themselves. Early in the afternoon the maids — of whom we were now advanced to keeping two — kindly remarked that 'the poor dear child ought to have a bit, anyhow,' and wheedled me into the kitchen, where I ate a slice of plum pudding. Shortly I began to feel that pain inside which in my frail state was inevitable, and my conscience smote me violently. At length I could bear my spiritual anguish no longer, and bursting into the study I called out: 'Oh! Papa, Papa, I have eaten of flesh offered to idols!' It took some time, between my sobs, to explain what had happened. Then my Father sternly said: 'Where is the accursed thing?' I explained that as much as was left of it was still on the kitchen table. He took my hand, and ran with me into the midst of the startled servants, seized what remained of the pudding, and with the plate in one hand and me still tight in the other, ran till we reached the dust-heap, when he flung the idolatrous confectionery onto the middle of the ashes, and then raked it deep down into the mass. The suddenness, the violence, the velocity of this extraordinary act made an impression on my memory which nothing will ever efface.

Edmund Gosse

Autumn term

9: THE WORM TURNS

A story for those who find Christmas just too much . . .

This is a story to please anyone who has got tired of too many Christmas songs on the radio, too many laughing plastic Father Christmases, too many cheap decorations . . . It is about a man called Professor Shandy who teaches in an American college. He feels that his neighbours overdo their Christmas decorations.

With a finesse born of much practice, Professor Shandy backed Mrs Ames off his front step and shut the door. This was the seventy-third time in eighteen years she'd nagged him about decorating his house. The tradition dated back, as Professor Shandy had taken the trouble to find out, no further than 1931, when the wife of the then president (of the college) . . . had found a box of Japanese lanterns . . . and decided to stage a Grand Illumination on Christmas Eve. The Grand Illumination had been such a smashing success that the college had repeated the event every year since . . . From near and far came tourists to bask in the spectacle . . . Pictures appeared in national magazines. However, the photographers always had to shoot one dark spot on the gala scene. This was the home of Peter Shandy . . .

Left to himself, Peter Shandy would willingly have made some concession to the event: a balsam wreath or a spray of holly on the front door, and a fat white candle guttering in the parlour window after dark. He rather liked Christmas. But altogether too many of Shandy's Christmases had been blighted by the overwhelming Christmas spirit around the Crescent. On this morning of 21 December . . . something snapped.

On the morning of 22 December, two men drove up to the brick house in a large truck. The professor met them at the door.

'Did you bring everything, gentlemen?'

'The whole works. Boy, you folks up here sure take Christmas to heart!'

'We have a tradition to maintain,' said Shandy. 'You may as well start on the spruce trees.'

All morning the workmen toiled. Expressions of amazed delight appeared on the faces of the neighbours and students. As the day wore on and the men kept at it, the amazement remained but the delight faded.

It was dark before the men got through. Peter Shandy walked them out to the truck. He was wearing his overcoat, hat and galoshes, and carrying a case.

'Everything in good order, gentlemen? Lights timed to flash on and off at six-second intervals? Amplifiers turned up to full volume? Steel-cased switch boxes provided with sturdy locks? Very well, then, let's flip on the power and be off . . .'

Precisely forty-eight hours later, on Christmas Eve, Professor Shandy stepped outside for a breath of air. Around him rolled the vast Atlantic. Above shone only the freighter's riding lights and a skyful of stars. The captain's dinner had been most enjoyable.

Back on the Crescent, floodlights would be illuminating the eight life-size reindeer mounted on the roof of the brick house. In its windows, sixteen Santa Claus faces would be leering above sixteen sets of artificial candles, each containing three red and two purple bulbs, each window outlined by a border of thirty-six more bulbs alternating in green, orange and blue.

He glanced at his watch and did rapid calculations in his head. At that precise point, the 742 outsize red bulbs on the spruce trees would have flashed on for the 28,800th time. The amplifiers must by now have blared out 2,536 renditions of 'I'm Dreaming of a White Christmas', 'I Saw Mommy Kissing Santa Claus' and 'All I Want For Christmas Is My Two Front Teeth.' They must be just now on the seventeenth bar of the 2,537th playing of 'I Don't Care Who You Are, Fatty, Get Those Reindeer Off My Roof.'

Professor Shandy smiled into the darkness. 'Bah, humbug,' he murmured and began to count the stars.

Charlotte MacLeod

10: THE MASSACRE OF THE INNOCENTS

(28 December)

This passage is taken from David Kossoff's Book of Witnesses *in which he describes Biblical events through the eyes of (imaginary) bystanders.*

Herod's Massacre of the Innocents is one of the blacker aspects of Christmas and is commemorated by the churches on 28 December. (See Matthew 2, verses 13-18.)

You'll remember that when Jesus was born at Bethlehem, the king of that area was a man called Herod. When he heard that a special baby, who was to be king, had been born, Herod was so jealous he gave orders for all babies under the age of two to be killed to prevent (as he thought) the special baby from growing up. Joseph however had been warned in a dream and the family had departed for Egypt. In this reading the events are described by a courtier of King Herod's.

You might say to me that Herod was mad. Possibly. But it was not a time of sanity and a certain madness is not unknown in great men. Also, it should be remembered, although it is difficult to believe, that Herod, Great Herod, never, ever, felt secure. He was suspicious, often rightly so, of everyone round him. Certainly he had little joy of his wife, the exquisite Mariamne. She was like ice. Admittedly, her life was, to say the least, difficult. When her younger brother, whom Herod had made high priest, became popular, Herod had him drowned, in his bath. Her grandfather, of eighty-seven, was put to death. Her sons were killed. Handsome, well-liked young men, with their mother's looks. There was so much death. Even Mariamne herself was killed.

Tragedy, tragedy. It almost turns into bizarre comedy the ghastly edict made by Herod that all boy babies under the age of two in Bethlehem should die to make certain that one particular baby was destroyed. This special baby that everybody seemed to be talking about.

Herod, being as I say a morbidly suspicious man, had built up, over the years, a very efficient informer system. At court we knew everything that went on in Judea. We knew about the crowd of shepherds looking for a baby born in a stable the morning after it had happened. We knew exactly how long the excitement would last; we'd had glad tidings from angels before. We'd had Messiahs by the dozen – and had regulations about how to get rid of them. Holy men and healers and miracle makers and magicians were thick upon the ground.

A report was given to Herod about the baby in the stable but I don't think he even read it. He was quite ill at the time, and very unbalanced. He was full of disease, bloated, disgusting. He was in pain, living on drugs, but hardly sleeping at all. He was afraid of the dreams, I think. He looked awful.

He was nearly seventy and looked a hundred. He had ruled in one way or another since he was fifteen. He had killed without mercy. Enemies; friends; his own flesh and blood. His hands were red. It was said at court that remorse, about Mariamne and his dead sons, was destroying his mind. His periods of lucidity were infrequent. Reports about shepherds and special babies were unlikely to be read.

But not long after the shepherds, wise men from far off places came to him, talking of a baby. Of a baby that was to be, so they said, 'King of the Jews'. They had seen signs, they said, a bright star, they said. And Great Herod, mighty king, was filled with a mad fear of a poor baby born in a stable, who was going to steal his kingdom. With a heavy and transparent cunning he told the wise men to find the child and bring him news so that he could do homage, prepare the way, make ready the throne.

He never saw the wise men again and he never found the baby. So he made the terrible order: 'Kill *all* the babies!' he said. 'All boy babies under two.' It was almost the last order he made. He was dead soon after. And never another word of the baby.

David Kossoff

Spring term

1: WINTER CELEBRATIONS

A presentation (arranged here for narrator and three readers) which describes some of our traditional mid-winter festivals.

Narrator: For many people, New Year's Day is the end of Christmas. On 2nd January, it's back to work. But it wasn't always like that. In olden times, Christmas was celebrated for twelve full days, right up to Twelfth Night – and that was a time for parties and dancing.

Reader 1: Some families had a twelfth cake, and whoever found the dried pea or bean that had been hidden inside it became king or queen for the night. On Twelfth Night, 1563, at the palace of Holyrood in Edinburgh, one of the maids found the bean and she was allowed to wear Mary, Queen of Scots' clothes and jewellery for the evening.

Narrator: An English visitor described what happened.

Reader 2: The queen of the bean was that day in a gown of cloth of silver; her head, her neck, her shoulders were so beset with precious jewels that more in our whole jewel-house could not be found! The cheer was great that night!

Narrator: The day after Twelfth Night is called Epiphany – and that's the day when Christians remember how the wise men came to the baby Jesus, bringing presents. And the Monday after Epiphany?

Spring term

Reader 1: Well, that's Plough Monday.

Reader 3: Plough Monday, the Monday after Twelfth Night, was the end of the medieval Christmas holiday. On that day, the plough was taken into the church to be blessed by the priest. And the farmworkers all prayed:

All readers: God speed the plough, and send us barley enough to make good ale to help us do our work.

Narrator: It may seem strange to us to pray for ale or beer, but in those times, it wasn't always safe to drink water and so ale was the everyday drink of country people; and so it was thought as natural to pray for ale as to pray for daily bread: bread and ale gave them strength to plough the land.

Reader 2: Then the ploughmen and boys, with their faces blackened, would drag the plough round the village demanding money. And if anyone refused to give them money, they threatened to plough up that person's front garden or lawn. And there was also much morris dancing in the streets that day.

Narrator: And another old custom was to go wassailling; and often the night for this was 17th January.

Reader 1: The idea is to go out on this evening with barrels of cider, guns and slices of bread – and sing a song to an apple tree!

Reader 3: Those taking part carry burning torches and gather round one of the best apple trees in the district. The men fire the guns up in the air, through the branches, and then sprinkle cider round its roots. Then they place a piece of bread soaked in cider in the fork of the tree. And then they sing.

All: Here's to thee, old apple tree,
Whence thou may'st bud and whence
   thou may'st blow;
Hats full, cups full, bushel

basket, sacks full,
And all my pockets full, too.
Hurray!

Narrator: In olden times, people were superstitious and thought this would frighten away any evil spirits and make sure there would be a good crop of apples. And the word 'wassail'? That's an old greeting: 'Was hail!' or:

All: 'We wish you good health!'

David Self

2: CHINESE NEW YEAR

The western or solar calendar has been used in China for all official dates since 1911, but the lunar calendar is still used by Chinese around the world to calculate the dates of the religious festivals. The timing of the Chinese New Year festival is therefore governed by the date of the new moon occurring between 21 January and 20 February. In China, the New Year festival is now celebrated as a Spring Holiday, a public holiday marked by family reunions.

Wherever they are around the world, the Chinese celebrate their New Year in special ways . . .

Chinese New Year is very much a family festival. Everybody tries to be with their parents, brothers and sisters for a special reunion dinner on New Year's Eve. Married women usually join their husband's family. Shortly before midnight, the front door is closed firmly with red paper seals to keep out any evil spirits. As morning dawns, grandfather breaks open the paper seals and firecrackers are let off to welcome in the New Year.

Everyone wears new clothes and visits close relatives. Children are even more polite than usual to their grandparents and the older members of the family. Those who have died are not forgotten either. Prayers are said for them and incense is burnt at the family altar. People exchange red packets of 'lucky money', called *lai see* (li ji). They give offerings to their favourite gods.

The next day more relatives and friends are visited. However, on the third day, known as 'Squabble Day', everyone avoids their relatives in case they quarrel! The fourth day is traditionally the time when married women can visit their families. The seventh day is 'Everyone's Birthday', when people celebrate being another year older.

Food plays an important part in Chinese New Year, as it does in most festivals. The Chinese are famous for the variety and delicious flavours of their cooking. New Year feasts are like banquets, with all kinds of meat, fish, noodles, sauces, soups and vegetables.

Not only is the food delicious, it is often used as a way of saying something or celebrating a particular idea. For example, it is the custom to bid farewell to the old year and welcome in the new one by eating a tasty porridge made from rice with eight different kinds of cereals, nuts, beans and fruits. This symbolizes a good harvest of all crops.

Some foods are special because their name or colour is lucky, in some way. Bowls of melon seeds, peanuts, dates and preserved fruits are always served to guests. These stand for good fortune, prosperity and long life.

In Hong Kong, New Year biscuits are made from moulds which stamp them with lucky mottoes such as 'Peace for old and young' and 'Heaven helps a good man'.

Of course, all the different regions of China have their own specialities, as do overseas Chinese communities. In North China, boiled dumplings stuffed with meat and cabbage are a great favourite. Elsewhere, sweet cakes from sticky rice flour are popular. Their glueyness is said to remind people of the way good friends and relatives stick together. Small offerings of rice and sweets may be made at family altars and temple shrines, along with fresh flowers and fruit.

Many families buy small kumquat trees for New Year. The branches are covered with tiny orange fruits at this season. Its Chinese name contains the lucky words 'gold' and 'orange'. These colours suggest wealth and riches. Golden oranges, satsumas and tangerines are popular at New Year for the same reason.

Gifts of food in beautifully wrapped parcels are often exchanged by friends and family. Nobody ever pays a visit empty-handed. It is considered polite to give a small present in return, as a way of suggesting that the visitors have been too generous, and of returning the good luck their gift has brought the household.

The poor are not forgotten either. Some large firms give away lucky money to those in need. Families remember those whose daily work they rely on, such as postmen and street cleaners, and give them small gifts of *lai see*.

Olivia Bennett

3: ROBERT BURNS
(Burns Night: 25 January)

Robert Burns (1759–1796) is often said to be Scotland's national poet. He began writing his dialect poems at the age of fourteen but they were not published until 1786 when he gained immediate fame and success. Burns is rare in being a writer celebrated in many countries. For example, he is admired in Russia while Burns Night is celebrated by Scots (and Sassenachs) all around the world.

Robert Burns is probably the most famous Scotsman who ever lived. All over the world, people gather each year to celebrate the anniversary of his birth, 25 January 1759. They admire his poetry, but that is not the only reason why they remember him.

In some ways, Burns is not a likely hero. He drank too much, and was too fond of girls, even after he was married. He was father to many illegitimate children whom he could not support. This was frowned upon by the churchgoing folk of his day. But that too is only part of his story.

Burns was born in a cottage at Alloway, in Ayrshire, the eldest son of a poor farmer. Even as children, Robert and his brother Gilbert had to work on the land doing jobs which were too hard for them, because their father could not afford a farmhand. They were often miserably cold and hungry, and despite much effort their farming was a failure. But their father wanted his sons to be educated and, although so poor, he joined with four of his neighbours to hire a teacher, who gave the boys a sound basic education. Burns went on learning all his life. His poems were written from a background of much reading and serious thinking.

Burns's father died in 1784. Two years later, Burns was so disheartened by his farming failures that he thought of emigrating to Jamaica. Meanwhile he had been writing poetry, and in 1786 a small book called 'Poems chiefly in the Scottish dialect' was published in Kilmarnock. It made him famous almost overnight, and when in 1787 a second edition was published in Edinburgh, he forgot about Jamaica. He went to Edinburgh instead!

He had a wonderful time in Edinburgh. Famous writers and university professors became his friends, and he was invited to parties where he mixed with fashionable ladies and gentlemen. Everyone wanted to know him, and all were impressed by his brilliant conversation and his simple good manners. Unfortunately none of his new friends helped him to find a secure job. Only one, a wealthy banker, tried to help by offering him the lease of Ellisland Farm, in Dumfriesshire. Once again, the farm failed.

Eventually, after the farm had used up all the money Burns had got from the Edinburgh edition of his poems, he gave up farming for ever. He found a poorly paid junior post as Customs and Excise Officer in Dumfries.

But there, worn out by ill health and anxiety, he died in 1796. He was ony thirty-seven.

Burns wrote many famous poems such as *Holy Willie's Prayer, Tam O'Shanter, Address to a Mouse* and *The Cotter's Saturday Night*. He also collected and wrote down many of Scotland's best-loved songs. However, he is remembered as a good kind of person, as well as a fine poet. In eighteenth-century Scotland there was much injustice. A few people were very rich; the rest were miserably poor. No one did much to help the poor, and the Church, which ought to have cared for them, supported the rich and harshly condemned the poor for sins which they could hardly help. Burns spoke out boldly against hypocrisy and unfairness. Even when he was in Edinburgh, mixing with fine society, he remembered the poor, and took their side against their masters. He supported the American colonists who wanted to break away from Britain in 1775, and he risked execution by writing *Ode for General Washington's birthday* in which he called King George III a tyrant. When the French Revolution started in 1789, he was not afraid to say that he wished the same could happen in Scotland. Only concern for the safety of his family made him eventually more careful of what he said in public. His revolutionary opinions did not make Burns popular. None of his Edinburgh friends wanted to know him, and in his last days he was very lonely. But nowadays he is admired as a champion of poor people, and among his best-known lines are those he wrote not long before he died:

> For a' that, and a' that
> It's comin' yet for a' that,
> That man to man, the warld o'er,
> Shall brothers be for a' that.

Eileen Dunlop and Antony Kamm

Spring term

4: WINTER WEATHER

A compilation for use in severe winter weather, perhaps especially in urban schools where it will explain the impact of heavy snow, etc, on rural communities.

You may enjoy it when it snows. Perhaps after a few days it becomes irritating, especially if it's fairly cold. But if you live right out in the countryside, snow is a real inconvenience. It changes your whole way of living.

Reader 1: For a month, an impassable hill and three miles of ice-packed road have cut us off from the relatively open main road which leads to town.
Here, in the country, we're living in a silent, all-white world. The fields are white with snow, the river is white with ice, the trees are white with frost. The whole countryside is gripped in the white silence of winter.

Reader 2: It grips hands, feet, whole body,
It reaches the heart by a quick route,
It makes portraits of faces, rearranging features
And always, always is quiet.

Soft, let the footsteps sink in the snow,
Let the voices disappear into whispers;
Think of the animals huddling in hibernation,
Of birds making small spurts for a crumb,
Of children hidden in mufflers.

Elizabeth Jennings

Reader 1: We normally have buses to town on only two days a week and those haven't reached us at all since the first fall of snow. All our links with the outside world hang on the kindness of the folk who live in the farm near the main road. Groceries, bread and the meat are left there and hauled the rest of the way by sledge. School holidays were extended by a week and even now half the children can't get to the nearest spot the school buses can reach.

Narrator: But what about the people who have to go out in the snow? Like the men whose job it is to keep the main roads and motorways clear? The men who drive the gritting lorries and the snow ploughs.

Reader 2: More snow is forecast for tonight – on top of a dozen falls in recent weeks – and once again the road men are out in the darkness, struggling against the blizzards to keep the high passes open. Up there in the biting cold it is often hard to tell whether it is snowing or not, for on most nights this winter the wind has come scourging out of the north-east, whipping the snow off the fells in a blinding fury and swirling it into the roads. So that as fast as one bit of road is cleared it is all blown over again and the road men have been denied even the satisfaction of a job well done.

These are the real heroes of the storm – these and the road scouts – and the lorry drivers, regretfully, are sometimes the villains. Their tradition, to get through at all costs, sounds noble enough, but too often the clumsy articulated vehicles prove unable to cope with the snow or ice, and the road may be blocked for hours to traffic which otherwise could have got through.

5: ST VALENTINE'S DAY
(14 February)

A reading for St Valentine's Day, outlining its history and associated customs.

You probably don't need telling which saint's day it is today. Some of you may already have received a Valentine's card. One or two of you have probably had several – and have been bragging about them unbearably . . . Many of you may have received none at all. (In my case . . .) Some of you may even have received one from a genuinely secret and unknown admirer. Anyway, this reading describes some of the Valentine's Day customs that have been observed in the past.

Spring term

St Valentine's Day is traditionally the day for people, and birds, to choose a sweetheart. Only if the weather happens to be mild are there signs of courtship in the bird world, for birds choose their mates according to the season rather than the date on the calendar. From time immemorial, however, young people have picked a partner and exchanged tokens of love on 14 February.

St Valentine was not a Christian Cupid, dedicated to striking the hearts of true lovers with a heavenly bow and arrow. Very little is known about him, except that he was martyred in Rome in the third century. The date of his death, rather than anything he did, is probably his only claim to being the patron saint of lovers. He is said to have died for his religious beliefs on 14 February – the Eve of Lupercalia, a Roman Festival of Youth.

The Romans brought their festivals to Britain, and although by the sixth century the Christian priests had managed to stamp out the wild Lupercalia celebrations, at least one of the customs survived right up until the eighteenth century. It was that of choosing a partner by lottery:

It is a ceremony, never omitted among the Vulgar, to draw lots which they term Valentines. The names of a select number of one sex are by an equal number of the other put into some vessel; and after that, everyone draws a name, which for the present is called their Valentine, and is also look'd upon as a good omen of their being man and wife afterwards.

H. Bourne, *Antiquitates Vulgares*, 1725

There was a strong element of chance in most St Valentine's Day customs. One common belief was that the first man seen by any woman on 14 February must be her Valentine, whether she liked him or not.

> Last Valentine, the day when birds of kind,
> Their paramours with mutual chirpings find,
> I early rose, just at the break of day,
> Before the sun had chas'd the stars away;

> Afield I went, amid the burning dew,
> To milk my kine, for so should housewives do,
> Thee first I spied: and the first swain we see,
> In spite of fortune shall our true love be.
>
> John Gay

Even married women were not exempt. In 1662 Samuel Pepys' wife went about with her hands in front of her eyes in case she was unlucky enough to catch sight of one of the painters decorating her house!

Unmarried girls believed that they would dream about their future husband on St Valentine's Eve. Before going to bed they said this prayer:

> Sweet guardian angels, let me have
> What I most earnestly do crave,
> A Valentine endowed with love,
> That will both kind and constant prove.

In an attempt to influence Fate, some girls ate boiled eggs, shell and all, having first replaced the yolk with salt. More likely to give them nightmares than sweet dreams! Others pinned bay leaves to their pillows; in the language of flowers bay means 'only death will part us'.

St Valentine's Day was a great time for giving presents, often anonymously, but by the nineteenth century these gifts had simply become Valentine cards, decorated with flowers and hearts, and at first, handmade.

Monday, St Valentine's Day. A pretty flower Valentine from Incognito, wrote the Reverend Francis Kilvert, in his diary for 1870.

'Incognito' is still the chief sender of Valentine cards. It means 'unknown', and guesswork is another traditional element of the day.

During the nineteenth century, when printing and postage became cheaper and easier, postal traffic on St

Valentine's Day was so heavy that London postmen demanded a special meals allowance to keep them going on their rounds. Sending Valentine cards is still popular, although some people prefer to publicly announce their devotion in the columns of the newspapers. Hearts are the most common symbol on Valentine cards, and fortune tellers promise their customers luck in love when the pack of cards turns up 'hearts'. 'To wear your heart on your sleeve' means to make no secret of your affections, to display your emotions in public (like those newspaper advertisers!). This stems from the days of chivalry when a knight would wear some token of his lady-love – her glove, for example – when he rode in a tournament.

Peter Watkins and Erica Hughes

6: CARNIVAL

(Shrovetide)

In many parts of the world, the period immediately before the Christian season of Lent is marked by a season of feasting: 'carne vale' or 'farewell to flesh/meat'. Mardi Gras ('Fat Tuesday') is observed in France (and America), Fasching in Germany, and Shrovetide in Britain. In Trinidad and Tobago, Carnival is the major festival of the year.

For us, Shrove Tuesday may mean pancakes and not much else. In other parts of the world, it means far more of a festival. For example, in the islands of Trinidad and Tobago in the West Indies, there are processions, steel bands, dances and fancy dress parades.

The biggest celebrations take place in Trinidad and Tobago's capital, Port-of-Spain. *Carnival* takes place on the Monday and Tuesday before Ash Wednesday, which is the first day of Lent. Lent is the name given to the forty days before the important Christian festival of Easter. It is a thoughtful time for Christians, when they traditionally fasted and gave up any sort of merry-making. So the last few days before Lent were often marked by wild feasts and celebrations, particularly in Catholic countries. In fact, it was Catholic Europeans who first brought *Carnival* to Trinidad.

The excitement of *Carnival* starts building up long before the festivities take place. There are lots of parties. From New Year's Eve onwards, the calypso singers and steelbands start composing and playing together in halls or practice rooms known as 'tents'. Each one wants to keep their ideas and tunes secret from the other bands. As a band may have more than twenty-five people hammering out the melody, keeping it a surprise isn't always easy.

Even before the tents are in full swing, the leaders of the costume bands are looking over designs and ideas. As *Carnival* gets closer, their preparations get more hectic. Coloured and shiny materials, sequins, glitter, feathers, glue, cotton thread, tissue paper, beads and paint disappear from the shops into people's homes and the workshops known as 'mas camps'.

On the Sunday, known as *Dimanche Gras*, the King and Queen of Carnival are crowned. At four o'clock the next morning a rocket goes off to announce the start of *Carnival* – but hardly anyone has gone to bed anyway! It's *J'Ouvert*, or *Jouvay*, as many Trinidadians call it. People dress up in their old *Carnival* costumes and join in the *Ol'Mas* fun. A day and night of dancing and music follows. On Tuesday the costume bands take over the streets. Rum, fruit juice and sweet and spicy snacks keep the dancers, singers and masqueraders going, right until the 'last lap' and the midnight hour. Suddenly it's Ash Wednesday and *Carnival* is over for another year.

'*Dimanche Gras*', '*J'Ouvert*', '*Ol Mas*', '*Carnival*'. All these words contain clues about the story of the festival and of Trinidad and Tobago. *Carnival* comes from the latin 'carne vale'. This means 'farewell to flesh'. Many

Spring term

Christians gave up meat or sweet things during Lent, as well as 'sins of the flesh' such as over-eating and wild singing and dancing. 'Dimanche' is Sunday in French. Playing *'mas'* and *'Ol Mas'* from 'masquerade', the French word for masked balls. *'Jouvay'* or *'J'Ouvert'* comes from 'le jour est ouvert' which means 'the day is open' in French – it is daybreak, and *Carnival* has begun!

Olivia Bennett

7: ST JOSEPH
(19 March)

One of the neglected characters of the New Testament is St Joseph; husband of Mary, the Mother of Jesus. He is mentioned only in Matthew, chapters one and two and in Luke, chapters one and two. In this passage, a Roman Catholic parish priest makes some further deductions.

[Perhaps after reading briefly from one of the Gospels]
  How do you imagine Joseph felt during the events of the first Christmas? What sort of man must he have been? We know very little more about him, except that he was some years older than Mary. But what else can we work out about him?

Today is the 'feast' of St Joseph; the husband of Mary and foster-father of Jesus Christ. By any standard that is a staggering responsibilty to have, and he was especially chosen for the task by God. It must make him one of the most important men in history, but I suspect few people ever think of him. True importance is measured by God's opinion of us and not by what we think of each other. Little is known of him from the Gospel except that he was a 'just' or upright man. Despite popular pictures of him as an old man, he was probably still a teenager when he was engaged to Mary. He was a working man, a carpenter by trade. No word of his is recorded, and what few facts we know of his life come obliquely from reference to others.

When he discovered that his fiancée was pregnant, he made no public fuss but decided to break off the engagement discreetly, so as to occasion her no hurt. When told, in a vision, that the conception was a direct action of God, he fully accepted the responsibility of caring for the Mother and Child. Without complaint, he took Mary to Bethlehem, where the Child was born, although the circumstances must have caused him great anxiety and inconvenience. Likewise, he took Jesus and Mary to Egypt at a nod from God, giving up his home and livelihood to do it. Equally humbly, he brought them back when God gave him the sign, and provided home and security for them in Nazareth, where he probably died at about the age of forty or so.

The Western Church was late in 'discovering' Joseph, but affection for him grows all the time. As he was the guardian of Jesus and Mary, the Church now adopts him as the Universal Protector. As he was a tradesman and teacher of Jesus in the art of carpentry, he is now regarded as the Patron of workers. Since he provided several homes for his wife and her Child, he is often invoked by those in search of a home of their own. As he presumably died in the arms of Jesus and Mary, he is looked upon as the Patron Saint of the dying.

One cannot help comparing Joseph's humility and heroic devotion to daily duty with the so-called great men of our own time. He was given what must be the most important duty of all time, but was content to live out his life in obscurity. We so often feel the need to draw attention to ourselves by our form of dress, or our titles, by our learning, or by our wealth. In this way, we imagine, we shall make our mark on others. We demand of ourselves and others instant wisdom, instant success, and instant influence. We arrogantly or angrily ask what right God has to make this or that demand of us. People like Joseph humbly acknowledge that God knows best, and simply get on with the job.

Spring term

But let's face it. The world is still full of unknown, simple folk who are hardworking and responsible, even when they feel themselves to be unappreciated by God, as well as by their fellow men. They actually provide the loving care which others only talk about. They produce the wealth which others squander or hoard. They enrich the lives of others but remain poor themselves. They are the 'just' or upright men and women whose value is known to God alone, and who in the long run make our world the marvellous place it is.

Father Robert Manley

8: MOTHERING SUNDAY
(Mid-Lent Sunday)

An explanation of the traditional Mothering Sunday customs.
N.B. Mothering Sunday occurs in the middle of the Christian season of Lent. The secular Mother's Day is observed on the second Sunday of May (except in this country where it has been superimposed on Mothering Sunday).

As you may or may not need reminding, Sunday is Mothering Sunday. Another name for it is Refreshment Sunday. It is also the middle of the season of Lent, a period when Christians used to fast and when many still voluntarily 'give something up', such as meat, chocolates, etc. Refreshment Sunday was a bit of a feast in the middle of the fast. But most of all it's a time to think about mothers.

The fourth Sunday in Lent is kept as Mothering Sunday. Mothers are given a pat on the back, and their young children bring them posies and flowers and cards they have made at school.

Originally it was not a human mother that was the focal point of Mothering Sunday. In its early years the Church required priests and people to visit the 'Mother Church' of the district on this day, and family gatherings may have developed from that.

Mothering Sunday, or Refreshment Sunday, provided a welcome break from the hardships of Lent. With a bit of luck, it coincided with the spell of mild weather which often occurs in March. Sons and daughters 'went a-mothering' and returned to the family home for the day. Before the days of legally enforced holidays, Simnel Sunday, as it was also called, was cherished as the only day when apprentices and 'living-in' servants could get home to see their mother, taking her a bunch of primroses or violets picked on the way, and the traditional Simnel cake.

There are three main kinds of Simnel cake, made in different parts of Britain: the star-shaped Devizes Simnel; the Bury Simnel, a flat spiced cake, thickest in the centre; and probably the best known, Shrewsbury Simnel, also eaten at Easter, with a layer of marzipan in the centre and eleven or twelve marzipan eggs on top – one for each month the young servant was away from home, perhaps.

There are various theories about how this fruit cake got its name. It goes back a long way in both England and France, and may well have developed from the Latin 'simila', meaning the fine wheat flour used for this sort of cake. The story about the servant girl whose Simnel cake was so heavy that her mother used it as a hassock or 'kneeler', makes you wonder if the flour was all *that* fine!

Mothering Sunday is sometimes confused with the American 'Mother's Day'. In 1907 an American woman, Anna Jarvis from Philadelphia, who had recently lost her own mother, suggested that one day in the year should be set aside for honouring all mothers whatever their colour or creed. The idea caught on, and within a few years the second Sunday in May was established as Mother's Day. Throughout the United States and Canada mothers are given presents, and carnations are worn in their honour – red for living mothers, white for the dead.

During the Second World War, American servicemen brought this festival to Britain. Shopkeepers particularly received it with enthusiasm as an opportunity for increasing the sale of cards, flowers and boxes of chocolates.

Peter Watkins and Erica Hughes

9: PASSOVER

The Jewish Passover festival occurs in the month of Nisan (March-April) and commemorates the liberation of the Jews from slavery in Egypt. The story is told in Exodus 12.

The most famous of all Jewish festivals is called the Passover. This is kept every year as a reminder each year of how the Jewish people ('the Children of Israel') were once kept as slaves in Egypt but eventually escaped. To remind them what happened, they eat special foods at this time of year: for example, unleavened bread. Various other foods are placed on the table for the main Passover meal:

A roasted or baked egg; a reminder of the festival sacrifice brought to the Temple in ancient times.

A roasted lamb bone; which represents the Passover lamb which used to be sacrificed in the Temple.

Bitter herbs; a reminder of the bitter lives of the slaves in Egypt. Horseradish is often used for this.

One or two other fresh vegetables (such as lettuce, watercress or cucumber); reminders that this is a spring festival.

A mixture of chopped apple, nuts, cinnamon and wine; a symbol of the mortar used by the slaves to make bricks in Egypt.

Finally, a dish of salt water is placed on the table. This represents the tears shed by the Jews during their long years of captivity.

Now a passage in which a Jewish rabbi, Rabbi Lionel Blue, explains their meanings:

When the children of Israel left Egypt they left in a hurry, like all refugees. There was no time for their bread to rise, so they ate it instead flat and unleavened. It is called the bread of poverty at the Passover meal, and if you are Christian, you probably eat a form of it, too, when you go to communion. You can buy a box of it – it is called *matzah* – at many supermarkets.

The bread of affliction makes a very tasty breakfast. Dip two slices in hot water and squeeze them dry. Mix the pieces into three beaten eggs with two pinches of salt and one tablespoon of sugar. Fry the mixture in hot oil until it sets. Put the frying pan under a hot grill and quickly brown the top. Scatter the matzah omelette with sugar and cinnamon and serve in wedges.

At the Passover table, foods are not what they seem, and their tastes are deceptive. There is a reminder of the slave labour in ancient Egypt – a memory of the mortar which the slave gangs used, as they suffered and died, building the pyramids of Pharaoh. You can make such a mortar yourself. Grate a peeled eating apple and mix it with chopped almonds and hazelnuts, a half teaspoon of cinnamon and some sweet red wine to make a paste. Jewish people put a spoonful of slave labour between two slices of the bread of affliction and eat it before the main course.

After the mortar you drink the tears of the Israelites. You place a hard boiled egg into the brine and you have a symbol and an *hors d'oeuvre* in one. New life – the egg – comes out of tears. I mash the new life into the salty paste and eat it with the bread of poverty.

Slavery in the ancient world was a bitter, bitter experience. That bitterness is present on the Passover table in the form of horseradish or horseradish pickle. And a very good relish it is too: if you eat a heaped tablespoon of it, it sharpens your appetite. I marvel at how Jews have turned their suffering and injustices into a menu of delight – making bitterness an *hors d'oeuvre* and finding humour from persecution. Here is a story I heard one recent Passover, at the end of the evening when the celebrants have drunk four glasses of the wine of redemption:

'From the Five Books of Moses we learn that only when the first person dared to plunge into the Red Sea did the waters actually part. How courageous that person must have been, say the commentators, but there is another folk explanation and it rings truer. When the Children of Israel got to the Red Sea, no one knew what to do. So someone pushed and said. 'You go first.' And another pushed and said, 'You go first,' and they all started pushing each other until someone fell into the Red Sea. And that is how the waters parted.'

Rabbi Lionel Blue

EASTER

10: PONTIUS PILATE

From about 6 CE, Judea was under direct Roman rule, governed by a 'prefect'. The Romans set up their headquarters at Caesarea, on the coast. The first three prefects governed for only three years each. Then a man called Gratus was made prefect and ruled for eleven years (about 15–26 CE). After much politicking, he appointed Caiaphas as high priest. Caiaphas hung onto the job for eighteen years (18–36 CE), mainly by supporting Gratus and his successor.

The Romans followed Herod's system to control the high priest. They took custody of his vestments. These were kept in the Antonia fortress which was permanently garrisoned by a cohort of auxiliary soldiers. After each festival the vestments would be packed up and sealed by the high priest and treasurers of the Temple. They were then deposited with the tribune in command of the garrison. The day before the next festival the treasurers would go to the Antonia, to inspect the seal and collect the garments again.

In 26 CE Tiberius replaced Gratus with the notorious Pontius Pilate.

Today we are going to hear something about the man who sent Jesus to be crucified: Pontius Pilate, the Roman governor or 'prefect' of Judea. He was a Spaniard and also a much-hated man. The most interesting thing about him is why was this man, who seemed to have no conscience at all, so keen to allow Jesus to go free – even at the risk of causing a riot in Jerusalem?

Pontius Pilate had arrived in Judea in 26 CE. He is described as greedy, vindictive and cruel. He should never have been prefect of Judea as he had nothing but contempt for Jewish customs. The governors before him had been careful not to offend the Jews. Pilate was deliberately provocative. The soldiers had been forbidden to carry their standards into Jerusalem because the images of the emperor on them offended against Jewish religious law. Pilate ordered his troops to take their standards into the city under the cover of darkness. The people found out what Pilate had done and an angry mob descended on Caesarea and besieged the prefect in his palace for five days. Only the timely removal of the standards prevented a more serious uprising and the massacre that would have followed.

Pilate's next mistake was unfortunate for he may have had the best of intentions. Jerusalem was always short of water and the governor decided to construct another aquaduct. His mistake was to pay for the building from the Temple treasury. The Jews of course were outraged. When next he visited Jerusalem, Pilate was engulfed by a shrieking mob. He had expected this. Some of his soldiers dressed in Jewish costume had mingled with the crowd. On the agreed signal the disguised soldiers attacked the demonstrators with clubs and killed several of them. Other such acts of violence are hinted at in the New Testament.

It was customary for the prefect to move from Caesarea to Jerusalem with his forces for the main feasts as there was always the possibility of a disturbance when large numbers of people gathered in the city. During the feasts the Roman troops in the Antonia fortress descended on to the Temple porticoes to discourage trouble makers.

The prefects were not the only rulers who went up to Jerusalem for the feasts. Antipas and Philip also made the trip. Therefore it was no coincidence that both Pilate and Antipas were in Jerusalem when Jesus was arrested. The chief priests accused Jesus of claiming to be Messiah. This was sufficient reason for Pilate to execute him. But for some reason he did not believe them and he did not want to get involved in a religious dispute. When he heard that Jesus was a Galilean he attempted to get the case transferred to Antipas. But Antipas did not want to get involved either and sent Jesus back to Pilate.

Peter Connolly

N.B. Pilate continued to provoke the Jews, so much that he was eventually stripped of his rank and re-called to Rome.

11: THE CRUCIFIXION

This passage is taken from David Kossoff's Book of Witnesses *in which he describes Biblical events through the eyes of (imaginary) bystanders.*

N.B. This may be read in two parts, the first part ending at the asterisk.

After Jesus had been condemned to be crucified by Pontius Pilate, he was led away to be scourged (or whipped) and then crucified. This is a description of those events, told as if by one of the Roman soldiers who carried out the punishment.

Not many people have seen a Roman punishment scourge. It's one of the worst whips ever invented. It can kill a man. It's designed to break skin and wrap round and tear. I've been asked why scourge a man who's going to be killed the same morning. Well, it wasn't the first time – and Pilate was hard. Also, he was fed up with the whole business. I didn't do the whipping, a great big sergeant from Syria did that, but I put the robe on. One of the lads found it somewhere. A purple robe, to make Jesus *look* like a king. When we put it on him, he looked like a corpse. He was naked, and that sergeant knew his job. Jesus could hardly stand. His back was like raw meat. I often dream of it. One of the boys had made a crown of twisted-together thorn stalks and he forced it down on Jesus's head. More blood. Then we stood him on a vegetable basket and marched round him and bowed and saluted and shouted in his face – and when his head dropped we slapped it up again. We gave him a big onion for an orb and a twig for a sceptre and we spat at him and laughed till we were weak. Till we cried.

I've cried many times since. In my sleep mostly. I can't say that the shame began right away, it didn't. As a soldier you do many things that you wouldn't in civilian life. But out of the service, by yourself, with time to look back, you see things differently. About eight years ago, when I'd been demobbed about a year, I met Peter the Fisherman, who made me a Christian. I was in a bad way and told him all about that night and my shame. Peter listened and then said, 'I know about the shame. On that night he was a stranger to you, a nothing, to be made sport of. On that night I'd known him three years and believed him to be the Son of God. I was his first follower and his friend. Yet on that night, in fear, I denied that I knew him. Three times.'

I think Peter said it to comfort me. It did a bit. But not much. Nothing does very much. You know, I haven't talked about that night for years. I think of it often; I dream about it, but I don't often talk about it. It's strange how talking about it somehow loosens the memory. All sorts of other things come back. As I told you, my feeling of shame about joining in that night didn't begin till some time after. We were a rough lot.

We were Roman occupation troops and we regarded the convicted prisoner as fair game. It broke the monotony.

So did a crucifixion.* We didn't like the job but if we were detailed that was it. Our duties were clear. There were regulations; a rulebook. The crosses were ordered normally three at a time – because normally three criminals were done together. There used to be a joke, made first, I was told, by Pilate. Seems he said, 'Do 'em in threes, nice company for each other.' It's possible; he was a cruel, hard man, was Pilate, with jokes to match. The prisoner carried his own cross, or at least dragged it with the cross bar over his shoulder. Very heavy the crosses were. A long, up-and-down, winding route would be worked out, so that as many people as possible would see the prisoner and read his crime, written on a board and carried by the lead corporal. Jesus's board just said, 'King of the Jews'. Another Pilate joke. When the Jewish elders asked him to change it, he refused and got very nasty.

Jesus was too weak to carry his cross. Not surprising, he'd been flogged half to death, so we pressed into service a man in the crowd. It was regulations; he couldn't refuse. There were regulations for everything. The distance apart of the crosses, the nailing of the hands and feet, the periods of watch, the crowd control, everything. There were also certain perks. Extra pay, extra drink ration – it could be a bloody business, the nailing part – and extra leave the following week. Also, we were entitled to the clothes and possessions of the prisoners. We would settle who got what by casting lots or gambling. Jesus had no possessions, and his clothes and sandals were poor stuff. We did better out of the two criminals we hung with him. They made a lot of noise those two, shouting and screaming, sometimes sensibly, sometimes like crazy or drunk men.

There were always women who offered drugged wine to those on the cross. Sisters of mercy. It was

Seasonal Readings

allowed in regulations. Jesus refused. He didn't say much. At one point I think he said a few words of comfort to the fellow on his left. There were some women a little way off who seemed to know him. None of his followers or disciples was there. They were all lying low, in hiding out of sight. We put the three prisoners up at nine in the morning. Fine, sunny morning. But at noon the sun went in and it got darker and darker. And very still and close. Most unusual. Frightening. Never before, or since. At about three o'clock all three had been quiet for some time. They'd been up six hours. Suddenly Jesus raised his head and looked up at the sky. I was quite near. Then he shouted at the top of his voice. His face was alight, his voice and body full of power. It was impossible. The crowd, in the weird twilight, were scared and nervous. My mates moved in a bit. Then Jesus shouted again, with the same lift of the head, the same power. 'It is finished!' he shouted. He died magnificently. I've never seen anything like it. One of the things that got him hung was saying he was the Son of God. At that moment I believed he was. I've believed it ever since.

David Kossoff

12: GOOD FRIDAY: THE ONE O'CLOCK NEWS

This news bulletin is intended to give a modern and realistic interpretation of what can seem to be a 'storybook' event. It may stimulate the writing of the hourly news bulletins that might have been 'broadcast' at other times during that day, or which cover other Biblical events.

Suppose radio had existed in the time of Jesus. This is how the lunchtime news might have sounded on the first Good Friday. Here is the news read by . . .

Early this morning, the Roman governor of Judea and Samaria, His Excellency Pontius Pilate, gave permission for the execution of the teacher and alleged revolutionary, Jesus of Nazareth. He also announced the release from prison of a man called bar-Abbas, condemned to death for the murder of Roman soldiers.

The announcement of the death sentence of Jesus of Nazareth came as something of a surprise as, earlier, the governor had spoken to the crowds outside the imperial palace, saying that he could see no reason to find him guilty. The crowds made no secret of their anger at this statement. Later came the new decision and Jesus was immediately led away to be whipped and crucified, according to Roman tradition. Large crowds followed him through the streets as he dragged the cross-beam of his own cross to the hill called Golgotha, outside the city wall. He is now on the cross: death is not expected for some hours. Two thieves are also being crucified today.

And now the main points of the rest of the news. A spokesman for the Zealots, the revolutionary movement fighting for the removal of all Romans from Judea, has welcomed the release of bar-Abbas. 'We could not have had better news at this holy season of the year,' he said.

Preparations for the Jewish Feast of the Passover go ahead throughout the city; the festival begins at six o'clock tonight.

And lastly, weathermen have as yet no explanation for the unnatural darkness which began about an hour ago. As listeners in Jerusalem will know, at the moment it is hardly light enough outside to read a scroll.

And that is the end of the news. More news in an hour.

David Self

Summer term

1: ROAD TO EMMAUS

This poem is loosely based on St Luke chapter 24, verses 13–32. It was written while the poet was still at school.

Three days after Jesus was put to death on the cross, his followers, or disciples, began to see him again. Some could not believe that he had risen from the dead, others believed at once. On one occasion he appeared to two of his disciples as they were walking along the road from Jerusalem to Emmaus. Oddly, they did not seem to recognize him.

Trio

The way was dark,
The night was lonely,
As two travellers struggled through their journey.
Presently they were joined by a third person
Who seemed to appear from nowhere.
The three made friends,
And soon got talking;
Talking about religion
And the Son of God.
At times the first two travellers were almost arguing,
While the third remained quiet –
(A young man with fair hair and beard.)
But the journey was too long to talk
All the time.
Then the lonely night and the dark way were silent.

Summer term

As the weary travellers neared the town
With its noise and lights
The late arrival disappeared
Just as quickly as he had come,
Leaving the two men
Amazed.
They searched the place about them,
But the person had disappeared
As imperceptibly as the silence.
That night at the inn
As the two travellers,
Tired and weary-limbed,
Were in their warm beds,
They thought of the silence and of the silent and
Strange young man who had joined them on the road.

Victor Harris

2: BALLAD OF THE BREAD MAN

Charles Causley's 'modernized' biography of Jesus is a suitable reading for the seasons of Christmas or Epiphany, but perhaps more especially for Holy Week and Easter. (It might also be used to introduce a project on the place of bread and 'the bread of life' in a study of Christianity.)

[*Begin with a seasonal introduction.*] . . . *This poem tells the life story of Jesus and ends by reminding us how, even after what happened at that first Easter, many people did not want to pay attention to him.*

>Mary stood in the kitchen
>>Baking a loaf of bread.
>
>An angel flew in through the window.
>>'We've a job for you,' he said.
>
>'God in his big gold heaven,
>>Sitting in his big blue chair,
>
>Wanted a mother for his little son.
>>Suddenly saw you there.'

Seasonal Readings

Mary shook and trembled,
   'It isn't true what you say.'
'Don't say that,' said the angel.
   'The baby's on its way.'

Joseph was in the workshop
   Planing a piece of wood.
'The old man's past it,' the neighbours said.
   'That girl's been up to no good.'

'And who was that elegant fellow,'
   They said, 'in the shiny gear?'
The things they said about Gabriel
   Were hardly fit to hear.

Mary never answered,
   Mary never replied.
She kept the information,
   Like the baby, safe inside.

It was election winter.
   They went to vote in town.
When Mary found her time had come
   The hotels let her down.

The baby was born in an annexe
   Next to the local pub.
At midnight, a delegation
   Turned up from the Farmers' Club.

They talked about an explosion
   That made a hole in the sky,
Said they'd been sent to the Lamb and Flag
   To see God come down from on high.

A few days later a bishop
   And a five-star general were seen
With the head of an African country
   In a bullet-proof limousine.

Summer term

'We've come,' they said, 'with tokens
   For the little boy to choose.'
Told the tale about war and peace
   In the television news.

After them came the soldiers
   With rifle and bomb and gun,
Looking for enemies of the state.
   The family had packed and gone.

When they got back to the village
   The neighbours said, to a man,
'That boy will never be one of us,
   Though he does what he blessed well can.'

He went round to all the people
   A paper crown on his head.
Here is some bread from my father.
   Take, eat, he said.

Nobody seemed very hungry.
   Nobody seemed to care.
Nobody saw the god in himself
   Quietly standing there.

He finished up in the papers.
   He came to a very bad end.
He was charged with bringing the living to life.
   No man was that prisoner's friend.

There's only one kind of punishment
   To fit that kind of a crime.
They rigged a trial and shot him dead.
   They were only just in time.

They lifted the young man by the leg,
   They lifted him by the arm,
They locked him in a cathedral
   In case he came to harm.

They stored him safe as water
  Under seven rocks.
One Sunday morning he burst out
  Like a jack-in-the-box.

Through the town he went walking.
  He showed them the holes in his head.
Now do you want any loaves? he cried.
  'Not today,' they said.

Charles Causley

3: THE SIKH UNIFORM
(13 April: Baisakhi)

A story told by the last of the Sikh gurus on the first Baisakhi day and therefore especially suitable for retelling on or near what many Sikhs regard as the most important festival of their year. (If it falls on a working day, it may be observed the following weekend.) Baisakhi marks the founding of the Khalsa, the brotherhood of all Sikh men and women, and it is from that date that Sikhs have worn the 'uniform' of the Five K's.

Members of the Sikh religion all wear a kind of uniform. You perhaps recognize Sikh men by their turbans but the true marks of their uniform are as follows:

kesh	uncut hair
kangha	comb
kara	bracelet
kaccha	shorts
kirpan	sword

It was on a particular day (called Baisakhi) nearly four hundred years ago that they were told by the tenth of their great teachers or gurus to wear this kind of 'uniform'. There are various reasons for wearing a uniform: it can give its wearer a sense of dignity and confidence, and it also lets people know what organization you belong to. This is the story told *by that Sikh guru, Guru Gobind Singh, to explain why Sikhs should wear their 'uniform' – and, by the way, remember that all Sikh men are called Singh (which means 'lion').*

There was once a donkey who lived the usual donkey's life. He was made to carry heavy loads, beaten by his master, given too little to eat and very little time for rest. One day, however, he was passing the house of a hunter. This man had been cleaning animal skins and had put some out to dry. The clumsy donkey brushed against them and one, that of a lion, fell on him, covering his head and back. Just then his master called him. As fearful as ever, the donkey reluctantly went to do his bidding. To the donkey's surprise his master turned and ran as he saw him enter the yard. The other animals, which had all despised the donkey, kept their distance. When he began to eat their food, which was much better than his, they did not complain. Even when he turned his attention to the vegetables the owner's wife had been about to prepare for their meal no one did anything.

After a while the donkey decided to wander from the yard, where everything was pretty boring, back into the town. As he did so the streets emptied. At the melon-seller's stall he stopped to steal a juicy piece, preparing his back for a heavy blow from a stick, but it never came. The stall holder just watched from a safe distance!

Eventually the donkey left the village for the scrubland beyond. He had a shock when he disturbed a tiger, and a bigger one when, instead of chasing him, it slunk away into the trees. Towards evening he decided to return to the safety of the village but found the gates closed and the watchman ready to throw stones at him. He feared the jungle at night but had no choice but to go there. He slept little and in the morning went cautiously to a pond to drink. Again the animals which might have threatened him made way for him.

For some months he lived this safe but solitary life. He began to long for company. One day he saw his master passing and ran from the woods towards him shouting for all he was worth. 'Hee Haw!' he cried repeatedly. This completely unnerved the man – he had never before encountered a braying lion. As he turned to flee something strange happened. When the donkey ran under a tree one of the branches removed the lion skin from its back. The master recognized the donkey, grabbed a stick and began beating it mercilessly. The perplexed animal couldn't understand what had happened and never could to its dying day.

There was little need for Guru Gobind Singh to explain the meaning of the story. Uniformed, the Sikh would command respect.

W. Owen Cole and Piara Singh Sambhi

4: SHAVUOT

Shavuot is a Jewish festival, the 'feast of weeks' or Pentecost. It is celebrated fifty days after Passover (just as Christians celebrate Pentecost or Whitsun fifty days after Easter). Shavuot commemorates the giving of the Law by God to Moses on Mount Sinai and also the wheat harvest or the 'harvest of the first fruits'. Shavuot occurs in May or June.

For Jewish people, Shavuot is a joyful festival when synagogues are decorated with flowers and dairy foods are eaten. It reminds Jews of two things. First, of the time when Moses was given the Law (including the Ten Commandments) by God at Mount Sinai. The Law or **Torah** *is the first five books of the Jewish Bible and the Christian Old Testament. Jews believe that by following the rules in the Torah they serve (and please) God. Secondly, Shavuot is a celebration of the harvest when the first crops of the year are gathered in.*

This is an explanation of Shavuot, written by a Jewish teacher.

Shavuot is the holiday on which we celebrate God's giving to us the Torah. We call this holiday the 'time of the giving of the Torah.' Not the 'receiving' of the Torah but the 'giving' of the Torah. A Hasidic Rabbi gave two reasons why:

First, we were 'given' the Torah only once, in Moses' time, on Shavuot, but every Jew in every generation 'receives' the Torah whenever he studies.

Second, while every Jew is 'given' the Torah equally, not every Jew 'receives' it equally. Some Jews understand it better than others; some Jews follow it more closely than others.

So we celebrate its giving, not its receiving.

That is one reason for Shavuot, but like all Jewish festivals, there is also a reason in nature. Shavuot is called in the Torah, *Hag ha-Katzir*, the Festival of the Grain Harvest. And it is *Hag ha-Bikkurim*, the Festival of the First Fruits. On Shavuot we celebrate the fulfilment of the promise of spring.

Shavuot means 'weeks'. It is celebrated seven weeks after Pesah. Pesah marks the beginning of the barley harvest. For seven weeks, through the days of the counting of the Omer, the barley harvest was completed and the wheat harvest begun. That harvest period ended with the Feast of (the Seven) Weeks – Shavuot. It's the story of spring turning into summer, of freedom ripening through law. On Shavuot, two loaves of bread, made from the newly harvested wheat, were brought to the Temple and offered as a gift to God.

It is a lovely season. The spring rains are over and the land is heavy with green. The heat of summer has not yet begun. Not only the grain had ripened in the Land of Israel: the grapes had turned purple; the first honey had been taken from the hive; other fruits were full and ready for plucking. These, too, were to be shared with God on Shavuot.

That the Jews shared things with God is one of the most important ideas of Shavuot. The Jews brought their first fruits to the Temple to give to God, not to pay their landlord, not because they had to. They came to share their first fruits with God as one partner shares with another.

In partnership, God and man make the earth live. God provides sun and rain and warmth. Man provides seed and skill and labour. Together, God and man produce the fruits of the earth. On Shavuot, man shares with God the produce of their joint work – and he remembers what he and God are trying to do for all men, everywhere.

Harry Gersh

5: SEASIDE HOLIDAY

A look at the traditional Victorian seaside holiday. (The passage has been arranged here for two narrators, and five readers.)

Nowadays summer holidays (for those who can afford them) are as likely to be in Spain as in Blackpool [or Brighton/ Yarmouth/Skegness]. It is not so long ago that only the very rich could afford to go abroad and it's not much more than a hundred years ago that ordinary people were first able to have a seaside holiday in this country. So what was a seaside holiday like a hundred years ago?

Narrator 1: The railways made it easy for ordinary people (if they had enough money) to visit the seaside. In 1820 it took six hours to bump along from London to Brighton on top of a stagecoach. The fare was twelve shillings. Forty years later the train service took less than half the time. The fare was eight shillings. Around the coast seaside towns grew in size.

Narrator 2: Some people went to the seaside just for the day. Factories organized outings like this one reported in a Blackburn paper:

Reader 1: Fares were a shilling there and back. A band was provided by Messrs Hopwood and two

Summer term

hundred loaves and from two to three hundredweight of cheese was stored in the horsebox.

Narrator 2: This sort of day trip was the highlight of the year for many people. It was their one escape from their home town to a different place where they were free from cares of home and work. Alfred Williams, who worked in Swindon, noticed that on the walls of the factory:

Reader 2: 'Roll on Trip' or 'Five Weeks to Trip' may be seen scrawled in big letters. 'Trip Day' is the most important day in the calendar at the railway town. For several months fathers and mothers, young men and juveniles have been saving up for the outing, whatever new clothes are bought for the summer are usually worn for the first time at 'Trip'.

Life in a Railway Factory, 1915

Narrator 1: Between 1863 and 1873 the numbers arriving by train at Blackpool Station increased four times. The town began to provide organized entertainments. In 1863 its North Pier was built for £13,500. In 1896 a gigantic wheel was put up. Growing numbers of these visitors came to stay for several days. Many seaside hotels were built in Victorian times though most visitors probably stayed in rented rooms in lodging houses. In some of these, people cooked their own meals. In others the landlady cooked food bought by the visitors.

Narrator 2: Landladies charged extra for doing washing and providing milk. Some charged for putting salt, pepper and sauce on the table. They also made money from day trippers who came to the door for hot water. Writing in *The Rochdale Observer* Trafford Clegg joked about how a landlady packed in visitors:

Reader 3: Plently of room, gentlemen, I have often had thirty people sleeping in the house and never more than seven in a bed. The parlour table holds five. Last summer I fitted a board over the scullery sink for two youngsters to sleep on and a hammock in the cellar steps with a breadth of carpet, and the clothes line. It was the coolest place in the house so I charged sixpence extra.

Quoted in J. K. Walton, *The Blackpool Landlady*, 1978

Narrator 1: By the 1860s Britain's summer beaches were crowded. Brighton and Margate, according to Elizabeth Stone, were:

Reader 4: ... crammed, but by decidedly unfashionable people. Look at these sands. They appear one moving mass of cabs, carts and carriages, horses, ponies, dogs, donkeys and boys; men, women, children and nurses, babies and bathing machines, little boys with spades, mamas with sewing and young ladies reading novels, young gentlemen with canes and eyeglasses. Then the hawkers [salesmen] are a most noisy and pressing fraternity here, nothing in the world that you can't buy from a puppy dog to a yard of cushion lace.

Chronicles of Fashion, 1845

Narrator 1: The *Yarmouth Guide* of 1877 warned visitors to beware of salesmen on the beach:

Reader 5: Take a seat and your troubles begin. 'Here's your chocolate creams.' 'Buns two a penny.' 'Yarmouth rock a penny a bar.' 'Apples penny a bag.' 'Nuts or pears.' 'Lemonade threepence a bottle.' 'Buy a bunch of grapes, Sir.' 'Walnuts eight a penny.' 'Milk a penny a glass.'

Narrator 2: Bathing was popular, but men and women were strictly separated and had to use different parts of the beach. Women, in particular, went into the sea from 'bathing machines'. When William Tayler went to Brighton with his employers he saw some of these machines:

Reader 1: There are numbers of old women have little wooden houses on wheels, and into these houses people goe that want to bathe, and then the house is pushed into the water and when the person has undressed, they get into the water and bathe, and then get into the wooden house again and dress themselves, and then the house is drawn on shore again.

Quoted in *Useful Toil*, 1974

Narrator 1: Women wore a large quantity of heavy clothing when they went bathing. Many men wore nothing at all. In Victorian times seaside towns tried to persuade men to wear swimming costumes. In 1873 the Reverend Francis Kilvert was given special swimming clothes for the first time:

Reader 2: At Seaton I had a bathe. A boy brought me to the machine door two towels, as I thought, but when I came out of the water and began to use them I found that one of the rags he had given me was a pair of very short red and white striped drawers to cover my nakedness. Unaccustomed to such things I had in my ignorance bathed naked and scandalized the beach. However some little boys who were looking on at the rude naked man appeared to be much interested in the spectacle and the young ladies who were strolling near seemed to have no objection.

Narrator 1: In the following year Kilvert was persuaded – like more and more Victorians – to wear a swimming costume:

Reader 2: At Shanklin one has to adopt the detestable custom of bathing in drawers. If ladies don't like to see men naked why don't they keep away from the sight? Today I had a pair of drawers given me which I could not keep on. The rough waves stripped them off and tore them down round my ankles. I took the wretched and dangerous things off and of course there were some ladies looking on as I came up out of the water.

Kilvert's Diary, 1870-79

Sydney Wood

A CALENDAR OF READINGS

The Christian calendar

The Christian calendar is a mixture of fixed dates (e.g. Christmas Day and most saints' days) and movable feasts.

The churches' year begins traditionally with Advent Sunday (the fourth Sunday before Christmas). Advent is a period of preparation leading up to the coming (or advent) of Jesus on Christmas Day. After the twelve days of the Christmas festival, Epiphany (6 January) marks the visit of the wise men to the infant Jesus.

The calendar dates of the spring festivals are governed by the date of Easter. Easter Sunday is the first Sunday after the full moon that occurs on the day of the spring equinox (21 March) or on any of the next twenty-eight days. Easter Sunday can therefore fall on any date between and including 22 March to 25 April. Easter in the Orthodox Church (e.g. in Greece) is calculated by another method.

Lent is a period of forty days, beginning with Ash Wednesday, which leads up to Easter. Traditionally a period of fasting of various degrees of severity, it is now seen more as a time of penitence and thoughtful preparation for Easter.

Holy Week is the week before Easter. It begins with Palm Sunday (the entry of Jesus into Jerusalem), goes through Maundy Thursday (the Last Supper), Good Friday (the Crucifixion) and so to Easter. The first Easter occurred at the Jewish Passover. As Passover is always on the 14th of the Jewish month of Nisan, the two festivals do not always coincide.

The end of the life of Jesus on earth is marked by Ascension Day (forty days after Easter, and always on a Thursday), and the coming of the Holy Spirit to the apostles at Whitsun or Pentecost is commemorated ten days later.

The Jewish calendar

The Jewish calendar is based on both lunar and solar movements. Because the lunar and solar years are of different lengths, an extra or 'leap' month is added to the calendar seven times in each nineteen years. This keeps the months (and festivals) in harmony with the seasons of the year but results in minor variations when compared with the Western calendar. Precise dates can be found at the front of most desk or office diaries. Note that Jewish holy days begin at dusk on the day before given dates.

The Hindu calendar

The Hindu calendar evolved in ancient India. It has twelve months linked to the phases of the moon. Hinduism has many holidays. Some are celebrated by the majority of Hindus, others only in certain communities or areas, and dates may differ from area to area.

Sikh festivals

Sikhs have two kinds of festivals: 'melas' (meetings or fairs) which re-interpret Hindu festivals, and 'gurpurds' which mark the anniversaries of the gurus.

Three of the major 'melas' are Hola Mohalla (the Sikh 'holi', a spring festival which occurs in February or March), Baisakhi (the anniversary of the khalsa) and Divali when Sikhs celebrate the release of Guru Hargobind from captivity in 1620.

The most important gurpurds are the birthdays of Guru Nanak and Guru Gobind Singh and the martyrdoms of Guru Arjan and Guru Tegh Bahadur.

Sikhs usually defer the celebration of a feast to the weekend closest to the actual anniversary.

This calendar indicates passages suitable for reading on particular dates and at special seasons. For the convenience of those who possess the complementary anthologies *Anthology for Assembly* and *The Assembly Handbook*, references are also included to suitable passages in those books. Their page numbers are prefaced *AA* for the former and *AH* for the latter book.

Autumn Term
Page numbers appear in brackets.

September
       Beginning of term   (25–7)
2   Great Fire of London   (122–7)
19   George Cadbury born 1839   (132–8)
29   Michaelmas   (*AH*187–8)
Also: Harvest   (173–8; *AA*151–2, 153; *AH*242–5)
       Rosh Hashanah (Jewish New Year)   (213–14; *AA*149–50; *AH*189)
       Yom Kippur (Day of Atonement)   (*AH*190)
       Sukkot   (*AA*152; *AH*190)
       Simhat Torah   (*AH*190)

October
3   Therese of Lisieux   (214–17)
4   St Francis of Assisi   (*AA*51–2)
4   Sputnik I launched 1957   (*AH*48–9)
24   United Nations Day   (*AA*154; *AH*102–3, 147–8, 245–8)
29   Wall Street Crash 1929   (*AH*65–7)
31   Hallowe'en   (*AA*156)
Also: Week of Prayer for World Peace (third week of the month)   (110–21; *AA*53–9; *AH*45–8, 143–4)
       Divali   (217–19; *AA*164; *AH*190–1)

November
1   All Saints' Day   (*AH*56–62)
2   All Souls' Day   (118–19; *AH*126–8, *AH*145–7)
5   Guy Fawkes Day   (*AH*191–3)
11   (Sunday nearest) Remembrance Sunday   (219–20; *AA*157–9; *AH*193–4)
11   St Martin   (220–3)
16   Guru Nanak's birthday   (161–3; *AA*142–4)
17   St Hugh of Lincoln   (223–8)
22   St Cecilia   (*AH*195–6)
Also: Advent (fourth Sunday before Christmas)   (*AA*160–1; *AH*15, 199–203)

Calendar of readings

December
6   St Nicholas   (*AA*162–3; *AH*196–8)
7–8   Pearl Harbour 1941   (*AH*47)
10   Declaration of Human Rights   (108–18; *AA*15–20, 42–3; *AH*103–5, 114–16)
11   Alexander Solzhenitsyn born 1918   (118–19; *AA*43–4; *AH*163)
28   Massacre of the Innocents   (233–5)
Also: Hannukah   (*AA*165)
       Christingle   (*AA*164)
End of term: Christmas   (228–35, 263–6; *AA*166–72; *AH*199–203)

Spring Term

January
6   Epiphany, Twelfth Night   (236; *AA*173; *AH*204–5)
       Plough Monday (Monday following Jan 6)   (237; *AA*174–5)
17   Wassailling   (237–8; *AH*207–8)
25   St Paul   (*AA*26–7, 176–7)
       Burns' Night   (240–2)
26   Australia Day   (*AH*104)
Also: Martin Luther King Day (third Monday)   (*AA*116–17)
       Week of Prayer for Christian Unity (third week)   (*AH*111–13, 181–3)
       Chinese New Year (late January-early February)   (238–40; *AH*206–7)
       World Leprosy Day (last Sunday in January)   (*AA*78–81)

February
2   Candlemas   (*AH*209)
7   Sir Thomas More born 1478   (181–5)
12   Abraham Lincoln's birthday   (35–6)
14   St Valentine's Day   (244–7)
20   Archbishop Luwum memorial service 1977   (*AH*60–2)
23   John Keats died 1821   (*AH*121)
Also: Shrovetide   (247–9; *AA*178; *AH*210–11)
       Ash Wednesday   (*AA*178; *AH*210)
       Ash Wednesday is also a 'give-up-smoking' day   (60–2; *AH*261–3)

Calendar of readings

Lent   (*AA*178–9; *AH*15, 273–5)
Purim (February–March)   (*AH*211–13)

March
17   St Patrick   (213–15)
19   St Joseph   (249–51)
29   Start of the Crimean War 1854   (*AH*45–7)
Also: Mothering Sunday (mid-Lent Sunday)   (23–5, 251–3; *AA*122–3, 180–1)
Passover (late March-early April)   (253–5; *AA*182–3; *AH*215–16)
Palm Sunday   (*AH*15)
Maundy Thursday   (*AH*217–18)
Good Friday   (255–61; *AA*184–9; *AH*178–9, 218–19, 264–6)
Easter   (262–6; *AA*190–5; *AH*220–2)
Easter in the Orthodox Church   (*AA*193–5)

April
5   End of financial/tax year   (*AH*254–7)
7   World Health Day   (57–9; *AA*109–10; *AH*105–6, 261–3, 270–3)
12   Yuri Gargarin, first man in space, 1961   (*AH*48)
13   Baisakhi   (266–8, *AH*222–4)

Summer Term

April
26   Daniel Defoe died 1730   (*AH*133–5)
28   Lord Shaftesbury born 1801   (*AH*58–60)
30   Iranian Embassy siege 1980   (*AH*141–3)

May
1   May Day, Labour Day   (*AA*196–7; *AH*224–5)
8   Mother Julian of Norwich   (*AH*56–8)
12   Florence Nightingale born 1820   (*AH*45–7)
23   Bay of Bengal floods, 1985   (93–100)
24   Commemoration of John and Charles Wesley (128–30)
29   Oak Apple Day   (*AH*231–2)
Also: Yom Ha'atzma'ut (Jewish Independence Festival, usually early in the month)   (163–72)
Christian Aid Week (third week of month)   (103–5;

Calendar of readings

        *AA*198–201; *AH*33–5, 275–8)
        Rogationtide (*AH*226–7)
        Ascension Day (Thursday, 40 days after Easter) (*AA*202; *AH*226)
        Pentecost (Christian) or Whitsun (*AA*202–3; *AH*229–31)
        Shavuot (Jewish Pentecost) (268–70)
        Wesak (May full moon) (*AH*227–9)

June
2   Jesse Boot born 1850 (138–41)
9   George Stephenson born 1781 (*AA*35–6)
15   World Children's Day (*AH*102–3)
24   Midsummer's Day; St John the Baptist (*AH*232–4)
27   Helen Keller born 1880 (*AH*135–6)
Also: Father's Day (third Sunday) (23–5; *AA*67–8)
      Hindu pilgrimages (*AH*234–5)

July
7   Sir Thomas More died 1535 (*AH*81–5)
15   St Swithin (*AA*16–18)
21   First moon walk 1969 (*AH*48–9)
End of term: Summer holidays (270–3; *AA*209–10; *AH*278–80)

The Muslim calendar

The Quran decrees the use of the lunar year, which is eleven days shorter than the solar year. In relation to the Western year, the Muslim year therefore starts 'earlier' each year and so, for example, the month of Ramadan can occur in any season.

The precise timing of a Muslim holy day can be calculated only a few days before its occurrence, and takes account of local sunrise and sunset times.

Muslim festivals
Al Hijra (New Year's Day) (191–3)
Ramadan (189–91; *AA*204–5; *AH*235–6)
Lailat-ul-Qadr (Commemoration of the start of the revelation of the Qu'ran) (186–9)
Eid ul-Fitr (*AH*236)
Eid ul-Adha (the last four days of the Hajj) (*AA*206–8; *AH*236)

Calendar of readings

Precise dates for the festivals of all the world faiths for any given year can be found in the *The Shap Calendar of Religious Festivals*, published annually by the Commission for Racial Equality, Elliot House, 10–12 Allington Street, London SW1E 5EH; distributed by Shap Working Party, 7 Alderbrook Road, Solihull, West Midlands B91 1NH.

Lefax (9 Murray Street, London NW1 9RE) publish 'filofax' size data sheets giving similar information.

Acknowledgements

The editor and publisher are grateful to the following copyright holders for permission to reproduce copyright material. Every effort has been made to trace owners of copyright material, but in some cases this has not proved possible. The publisher would be glad to hear from any others.

Amnesty International for an excerpt from 'Terror in Iran' published in *Amnesty* No. 1, February 1983; for 'Prisoner of Conscience'; and for 'First they came for the Jews . . .' by Pastor Niemöller quoted in *In Prison and You Came to Me*; Atheneum Publishers Inc for 'Teevee' by Eve Merriam published in *Catch a Little Rhyme*; BBC for excerpts from 'Sympathy' by Lesley Davies from the School Radio series *Speak* broadcast on May 10, 1976; for 'War Report' by Christopher Wain from the School Radio series *A Service for Schools* broadcast on March 14, 1985; BBC Enterprises Ltd for excerpts from *Bright Blue* by Rabbi Lionel Blue; Behrman House Inc for an excerpt from *When a Jew Celebrates* by Harry Gersh; Blackie & Sons Ltd for excerpts from *Worlds of Difference* by Martin Palmer and Esther Bisset; The Bodley Head for an excerpt from *The Eighteenth Emergency* by Betsy Byars; for an excerpt from *A Star for the Latecomer* by Bonnie and Paul Zindel; for the prose poem 'We Will Never Die' by Alexander Solzhenitsyn in *Stories and Prose Poems*; B T Batsford for 'England's first woman doctor' by Eva Bailey in *Disease and Discovery*; British Council of Churches for prayers from British Council of Churches Human Rights Day Service 1980; Jonathan Cape Ltd for an excerpt from *Run for Your Life* by David Line; for 'Dividing the Camels' by Idries Shah from *Thinkers of the East*; for excerpts from 'Harrison Bergon' by Kurt Vonnegut Jnr in *Welcome to the Monkey House*; Chambers Publishers for 'Why people smoke' from *Smoking: What's In It For You?* by Sue Armstrong; Chatto & Windus Ltd for an excerpt from *The Rebel* by D. J. Enright (agents: Watson, Little Ltd); *Christian Aid News* for 'How Much is a Packet of Rice?' by Derrick Knight from the article

Acknowledgements

'Poor Peasants Passed by in Rice Revolution', *Christian Aid News* July/September 1986; William Collins Ltd for excerpts from 'Home for the Dying' from *Something Beautiful for God*, Malcolm Muggeridge interviewing Mother Teresa; for excerpts from *A Precocious Autobiography* by Yevgeny Yevtushenko; for the excerpts 'The Massacre of the Innocents' and 'The Crucifixion' from *The Book of Witnesses* by David Kossoff; Curtis Brown for 'In the Street' by Roger Bush from *Prayers for Pagans*; the extract taken from *What Christians Believe* by David Cox published and copyright 1963 by Darton, Longman and Todd Ltd and is used by permission of the publishers; David Higham Associates Ltd for 'Silence of Winter' in *Collected Poems* by Elizabeth Jennings published by Macmillan; Dryad Press Ltd for an excerpt from *Acid Rain* by Philip Neal; for an excerpt from *Time for Trees* by Joy Palmer; Dublin Evening Herald for excerpts from 'Cry for My Lost Son', Tuesday May 13, 1986; Edward Arnold (Publishers) Ltd for 'I say my prayers when it's calm . . .' and for 'Thoughts on Remembrance Sunday' by Michael Davis quoted in *Words for Worship* compiled by Christopher Campling and Michael Davis; Exley Publications Ltd for 'Prince Charming' from *Challenges* by M. Bingham, S. Edmondson and S. Stryker; Faber & Faber Ltd for 'warty bliggens the toad' from *Archy and Mehitabel* by Don Marquis; The Flora Project for Heart Disease Prevention for excerpts from *Henry the Heart's Healthy Hints*; W. Foulsham & Co Ltd for an excerpt from *What About Drugs?* by Angela Cotton; for the excerpt 'Drugs: A Case History' from *What About Drugs?* by Angela Cotton; Grevatt & Grevatt for 'The Blind Men and the Elephant' by Siew-Yue Killingley quoted in *A Handbook of Hinduism for Teachers* edited by Dermot Killingley; The Guardian for an excerpt from *Country Diary* 1963 by A. H. G.; Hamish Hamilton Ltd for 'The Bear Who Let It Alone' from *Fables For Our Times* by James Thurber; and 'The Tiger Who Would Be King' from *Further Fables For Our Times* by James Thurber; Harcourt Brace Jovanovich Ltd for 'Who do you think you are' from *The People, Yes* by Carl Sandburg; for 'What kind of liar are you?' from *The People, Yes* by Carl Sandburg; William Heinemann Ltd for an excerpt from *If Only I Could Walk* by Myra Schneider; Hodder & Stoughton Ltd for excerpts from *The Friendship Factor* by Alan Loy McGinnis; The Hogarth Press for an excerpt from *An Autobiography* by Edwin Muir; Indiana University Press for 'Africa's Plea' by Roland Tombekai Dempster in *Poems for Black Africa*; The Islamic Foundation for 'Be My Guest' from *Love Your Brother, Love Your Neighbour* by Khurrah Murad; for an excerpt from *Marvellous Stories from the Life of Muhammad* by Mardijah Aldrich Tarantino; John Murray (Publishers) Ltd for excerpts from *Living in Victorian Times* by Sydney Wood; Lion Publishing plc for 'A Wesleyan childhood'

Acknowledgements

from the *Journal of John Wesley* abridged by Christopher Idle; Longman Group Ltd for an excerpt from *Children of the Gods* by Kenneth McLeish; Macmillan Children's Books for 'First Day' from *Dragon in the Garden* by Reginald Maddock; for 'The Trial of Tomorrow' by Guy Burt from *Young Words*; Macmillan Education Ltd for 'David Conquers Jalud' by Abdul Rahman Rukaini from *Stories of the Prophets of Islam: Daud, Sulaiman and Ayub*; for an excerpt from *Festival! Chinese New Year* by Olivia Bennett; for an excerpt from *Festival! – Carnival* by Olivia Bennett; for 'The Ballad of the Bread Man' by Charles Causley from *Charles Causley: Collected Poems 1951–1975*; Julia MacRae Books for excerpts from *Here's the Year* by Peter Watkins and Erica Hughes; the estate of the late Father Robert Manley for 'The Old Woman at the Bus Stop' and 'St Joseph' from *Motley Miscellany*; *Newsweek* for the excerpt 'We have never been free . . .' from *Newsweek*, May 10, 1971; for excerpts from 'Aftershocks of a deadly cyclone' from *Newsweek*, June 10, 1985; *Oxfam News* for 'Drought in Ethiopia' from the article 'Bleak Outlook if Aid Ceases' by Paddy Coultes in *Oxfam News*, winter 1984; Oxford University Press for an excerpt from *Brother in the Land* by Robert Swindells; for 'Trio' by Victor Harris in *Every Man Will Shout* compiled by Roger Mansfield, edited by Isobel Armstrong; for excerpts from *Living in the Time of Jesus of Nazareth* by Peter Connolly; Pavilion Books for 'The Mango Tree' by Madhur Jaffrey from *Seasons of Splendour*; Penguin Books Ltd for three fables from *Fables of Aesop* translated by S. A. Handford, copyright © S. A. Handford, 1954; for excerpts from *You and All the Others* by Bill Stewart; Religious and Moral Education Press for excerpts from *Divali* by Howard Marsh; for an excerpt from *Baisakhi* (The Living Festivals Series) by W. Owen Cole and Piara Singh Sambhi; Richard Drew Publishing Ltd for an excerpt from *Scottish Heroes and Heroines* by Eileen Dunlop and Antony Kamm; E. H. Robertson for an excerpt from *Paul Schneider: The Pastor of Buchenwald* by E. H. Robertson, published by SCM Press Ltd; The Salvation Army for excerpts from the article 'Emergency Service!' by Captain Joe Burlison published in *All the World* Vol. 25, No. 6, April–June 1983; for the excerpt 'The Soup Run' from a Salvation Army Information leaflet; for 'Army Without Guns' by Cyril Barnes from a Salvation Army booklet; SCM Press Ltd for an excerpt on Sir Christopher Wren taken from *Listen on Wednesday* by John G. Williams; Shelter for publicity material by David Moore; The Sikh Missionary Society for an excerpt from *The Guru's Way* by G. S. Sidhu, G. S. Sivia and Kirpal Singh; *Time Magazine* for 'Yakub Ali's Story' from *Trail of Tears and Anguish* published in *Time*, June 10, 1985; Unwin Hyman for 'Paperboy wanted/Equal rights' by Bernard Ashley from *Openings* by Roy Blatchford; Valentine

Acknowledgements

Mitchell & Co for excerpts from *Hannah Senesh: Her Life and Diary* translated by Marta Cohn, copyright © Nigel March; Viking Penguin Inc for 'The Creation' by James Weldon Johnson, copyright © Grace Nail Johnson, 1955; Virago Press for excerpts from *Ordinary Lives: One Hundred Years Ago* by Carol Adams; Wayland Publishers Ltd for excerpts from *Addiction in the News* by Vanora Leigh.

Index

Authors

Adams, Carol, 141–6
Aesop, 39–40
Amnesty International, 108–110, 110–11
Armstrong, Sue, 60–2
Ashley, Bernard, 73–7

Bailey, Eva, 130–2
Barnes, Cyril, 181–2
Bennett, Olivia, 238–40, 247–9
Bingham, Mindy, 202–204
Bisset, Esther, 147–9
Blue, Rabbi Lionel, 213–14, 253–5
British Council of Churches, 116–18
Burlison, Captain Joe, 83–5
Burt, Guy, 206–9
Bush, Roger, 183
Byars, Betsy, 71–3

Causley, Charles, 263–6
Christian Aid, 103–5
Cohn, Marta, 163
Cole, W. Owen, 266–8
Connolly, Peter, 255–7
Cotton, Angela, 63–4, 64–6
Coulter, Paddy, 100–103
Cox, David, 151–3

Dafne, Reuven, 164–6, 171–2

Davies, Lesley, 29–32
Davis, Michael, 219–20
Dempster, Roland Tombekai, 19
Dunlop, Eileen, 240–2

Edmondson, Judy, 202–204
Enright, D. J., 20–1

Flora Project for Heart Disease Prevention, 57–9

Gersh, Harry, 268–70
Gosse, Edmund, 229–30

Harris, Victor, 262–3
Hughes, Erica, 244–6, 251–3

Jaffrey, Madhur, 43–5
Jennings, Elizabeth, 243
Johnson, James Weldon, 152–5

Kamm, Antony, 240–2
Keitlen, Tomi, 51–3
Knight, Derrick, 103–105
Kossoff, David, 233–5, 257–60

Lawrence, Howard, 113–16
Leigh, Vanora, 81–3
Line, David, 27–9

MacLeod, Charlotte, 231–3

Maddock, Reginald, 25–7
Manley, Father Robert, 45–7, 249–51
marquis, don, 48–50
Marsh, Howard, 217–19
McGinnis, Alan Loy, 34–6
McLeish, Kenneth, 149–51
Merriam, Eve, 78
Muggeridge, Malcolm, 105–107
Muir, Edwin, 21–2
Murad, Khurram, 197–200

Neal, Philip, 90–2
Newsweek, 96–7, 97–100, 113–16
Niemöller, Pastor Martin, 112–13

OXFAM, 100–103

Palgi, Yoel, 166–8, 169–70
Palmer, Joy, 55–7, 228–9
Palmer, Martin, 147–9
Pepys, Samuel, 122–7

Robertson, E. H., 111–12
Rukaini, Abdul Rahman, 200–201

Salvation Army, 83–5, 88–90, 181–2
Sambhi, Piara Singh, 266–8
Sandburg, Carl, 17–18
Schneider, Myra, 53–5

Self, David, 132–8, 138–41, 156–9, 159–60, 173–8, 186–9, 189–91, 191–3, 193–7, 214–17, 220–3, 223–8, 236–8, 260–1
Senesh, Hannah, 164, 172
Shah, Idries, 41–3
Shelter, 85–8
Sidhu, G. S., 161–3
Singh, Kirpal, 161–3
Sivia, G. S., 161–3
Solzhenitsyn, Alexander, 118–19
Stewart, Bill, 23–5, 32–4
Stryker, Sandy, 202–204
Swindells, Robert, 209–11

Tarantino, Mardijah Aldrich, 184–6
Teresa, Mother, 105–107
Thurber, James, 40–1, 47–8
Time, 93–5

Vonnegut, Kurt, Jnr, 204–206

Wain, Christopher, 160–1
Watkins, Peter, 244–6, 251–3
Wesley, Susannah, 128–30
Williams, John G., 127–8
Wood, Sydney, 270–3

Yevtushenko, Yevgeny, 36–8, 119–21

Zindel, Bonnie and Paul, 79–81

Index of authors and topics

Topics

This index is intended to help assembly leaders to make links between related passages. It does not include references to topics that can be located from the contents list or from the list of festivals and anniversaries (pages 275–81).

Chinese beliefs, 147–9, 156–9, 238–40
Christianity, 151–5, 173–83, 220–8, 233–5, 249–53, 255–66

Ecology, 55–7, 90–2, 100–103

Family, 23–5, 43–5, 128–30, 251–3

Handicaps, 51–5
Health, 17–18, 57–9, 60–70, 103–105, 130–2, 138–41
Hinduism, 43–5, 155–6, 217–19
Homelessness, 85–90, 93–100, 105–107
Human nature, 18–22, 29–38, 48–50, 183

Islam, 41–3, 184–201

Judaism, 113, 157–61, 163–72, 213–14, 253–5, 268–70
Justice, 27–9

Parables, 39–50, 173–8, 179–80, 193–7, 197–200

Rights, 19, 73–7, 108–18

Salvation Army, 83–5, 88–90, 181–2
School, 25–7
Sikhism, 161–3, 266–8

Winter, 228, 236–8, 243–4